Junior Dictionary

Collins

Collins Junior Dictionary

First published 2000

© HarperCollins*Publishers* Ltd 2000

10 9 8 7 6 5 4 3 2 1

ISBN 0 00 316155 2 hardback
ISBN 0 00 316156 0 paperback

A catalogue record for this book is available from the British Library.

Published by Collins
A division of HarperCollins*Publishers* Ltd
77–85 Fulham Palace Road
Hammersmith
London W6 8JB

www.**Collins**Education.com
On-line Support for Schools and Colleges

www.**fireandwater**.com
Visit the book lover's website

Compiler	Evelyn Goldsmith
Literacy consultants	Kay Hiatt, Rosemary Boys
Numeracy consultant	Jan Henley
Science consultant	Rona Wyn Davies
Cover designer	Susi Martin
Design	Neil Adams, Grasshopper Design Co.
Illustrators	Tim Archbold, Tamsin Cook, Felicity House, Pat Murray, Sarah Wimperis, Sue Woollatt (all of Graham-Cameron Illustration)

Photos
All commissioned photos by Steve Lumb.

The publishers wish to thank the following for permission to use photographs:
Cover photos by NASA (planet) and Bruce Coleman (moth).
Andes Press: p. 61 Diwali; **Art Directors & Trip**: p. 7 acorn, p. 8 aeroplane, p. 12 antelope, p. 29 bridge, p. 31 butterfly, p. 32 cactus, p. 34 carnival, p. 48 coral, p. 62 dragonfly, p. 64 duck, p. 65 Earth, p. 65 eclipse, p. 68 erupt, p. 69 evergreen, p. 86 giraffe, p. 95 harvest, p. 101 horse, p. 102 hurricane, p. 103 illuminations, p. 107 ivy, p. 113 ladybird, p. 115 leaves, p. 128 mill, p. 147 pagoda, p. 172 ray, p. 174 reflection, p. 178 rhinoceros, p. 180 rose, p. 209 statue, p. 223 thatched, p. 230 tractor; **BBC**: p. 213 studio; **Biofotos/Heather Angel**: p. 18 badger, p. 57 desert, p. 81 fox, p. 158 polar bear; **Oxford Scientific Films**: p. 13 ape, p. 14 aquarium, p. 32 camel, p. 38 cheetah, p. 52 crystal, p. 85 gerbil, p. 88 gorilla, p. 103 iceberg, p. 108 jellyfish, p. 148 panda, p. 157 plough, p. 171 rainbow, p. 191 shark, p. 206 springbok, p. 218 swan, p. 226 tiger, p. 253 x-ray; **Papilio**: p. 25 bluebells, p. 56 deer, p. 117 lighthouse.

All other photos and illustrations © HarperCollins*Publishers* Ltd 2000.

Acknowledgements
The publishers would like to thank all the teachers, staff and pupils who contributed to this book:

Models
Lauren Carroll
Stacey Cleary
Tom Crane
Katherine Davis
William Davis
Ruby Feroze
Elizabeth Fison
Jesse Johnson
Ismael Khan
Margaret Omoboade
Zina Patel
Dunia Pavlovic
Petra Pavlovic
Milo Petrie-Foxell
Dexter Sampson
Mauri-Joy Smith
Tom Symonds
Rosie Ward

Schools
Aberhill Primary, Fife; ASDAC, Fife; Canning St Primary, Newcastle upon Tyne; Cowgate Primary, Newcastle upon Tyne; Crombie Primary, Fife; the Literacy Team at Dryden Professional Development Centre, Gateshead; Dunshalt Primary, Fife; Ecton Brook Lower, Northampton; English Martyrs RC Primary, Newcastle upon Tyne; Hotspur Primary, Newcastle upon Tyne; John Betts Primary, London; Lemington First, Newcastle upon Tyne; LMTC Education Development Centre, Northumberland; Melcombe Primary, London; Methilhill Primary, Fife; Newcastle Literacy Centre, Newcastle upon Tyne; Northampton High, Northampton; Pitcoudie Primary, Fife; Pitreavie Primary, Fife; Ravenswood Primary, Newcastle upon Tyne; St Andrew's CE Primary, London; Simon de Senlis Lower, Northampton; Sinclairtown Primary, Fife; Standens Barn Lower, Northampton; Touch Primary, Fife; Towcester Infants, Northampton; Wooton Primary, Northampton.

Printed in Great Britain by Scotprint Book Printers, Haddington, East Lothian

Contents

Using this dictionary

A dictionary tells you what a word means and how to spell it. The words in a dictionary are listed in alphabetical order.

How to find a word

Look up the word **fossil**. What letter does it begin with? Use the **alphabet line** at the side of the page. The green box tells you that the words on this page start with **f**.

Think about the second letter of the word. You are looking for a word beginning with **fo**. Use the **guide word** at the top of the page. A guide word at the top left tells you the *first word* on that page. A guide word at the top right tells you the *last word* on that page. The guide word for this page is **frequent** – it starts with **fr**. Does **fo** come before **fr**?

When you think you have the right page, look at the blue words. These are called **headwords**. The headwords are in alphabetical order. If you run your finger down the headwords on this page, you will see more than one that begins with **fo**. Think about the next letter or letters in your word and look for a headword that begins with **fos**.

Keep looking until you find the word **fossil**.

① **headword**

⑦ **phrase**

③ **part of speech**

④ **definition**

⑨ **irregular form**

⑥ **photo**

⑩ **more information**

frequent ····· **guide word**

forward
ADVERB If you move **forward** or **forwards**, you move the way you are facing.
look forward PHRASE If you **look forward** to something, you want it to happen.

fossil **fossils**
NOUN A **fossil** is the hardened remains of a prehistoric animal or plant that are found inside a rock.

fought
VERB **Fought** is the past tense of **fight**.

foul **fouler, foulest**
ADJECTIVE If something is **foul**, it is extremely unpleasant.

found
VERB **Found** is the past tense of **find**.

foundation **foundations**
NOUN The **foundations** of a building are the solid layers of material put below the ground to support it.

fountain **fountains**
NOUN A **fountain** is a jet or spray of water forced up into the air by a pump.

fox **foxes**
NOUN A **fox** is a wild animal like a dog, with reddish-brown fur and a thick tail.

fraction **fractions**
NOUN **1** In maths, a **fraction** is a part of a whole number, for example ½.
See *Fractions* on page 272.
NOUN **2** A **fraction** is also a tiny part of something.

fracture **fractures**
NOUN A **fracture** is a crack or break in something, especially a bone.

fragile
ADJECTIVE Something that is **fragile** is easily broken or damaged.

fragment **fragments**
NOUN A **fragment** of something is a small piece or part of it.

frame **frames**
NOUN A **frame** is the part surrounding something like a window or picture, or the lenses of a pair of glasses.

freckle **freckles**
NOUN **Freckles** are small, light brown spots on someone's skin.

free
ADJECTIVE **1** If a person or animal is **free**, they can go where they want.
Tom opened the cage and set the bird free.
ADJECTIVE **2** If something is **free**, it does not cost anything.
freedom NOUN

freeze **freezes, freezing, froze, frozen**
VERB **1** If a liquid **freezes**, it becomes solid because the temperature is low.
VERB **2** If you **freeze** something, you store it at a very low temperature.

freezer **freezers**
NOUN A **freezer** is a refrigerator for freezing and storing food.

frequent
ADJECTIVE If something is **frequent**, it happens often.
frequency NOUN **frequently** ADVERB

a
b
c
d
e
Ff ··· **alphabet line**
g
h
i
j
k
l
m
n
o
p
q
r
s
t
u
v
w
x
y
z ····

⑥ **illustration**

⑤ **example sentence**

② **other forms**

⑧ **related words**

81

4

Finding out about a word

(1) The headword is the word you are looking up.

(2) On the same line as the headword, you will see how to spell other forms of the word, such as plural nouns, verb tenses or other adjective forms, called comparatives and superlatives.

(3) Next you will see the part of speech. This tells you what type of word the headword is, such as a noun, verb, adjective, adverb or pronoun.

(4) After the part of speech, you will find the definition. The definition tells you what the word means. The definitions are numbered if there is more than one. Each definition has its own part of speech.

(5) Some words have an example sentence in *italics*. This shows you how the word might be used in speech or writing.

(6) Some words have a photo or other illustration to help you read the word and understand its meaning.

(7) A phrase may also be included. For example, under the word **forward**, you will also find the definition of the phrase **look forward**.

(8) Sometimes, other related words are given at the end, with their parts of speech. These tell you, for example, the noun or adverb form of the word.

(9) An irregular form of a word is a plural noun or verb tense which does not follow the usual spelling rules. You can find many irregular forms in this dictionary.

(10) Some definitions tell you where to look for more information, such as another headword, or the pages at the back of the dictionary.

Other features of this dictionary

● **Pronunciation** is how you say a word. Some words can be spelled the same, but sound different and mean different things – these words are called homographs. This dictionary gives you pronunciation help for some words, including homographs. For example:

tear **tears, tearing, tore, torn**
(*rhymes with* **fear**) NOUN **1** Tears are the drops of liquid that come out of your eyes when you cry.
(*rhymes with* **fair**) VERB **2** If you **tear** something, such as paper or fabric, you pull it apart.

● Some definitions include a label, such as FORMAL, INFORMAL or TRADEMARK. This tells you a little more about the word or how it is used. For example:

Rollerblade **Rollerblades**
NOUN; TRADEMARK **Rollerblades** are roller skates which have the wheels set in one straight line on the bottom of the boot.

Picture pages, word banks and number banks

There are special topic pages at the back of this dictionary to support your writing.

Picture pages have labelled illustrations of things such as fruit and vegetables, parts of the body, different types of animals, and shapes and colours.

Other pages help you understand parts of speech, punctuation, and prefixes and suffixes.

Word banks and **number banks** help you learn and spell time words, weather words, synonyms and antonyms, confusable words, abbreviations, measures, numbers and fractions.

b
c
d
e
f
g
h
i
j
k
l
m
n
o
p
q
r
s
t
u
v
w
x
y
z

Aa

abacus **abacuses**

NOUN An **abacus** is a frame with beads that slide along rods. It is used for counting.

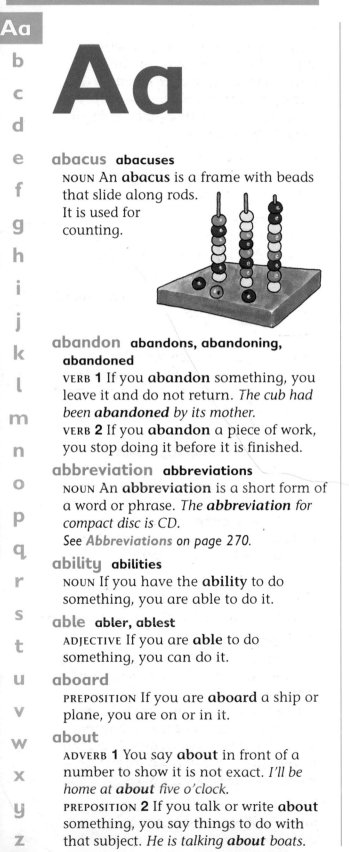

abandon **abandons, abandoning, abandoned**

VERB **1** If you **abandon** something, you leave it and do not return. *The cub had been abandoned by its mother.*

VERB **2** If you **abandon** a piece of work, you stop doing it before it is finished.

abbreviation **abbreviations**

NOUN An **abbreviation** is a short form of a word or phrase. *The abbreviation for compact disc is CD.*
See *Abbreviations* on page 270.

ability **abilities**

NOUN If you have the **ability** to do something, you are able to do it.

able **abler, ablest**

ADJECTIVE If you are **able** to do something, you can do it.

aboard

PREPOSITION If you are **aboard** a ship or plane, you are on or in it.

about

ADVERB **1** You say **about** in front of a number to show it is not exact. *I'll be home at about five o'clock.*

PREPOSITION **2** If you talk or write **about** something, you say things to do with that subject. *He is talking about boats.*

above

PREPOSITION If something is **above** something else, it is over it, or higher up.

abroad

ADVERB When you go **abroad**, you go to a different country.

absent

ADJECTIVE If someone is **absent**, they are not here.

absolutely

ADVERB You can use **absolutely** to make what you are saying sound stronger. *You must stay absolutely still.*

absorb **absorbs, absorbing, absorbed**

VERB If something **absorbs** a liquid, it soaks it up or takes it in.

absurd

ADJECTIVE Something that is **absurd** seems silly, because it is quite different from what you would expect. *It's absurd to wear your jumper in this heat.*

abuse

NOUN **Abuse** is cruel treatment of someone.

accelerate **accelerates, accelerating, accelerated**

VERB When someone **accelerates**, they speed up.

accept **accepts, accepting, accepted**

VERB If you **accept** something you have been offered, you say yes to it.

accident **accidents**

NOUN An **accident** is something nasty that happens by chance. *He broke his leg in a climbing accident.*

accidentally ADVERB

account accounts

NOUN **1** An **account** is something written or spoken that tells you what has happened.
NOUN **2** An **account** is also money that you keep at a bank.

accurate

ADJECTIVE An **accurate** measurement or description is exactly right.

ache aches

NOUN An **ache** is a dull, lasting pain.

achieve achieves, achieving, achieved

VERB If you **achieve** something, you usually get it by hard work.
achievement NOUN

acid acids

NOUN Some **acids** give food a sharp, sour taste. Lemons and vinegar contain acid. Strong acid can burn your skin.

acid rain

NOUN **Acid rain** is rain that is mixed with dirty gases in the air. It can damage buildings, trees and fish.

acorn acorns

NOUN An **acorn** is a nut. Acorns grow on oak trees.

acrobat acrobats

NOUN An **acrobat** is someone who does difficult and exciting tricks, like balancing on a high wire.

across

PREPOSITION If you go **across** something, you go from one side to the other.

act acts, acting, acted

VERB **1** When you **act**, you do something. *He had to act quickly to put out the fire.*
VERB **2** If you **act** in a play or film, you have a part in it.
NOUN **3** An **act** is something that you do.

action actions

NOUN An **action** is a movement of part of your body.

active

ADJECTIVE **1** Someone who is **active** moves about a lot, or is very busy.
ADJECTIVE **2** In grammar, a verb in the **active** voice is one where the subject does the action, rather than having it done to them. See **voice**.

activity activities

NOUN **Activity** is when there are a lot of things happening.

actor actors

NOUN An **actor** is a man or woman whose job is to act in plays or films.

actress actresses

NOUN A female actor is sometimes called an **actress**. See **actor**.

actual

ADJECTIVE You describe something as **actual** when you mean it is real. *The shop said the paint was red, but the actual colour was pink.*
actually ADVERB

adapt adapts, adapting, adapted

VERB **1** If you **adapt** to something new, you change in some way that helps you.
VERB **2** If you **adapt** something, you change it to suit your needs. *The book was adapted to make a film.*

adaptable

ADJECTIVE Someone who is **adaptable** can change to deal with new situations.

add adds, adding, added

VERB **1** If you **add** something, you put it with whatever you have already. *Put flour in the bowl and add an egg.*
VERB **2** If you **add** numbers of things together, you find out how many you have. The sign + means add. *I have two marbles in the bag. If I add these three, it makes five altogether.* 2 + 3 = 5

addition

NOUN **Addition** is adding numbers or things together.

address

b
c
d
e
f
g
h
i
j
k
l
m
n
o
p
q
r
s
t
u
v
w
x
y
z

address addresses

NOUN Your **address** is the name or number of your house, and the street and town where you live.

Sunday 26th March

Dear Kids,
Today we climbed to the top of this canyon, and then down again. Grandad is asleep now. It is very hot. Hope you are all well.
Lots of Love
Grandma

Becci, Joe, Tom and Dan
4 Fore Street
Porthleven
Cornwall
U.K.

KINGS CANYON, WATARRKA NATIONAL PARK, NORTHERN TERRITORY AUSTRALIA

adjective adjectives

NOUN An **adjective** is a word that describes someone or something. "Beautiful" and "green" are adjectives. *See Adjective on page 263.*

admire admires, admiring, admired

VERB **1** When you **admire** someone, you think very highly of them.
VERB **2** When you **admire** something, you enjoy looking at it. *They stopped the car to admire the view.*

admit admits, admitting, admitted

VERB **1** If you **admit** something, you agree that it is true.
VERB **2** If people are **admitted** to a place, they are allowed to go in.

adopt adopts, adopting, adopted

VERB If a person **adopts** a child, they make the child their own by law.

adore adores, adoring, adored

VERB If you **adore** someone, you love them very much.

adult adults

NOUN An **adult** is a grown-up person or animal.

advance advances, advancing, advanced

VERB If someone **advances**, they move forward. *The army advanced nine miles in one day.*

advantage advantages

NOUN An **advantage** is something that helps you do better than other people. *His long legs gave him an advantage in the race.*

adventure adventures

NOUN If you are having an **adventure**, you are doing something exciting.

adverb adverbs

NOUN An **adverb** is a word that answers questions like how, when, where and why. In the sentence "The girl came quietly into the room", the word "quietly" is an adverb telling you how the girl came in.
See Adverb on page 263.

advertise advertises, advertising, advertised

VERB If you **advertise** something, you tell people about it through newspapers, posters or TV.

advertisement advertisements

NOUN An **advertisement** is a notice in the paper, or on a poster or TV, about a job or things for sale.

advice

NOUN If you give someone **advice**, you say what you think they should do.

advise advises, advising, advised

VERB When you **advise** someone, you tell them what you think they should do.

aerial aerials

NOUN An **aerial** is a wire that sends or receives radio or television signals.

aeroplane aeroplanes

NOUN An **aeroplane** is a flying vehicle with wings and one or more engines.

blindfold **blindfolds**

NOUN A **blindfold** is a strip of cloth tied over someone's eyes so that they cannot see.

blink **blinks, blinking, blinked**

VERB When you **blink**, you shut your eyes and open them again quickly.

blister **blisters**

NOUN A **blister** is a small bubble on your skin, containing watery liquid. Blisters are caused by a burn or rubbing.

blizzard **blizzards**

NOUN A **blizzard** is a bad snowstorm with strong winds.

block **blocks, blocking, blocked**

NOUN **1** A **block** of flats or offices is a large tall building.

NOUN **2** A **block** of something like stone or wood is a large rectangular piece of it.

VERB **3** To **block** means to get in the way.

block graph **block graphs**

NOUN A **block graph** is used to show information clearly, by using blocks to make columns.

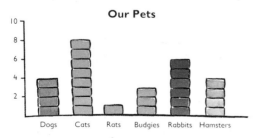

blood

NOUN **Blood** is the red liquid that your heart pumps round inside your body.

bloom **blooms, blooming, bloomed**

VERB When a plant **blooms**, its flowers open.

blossom

NOUN **Blossom** is the flowers that appear on a tree before the fruit.

blot **blots**

NOUN A **blot** is a mark made by a drop of liquid, especially ink.

blouse **blouses**

NOUN A **blouse** is a kind of shirt worn by a girl or a woman.

blow **blows, blowing, blew, blown**

VERB **1** When the wind **blows**, the air moves faster.

VERB **2** If you **blow**, you send out a stream of air from your mouth.

NOUN **3** A **blow** is a hard hit.

blue **bluer, bluest**

ADJECTIVE Something that is **blue** is the colour of the sky on a sunny day. *See* **Colours** *on page 271.*

bluebell **bluebells**

NOUN A **bluebell** is a flower that often grows wild in woods in Europe.

blunt **blunter, bluntest**

ADJECTIVE **1** A **blunt** knife is not sharp.

ADJECTIVE **2** Something that is **blunt** has a rounded, rather than pointed, end. *My pencil's **blunt**.*

blur **blurs**

NOUN A **blur** is a shape that you cannot see clearly. *The car went past so fast it was just a **blur**.*

blurred ADJECTIVE   **blurry** ADJECTIVE

blurb **blurbs**

NOUN A **blurb** is a short piece written to attract people's interest. There is usually a blurb on the back of a book. *The **blurb** says this book is exciting.*

a
Bb
c
d
e
f
g
h
i
j
k
l
m
n
o
p
q
r
s
t
u
v
w
x
y
z

blush blushes, blushing, blushed
VERB When you **blush** you become red in the face, usually because you are embarrassed.

boar boars
NOUN A **boar** is a male pig.

board boards
NOUN A **board** is a flat, thin piece of wood.

boast boasts, boasting, boasted
VERB If you **boast**, you talk too proudly about something.

boat boats
NOUN A **boat** is a small vessel for travelling on water. See **ship**.

body bodies
NOUN 1 Your **body** is every part of you. Some animals, like elephants, have very large bodies.
See **Your body** on page 258.
NOUN 2 You can say **body** when you mean just the main part of a person, not counting head, arms and legs.
NOUN 3 A **body** is a dead person.

bog bogs
NOUN A **bog** is an area of land that is always wet and spongy.

boil boils, boiling, boiled
VERB 1 When liquid **boils** it gets very hot. It bubbles and steam rises from it.
VERB 2 If you **boil** food, you cook it in boiling water.
NOUN 3 A **boil** is a painful red swelling on the skin.

bold bolder, boldest
ADJECTIVE 1 Someone who is **bold** is not afraid of risk or danger.
ADJECTIVE 2 Letters that are in **bold** type are thicker than ordinary printed letters.

bolt bolts, bolting, bolted
NOUN 1 A **bolt** is a long round metal pin with a flat end. It screws into a nut to fasten things.

NOUN 2 A **bolt** is a metal bar that you can slide across to keep a door shut.
VERB 3 If you **bolt** a door or window, you lock it with a bolt.
VERB 4 When a person or animal **bolts**, they suddenly run very fast.

bomb bombs
NOUN A **bomb** is a weapon which explodes and damages a large area.

bone bones
NOUN Your **bones** are the hard parts inside your body which make up your skeleton.

bonfire bonfires
NOUN A **bonfire** is a fire lit outdoors, usually to burn garden rubbish.

bonnet bonnets
NOUN 1 A **bonnet** is the metal cover over a car's engine.
NOUN 2 A **bonnet** is also a baby's or woman's hat tied under the chin.

book books, booking, booked
NOUN 1 A **book** is a number of pages held together inside a cover.
VERB 2 If you **book** something, you ask someone to keep it for you. *We booked seats at the cinema.*

boot boots
NOUN 1 Boots are strong shoes that cover your ankle and sometimes your calf.
NOUN 2 The **boot** of a car is a space for luggage.

border borders
NOUN 1 A **border** is the line dividing two countries.
NOUN 2 A **border** is a strip along the edge of something, usually as a decoration.

bore bores, boring, bored
VERB 1 If somebody **bores** you, you do not find them interesting.
VERB 2 If you **bore** a hole in something, you make a hole with a drill.
VERB 3 Bore is the past tense of **bear**.

bored

ADJECTIVE When you are **bored**, you feel tired and impatient because you have nothing interesting to do.

boredom NOUN

boring

ADJECTIVE Something **boring** is so dull that you have no interest in it.

born

VERB When a baby is **born**, it comes out of its mother's body.

borrow **borrows, borrowing, borrowed**

VERB When you **borrow** something, someone lets you have it for a while but they expect you to give it back later.

boss **bosses**

NOUN Someone's **boss** is the head of the place where they work.

bossy

ADJECTIVE A **bossy** person likes to tell others what to do.

both

ADJECTIVE OR PRONOUN You use **both** when you are talking about two things or people. *She wanted **both** pairs of jeans.*

bother **bothers, bothering, bothered**

VERB **1** If something **bothers** you, it annoys you or makes you feel worried.

VERB **2** If you **bother** about something, you care about it and take trouble over it.

bottle **bottles**

NOUN A **bottle** is a container for keeping liquids in. Bottles are usually made of glass or plastic.

bottom **bottoms**

NOUN **1** The **bottom** of something is the lowest part of it.

NOUN **2** Your **bottom** is the part of your body that you sit on.

bought

VERB **Bought** is the past tense of **buy**.

boulder **boulders**

NOUN A **boulder** is a big rounded rock.

bounce **bounces, bouncing, bounced**

VERB When something **bounces**, it springs back in the opposite direction as soon as it hits something hard.

bound **bounds, bounding, bounded**

VERB **1** When animals or people **bound**, they move quickly with large leaps.

ADJECTIVE **2** If something is **bound to** happen, it is sure to happen.

boundary **boundaries**

NOUN The **boundary** of an area of land is its outer limit.

bow **bows, bowing, bowed**

(*rhymes with* **low**)

NOUN **1** A **bow** is a kind of knot with two loops used to tie laces and ribbons.

NOUN **2** A **bow** is also a weapon used for shooting arrows.

NOUN **3** The **bow** for a stringed musical instrument is a long piece of wood with horsehair stretched along it.

(*rhymes with* **now**) VERB **4** When you **bow**, you bend your body forward.

bowl **bowls**

NOUN A **bowl** is an open container used for holding liquid or serving food.

box **boxes**

NOUN A **box** is a container with straight sides, made from something stiff, like cardboard, wood or plastic.

boy **boys**

NOUN A **boy** is a male child.

bracelet **bracelets**

NOUN A **bracelet** is a band or chain which is worn round the wrist or arm as an ornament.

bracket **brackets**

NOUN **Brackets** are a pair of written marks ( ) placed round words that are not part of the main text.
See Punctuation on page 264.

Braille

NOUN **Braille** is a form of writing using raised dots that blind people can read by touching the dots with their fingers.

brain **brains**

NOUN Your **brain** is inside your head and controls your whole body. It lets you think, feel and remember.

brainstorm **brainstorms, brainstorming, brainstormed**

VERB When people **brainstorm**, they get together to develop ideas. *This morning we are* **brainstorming** *words about dogs.*

brake **brakes**

NOUN The **brake** is the part of a vehicle that slows it down or stops it.

bramble **brambles**

NOUN A **bramble** is a wild bush with thorns. The fruit are called blackberries.

branch **branches**

NOUN A **branch** is part of a tree that grows out from the trunk.

brass

NOUN **Brass** is a yellow metal made from copper and zinc. It is used for making things like ornaments and some musical instruments.

brave **braver, bravest**

ADJECTIVE If you are **brave**, you show you can do something even if it is frightening.
bravely ADVERB   **bravery** NOUN

bread

NOUN **Bread** is a very common food, made with flour and baked in an oven.

breadth

NOUN The **breadth** of something is the distance that it measures from one side to the other.

break **breaks, breaking, broke, broken**

VERB **1** If you **break** something, it splits into pieces or stops working.
VERB **2** If you **break** a rule or a promise, you fail to keep it.

breakdown **breakdowns**

NOUN If someone's car has a **breakdown**, it stops working during a journey.

breakfast **breakfasts**

NOUN **Breakfast** is the first meal of the day.

breast **breasts**

NOUN **Breasts** are the two round parts on the front of a woman's body, which can produce milk to feed a baby.

breath

NOUN Your **breath** is the air that you take into and let out of your lungs.

breathe **breathes, breathing, breathed**

VERB When you **breathe**, you take air into your lungs through your nose or mouth, and then let it out again.

breed **breeds**

NOUN A **breed** of an animal is a particular kind. For example, a labrador is a breed of dog.

breeze **breezes**

NOUN A **breeze** is a gentle wind.

brick **bricks**

NOUN A **brick** is a block used for building. It is made of baked clay.

bride **brides**

NOUN A **bride** is a woman on or near her wedding day.

bridegroom bridegrooms

NOUN A **bridegroom** is a man on or near his wedding day.

bridesmaid bridesmaids

NOUN A **bridesmaid** is a woman or girl who helps a bride on her wedding day.

bridge bridges

NOUN A **bridge** is something built over things like rivers, railways or roads, so that people or vehicles can get across.

brief briefer, briefest

ADJECTIVE Something that is **brief** lasts only a short time.
briefly ADVERB

briefcase briefcases

NOUN A **briefcase** is a flat case used for carrying papers.

bright brighter, brightest

ADJECTIVE **1** Bright colours are clear and easy to see.
ADJECTIVE **2** A light that is **bright** shines strongly.
ADJECTIVE **3** Someone who is **bright** is quick at learning or noticing things.

brilliant

ADJECTIVE **1** A **brilliant** colour or light is extremely bright.
ADJECTIVE **2** Someone who is **brilliant** is extremely clever or skilful.

brim brims

NOUN **1** If you fill a cup to the **brim**, you fill it right up to the top.
NOUN **2** The **brim** of a hat is the part that sticks outwards from the head.

bring brings, bringing, brought

VERB **1** If you **bring** someone on a visit, they come with you.
VERB **2** If you **bring** something, you have it with you when you arrive.

bristle bristles

NOUN The **bristles** of a brush are the thick hairs or thin pieces of plastic which are fixed to the main part of it.

brittle

ADJECTIVE If something is **brittle**, it is hard but easily broken.

broad broader, broadest

ADJECTIVE Something such as a road or river that is **broad** is very wide.

broadcast broadcasts

NOUN A **broadcast** is a programme or announcement on radio or television.

broke

VERB Broke is the past tense of **break**.

broken

VERB Broken is the past participle of **break**.

brooch brooches

NOUN A **brooch** is a small piece of jewellery which is worn pinned to a dress, blouse or coat.

broom brooms

NOUN A **broom** is a kind of brush with a long handle.

brother brothers

NOUN Someone's **brother** is a boy or man who has the same parents as they have.

brought

VERB Brought is the past tense of **bring**.

brown browner, brownest

ADJECTIVE Something that is **brown** is the colour of earth or of wood.
See *Colours* on page 271.

bruise bruises

NOUN A **bruise** is a purple mark on your skin where something has hit it.

a
Bb
c
d
e
f
g
h
i
j
k
l
m
n
o
p
q
r
s
t
u
v
w
x
y

brush

brush brushes

NOUN A **brush** is a lot of bristles fixed to a handle. Different brushes are used for jobs like cleaning your teeth or painting.

bubble bubbles

NOUN A **bubble** is a ball of air or gas. You can make bubbles with soapy water. Fizzy lemonade has bubbles, too.

bucket buckets

NOUN A **bucket** is a container with a handle, often used for carrying water.

buckle buckles

NOUN A **buckle** is a fastening on the end of a belt or strap.

bud buds

NOUN A **bud** is a small lump on a plant which will open into a leaf or flower.

Buddhist Buddhists

NOUN A **Buddhist** is someone who follows the teachings of Buddha.

budgerigar budgerigars

NOUN Budgerigars are small brightly-coloured birds, often kept as pets.

buffalo buffaloes

NOUN A **buffalo** is an animal like a large cow with long curved horns.

bug bugs

NOUN 1 A **bug** is an insect.
NOUN 2 A **bug** is also an illness, such as a flu bug or a stomach bug.

build builds, building, built

VERB If you **build** something, you make it by joining things together.

builder builders

NOUN A **builder** is a person whose job is to build houses and other buildings.

building buildings

NOUN A **building** is a place like a house that has walls and a roof.

bulb bulbs

NOUN 1 A **bulb** is the glass part of a lamp that gives out light.
NOUN 2 A **bulb** is also a root shaped like an onion. Many spring flowers such as daffodils and tulips grow from bulbs.

bulge bulges, bulging, bulged

VERB If something **bulges**, it sticks out in a lump. *His pockets **bulged** with conkers.*

bull bulls

NOUN A **bull** is a male cow, elephant or whale.

bulldozer bulldozers

NOUN A **bulldozer** is a tractor with a steel blade on the front. It is used for moving large amounts of earth or stone.

bullet bullets

NOUN 1 A **bullet** is a small piece of metal fired from a gun.
NOUN 2 A **bullet point** is a heavy dot used to draw attention to a piece of text.

bully bullies

NOUN A **bully** is someone who hurts or frightens other people.

bump bumps, bumping, bumped

VERB 1 If you **bump** into something, you hit it while you are moving.
NOUN 2 If you hear a **bump**, it sounds like something falling to the ground.
NOUN 3 A **bump** is a raised uneven part on a surface such as a road.

bumper bumpers

NOUN Bumpers are bars on the front and back of a vehicle that protect it if there is an accident.

bun buns

NOUN A **bun** is a small round cake.

bunch bunches

NOUN A **bunch** is a group of things together, like flowers or grapes. *See Collective nouns on page 262.*

bundle bundles

NOUN A **bundle** is a number of small things that have been tied together.

bungalow bungalows

NOUN A **bungalow** is a house with all its rooms on one floor.

bunk beds

NOUN **Bunk beds** are two single beds fixed one above the other.

burger burgers

NOUN A **burger** is a flat piece of minced meat. It is often eaten in a bread roll.

burglar burglars

NOUN A **burglar** is someone who breaks into buildings to steal things.

burn burns, burning, burned or burnt

VERB **1** If something is **burning**, it is being spoiled or destroyed by fire.

VERB **2** People often **burn** fuel, such as coal, to keep warm.

NOUN **3** A **burn** is an injury caused by heat or fire.

burrow burrows

NOUN A **burrow** is a hole in the ground that an animal lives in.

burst bursts, bursting, burst

VERB When something like a balloon or tyre **bursts**, it splits open suddenly.

bury buries, burying, buried

VERB If you **bury** something, you put it in a hole in the ground and cover it.

bus buses

NOUN A **bus** is a large motor vehicle. People pay to go on buses.

bush bushes

NOUN A **bush** is a large woody plant with lots of branches. It is smaller than a tree.

business businesses

NOUN **1** **Business** is the work of making, buying and selling things or services.

NOUN **2** A **business** is a group of people who make and sell things.

bus stop bus stops

NOUN A **bus stop** is a place where people can get on or off buses.

busy busier, busiest

ADJECTIVE **1** When you are **busy**, you are working hard on something.

ADJECTIVE **2** A place that is **busy** is full of people doing things or moving about.

but

CONJUNCTION You use **but** to join two parts of a sentence when the second part is unexpected. *Megan likes most green vegetables,* **but** *she won't eat broccoli.*

butcher butchers

NOUN A **butcher** is a shopkeeper who cuts up meat and sells it.

butter

NOUN **Butter** is a yellow fat made from cream. You spread it on bread or use it for cooking.

butterfly butterflies

NOUN A **butterfly** is an insect with four large wings which flies during the day. See *Insects* on page 259.

button buttons

NOUN **1** A **button** is a small disc used to fasten clothes.

NOUN **2** A **button** is also a part of a machine that you press to make it work.

buy buys, buying, bought

VERB When you **buy** something, you get it by paying money for it.

buzz buzzes, buzzing, buzzed

VERB If something **buzzes**, it makes a "zzz" sound like a bee.

a
Bb
c
d
e
f
g
h
i
j
k
l
m
n
o
p
q
r
s
t
u
v
w
x
y
z

a
b
Cc
d
e
f
g
h
i
j
k
l
m
n
o
p
q
r
s
t
u
v
w
x
y
z

Cc

cab cabs
NOUN **1** The **cab** is the place where the driver sits in a bus, truck or train.
NOUN **2** A **cab** is another word for a taxi.

cabbage cabbages
NOUN A **cabbage** is a vegetable that looks like a large ball of leaves.
See *Vegetables* on page 256.

cabin cabins
NOUN **1** A **cabin** is a room in a ship, boat or aeroplane for passengers or crew.
NOUN **2** A **cabin** is also a small house in a wild place such as a forest.

cable cables
NOUN **1** A **cable** is a thick rope or chain.
NOUN **2** A **cable** is also a bundle of wires with a rubber covering, which carries electricity.
NOUN **3 Cable television** is a system in which the signals are sent along wires.

cactus cactuses
or **cacti**
NOUN A **cactus** is a plant with spines. It can grow in hot, dry places like deserts.

café cafés
NOUN A **café** is a place with tables and chairs where you buy drinks and snacks.

cage cages
NOUN A **cage** is a box or room with bars in which birds or animals are kept.

cake cakes
NOUN A **cake** is a sweet food made with flour, sugar, fat and eggs, and baked in an oven.

calculate calculates, calculating, calculated
VERB If you **calculate** something in maths, you work it out.

calculation calculations
NOUN A **calculation** is something you work out in maths.

calculator calculators
NOUN A **calculator** is a small electronic machine which you can use to give you the answer to different calculations.

calendar calendars
NOUN A **calendar** is a list of the months, weeks and days in a year.

calf calves
NOUN **1 Calves** are young cows, elephants and whales.
See *Young animals* on page 260.
NOUN **2** Your **calf** is the part at the back of your leg between the knee and ankle.

call calls, calling, called
VERB **1** If you **call** someone, you shout for them, or telephone them.
VERB **2** If you **call** someone something, you give them a name.
VERB **3** If an animal or thing is **called** something, that is their name.

calm calmer, calmest
ADJECTIVE **1** If you are **calm**, you do not seem worried or excited.
ADJECTIVE **2** If the sea is **calm**, it is smooth and still because there is no wind.

came
VERB **Came** is the past tense of **come**.

camel camels
NOUN A **camel** is a large animal which carries people and things in the desert.

camera cameras
NOUN A **camera** is a piece of equipment you use to take pictures.

camouflage camouflages, camouflaging, camouflaged

VERB To **camouflage** something is to hide it by giving it the same colour or appearance as its surroundings.

camp camps

NOUN A **camp** is a place where people stay in tents.

can could; cans

VERB **1** If you **can** do something, you are able to do it. *I can swim.*

NOUN **2** A **can** is a metal container for something like food, drink or paint.

canal canals

NOUN A **canal** is a narrow stretch of water made for boats to travel along.

cancel cancels, cancelling, cancelled

VERB If you **cancel** something that has been planned, you stop it from happening.

candle candles

NOUN A **candle** is a wax stick with a string called a wick inside. You light the wick and it burns to give light.

cane canes

NOUN **1** A **cane** is the long hollow stem of a plant such as bamboo.

NOUN **2** A **cane** is a tall narrow stick used to support things.

cannot

VERB **Cannot** is the same as **can not**.

canoe canoes

NOUN A **canoe** is a small light boat, moved with a paddle.

can't

VERB **Can't** is a contraction of **cannot**.

canvas

NOUN **Canvas** is strong cloth, used for making things like tents and sails.

canyon canyons

NOUN A **canyon** is a narrow valley with very steep sides, often with a river.

cap caps

NOUN **1** A **cap** is a soft flat hat with a peak at the front.

NOUN **2** A **cap** is also a small flat lid on a bottle or container.

capable

ADJECTIVE If a person is **capable** of doing something, they are able to do it. *He's capable of doing better.*

capacity capacities

NOUN The **capacity** of something is the largest amount it can hold, produce or carry. *The capacity of this jug is one litre.*

capital capitals

NOUN **1** The **capital** is the main city in a country. *Paris is the capital of France.*

NOUN **2** A **capital** is a big letter of the alphabet, such as A, B and C. Capital letters are also called upper-case letters. See **lower-case**.

See *Punctuation* on page 264.

captain captains

NOUN **1** A **captain** is the person in charge of a ship or an aeroplane.

NOUN **2** A **captain** is the person who leads a team in sports like football.

caption captions

NOUN A **caption** is the words printed underneath a picture which explain what the picture is about.

capture captures, capturing, captured

VERB If you **capture** somebody, you take them prisoner.

car cars

NOUN A **car** is a road vehicle with wheels and an engine. It needs a driver and has room for passengers.

a b **Cc** d e f g h i j k l m n o p q r s t u v w x y z

caravan

caravan **caravans**
NOUN A **caravan** is a vehicle pulled by a car in which people live or spend their holidays.

card **cards**
NOUN **1** Card is strong, stiff paper.
NOUN **2** A greetings **card** usually has a picture on the front and is sent to people on special days such as birthdays.
NOUN **3** Playing **cards** are small pieces of card with numbers or pictures on them. They are used for card games.

cardboard
NOUN Cardboard is thick, stiff paper.

cardigan **cardigans**
NOUN A **cardigan** is a knitted jacket. You fasten it at the front with buttons.

care **cares, caring, cared**
VERB **1** If you **care** about something or someone, you think they are important.
VERB **2** If you **care** for a person or animal, you look after them.
NOUN **3** If you do something with **care**, you take trouble over it.

career **careers**
NOUN Someone's **career** is the work they do, which they hope to do for a long time. *John wants a **career** in teaching.*

careful
ADJECTIVE If someone is **careful**, they try to do things safely and well.

careless
ADJECTIVE If you are **careless**, you do not pay attention to what you are doing.

caretaker **caretakers**
NOUN A **caretaker** is a person who looks after a large building such as a school.

cargo **cargoes**
NOUN Cargo is the goods carried on a ship or plane.

carnival **carnivals**
NOUN A **carnival** is a sort of party in the streets. There is usually music and dancing, and people dress up and decorate cars and trucks.

carpenter **carpenters**
NOUN A **carpenter** is a person who works with wood, usually for furniture.

carpet **carpets**
NOUN A **carpet** is a thick covering for a floor, often made of wool.

carriage **carriages**
NOUN **1** A **carriage** is one of the vehicles that make up a passenger train.
NOUN **2** A **carriage** is also a vehicle with wheels, pulled by horses.

carrot **carrots**
NOUN A **carrot** is a long thin orange vegetable that grows under the ground. *See **Vegetables** on page 256.*

carry **carries, carrying, carried**
VERB When you **carry** something, you pick it up and take it with you.

cart **carts**
NOUN A **cart** is a heavy wooden vehicle pulled by horses or cattle on farms.

carton **cartons**
NOUN A **carton** is a strong cardboard or plastic box for holding food or drink.

cartoon **cartoons**
NOUN **1** A **cartoon** is a film where the characters are drawn instead of being real people.
NOUN **2** A **cartoon** is also a funny drawing in a magazine, newspaper or book.

cartwheel cartwheels

NOUN A **cartwheel** is a movement. You put your hands on the floor and move your legs round in a circle until you land on your feet again.

carve carves, carving, carved

VERB **1** If you **carve** an object, you cut it out of something like stone or wood.
VERB **2** If someone **carves** a piece of meat, they cut slices from it.

case cases

NOUN A **case** is a box for keeping or carrying things in.

cash

NOUN **Cash** is coins and paper money.

cassette cassettes

NOUN A **cassette** is a small flat container with magnetic tape inside, which is used for recording and playing back sounds.

cast casts, casting, cast

NOUN **1** The **cast** of a play or film is all the people who act in it.
NOUN **2** A **cast** is an object made by pouring liquid plaster or metal into a container and leaving it to harden.
VERB **3** If something **casts** a shadow onto a place, it makes a shadow fall there.
VERB **4** If someone like a witch **casts** a spell on someone or something, they do magic that affects that person or thing.

castle castles

NOUN A **castle** is a large building with walls or ditches round it to protect it from attack.

cat cats

NOUN A **cat** is a small furry animal, often kept as a pet. There are also larger, wild cats, such as lions and tigers.

catalogue catalogues

NOUN A **catalogue** is a list of things for sale or for looking at.

catch catches, catching, caught

VERB **1** If you **catch** something, you take hold of it while it is moving.
VERB **2** If you **catch** a bus or train, you get on it to go somewhere.
VERB **3** If you **catch** something like measles, you get that illness.

catching

ADJECTIVE An illness that is **catching** can spread very quickly.

category categories

NOUN A **category** is a set of things with a particular feature or quality in common.

caterpillar caterpillars

NOUN A **caterpillar** is a very small animal like a worm with legs, that will change into a butterfly or moth.

cathedral cathedrals

NOUN A **cathedral** is a large, important church.

cattle

NOUN Bulls and cows are called **cattle**.

caught

VERB **Caught** is the past tense of **catch**.

cauliflower cauliflowers

NOUN A **cauliflower** is a round white vegetable with green leaves on the outside.
See *Vegetables* on page 256.

cause causes, causing, caused

VERB To **cause** something means to make it happen.

cautious

ADJECTIVE Someone who is **cautious** acts carefully to avoid possible danger.

cave

cave caves
NOUN A **cave** is a large hole in the side of a hill or cliff, or under the ground.

CD CDs
NOUN CD is an abbreviation of **compact disc**.

CD-ROM CD-ROMs
NOUN **CD-ROM** is an abbreviation of **compact disc read-only memory**. It is a disc which can be played on a computer to show sounds and pictures.

ceiling ceilings
NOUN The **ceiling** is the inside roof of a room.

celebrate celebrates, celebrating, celebrated
VERB If you **celebrate** something, you do something enjoyable like having a party, to show it is a special occasion.

celery
NOUN **Celery** is a vegetable with long, pale green stalks.
See *Vegetables* on page 256.

cell cells
NOUN **1** Animals and plants are made from tiny parts called **cells**.
NOUN **2** A **cell** is also a small room where a prisoner lives.

cellar cellars
NOUN A **cellar** is a room under a house where you can store things.

Celsius
ADJECTIVE You use degrees **Celsius** to measure temperature. In the Celsius scale, 0 degrees (0°C) is the freezing point of water and 100 degrees (100°C) is its boiling point.

cement
NOUN **Cement** is a grey powder which is mixed with sand and water and used to make bricks stick together.

cemetery cemeteries
NOUN A **cemetery** is a place where dead people are buried.

centigrade
ADJECTIVE **Centigrade** means the same as **Celsius**.

centimetre centimetres
NOUN A **centimetre** (cm) is a measure of length. It is the same as 10 millimetres.

centipede centipedes
NOUN A **centipede** is a tiny animal like a worm, but with lots of legs.

central
ADJECTIVE Something that is **central** is in the middle of an object or an area.

centre centres
NOUN **1** The **centre** of anything is the middle of it.
NOUN **2** A **centre** is a place where people can go for a particular purpose, for example sports.

century centuries
NOUN A **century** is a period of 100 years. The 21st century is the time between 2000 and 2099.

cereal cereals
NOUN **1** Cereal is a plant which has seeds called grain that can be used for food.
NOUN **2** Cereal is also a food made from grain that is often eaten for breakfast.

ceremony ceremonies
NOUN A **ceremony** is a set of formal actions performed at a special occasion such as a wedding.

certain

ADJECTIVE If you are **certain** of something, you are sure it is true.

certificate **certificates**

NOUN A **certificate** is a piece of paper which says that something important like a birth or marriage took place.

chain **chains**

NOUN A **chain** is made from rings of metal joined together in a line.

chair **chairs**

NOUN A **chair** is a seat with a back, for one person.

chalk

NOUN **Chalk** is a soft white rock. It can be made into sticks for writing on blackboards.

champion **champions**

NOUN A **champion** is a person who has beaten everyone else in a contest.

chance **chances**

NOUN 1 If there is a **chance** that something will happen, it might happen.

NOUN 2 If you are given a **chance** to do something, you are allowed to do it if you want to.

by chance PHRASE If something happens **by chance**, it has not been planned.

change **changes, changing, changed**

VERB 1 When something **changes**, it becomes different.

VERB 2 When you **change** your clothes, you put on different ones.

NOUN 3 If there is a **change** in something, it is different in some way.

NOUN 4 **Change** is the money you are given when you pay more than the right amount for something.

channel **channels**

NOUN 1 A **channel** is a passage for water or other liquid.

NOUN 2 Television companies use **channels** to broadcast programmes.

chaos

NOUN **Chaos** is a state of complete confusion, where nothing is organized.

chapter **chapters**

NOUN A **chapter** is a part of a book.

character **characters**

NOUN 1 The **characters** of a book, film or play are the people it is about.

NOUN 2 Someone's **character** is the sort of person they are. *She has a kind character*.

charge **charges, charging, charged**

VERB 1 If someone **charges** you money, they ask you to pay for something.

VERB 2 If something or someone **charges** towards you, they rush forward.

in charge PHRASE If you are **in charge** of something, you are the person looking after it.

charity **charities**

NOUN A **charity** is an organization which raises money for a particular cause, such as people in need.

charm **charms**

NOUN 1 A **charm** is a small ornament that is fixed to a bracelet or necklace.

NOUN 2 A **charm** is also a magical spell or an object that is supposed to bring good luck.

chart **charts**

NOUN 1 A **chart** is a sheet of paper that shows things like dates or numbers.

NOUN 2 A **chart** can also be a map of the sea or of the stars.

chase **chases, chasing, chased**

VERB If you **chase** someone, you run after them to try and catch them.

chat **chats**

NOUN A **chat** is a friendly talk about things that are not very important.

a
b
Cc
d
e
f
g
h
i
j
k
l
m
n
o
p
q
r
s
t
u
v
w
x
y
z

cheap

cheap **cheaper, cheapest**
ADJECTIVE Something **cheap** costs very little, or less than you might expect.

cheat **cheats, cheating, cheated**
VERB When someone **cheats**, they lie or do unfair things to get what they want.

check **checks, checking, checked**
VERB 1 If you **check** something, you make sure it is correct or safe.
NOUN 2 A **check** is a pattern of squares.

checkout **checkouts**
NOUN A **checkout** is the place in a supermarket where you pay.

cheek **cheeks**
NOUN Your **cheeks** are the sides of your face below your eyes.

cheer **cheers, cheering, cheered**
VERB When you **cheer**, you shout to show you are pleased about something or to encourage a person or team.

cheerful
ADJECTIVE Someone who is **cheerful** shows they are feeling happy.

cheese **cheeses**
NOUN **Cheese** is a food made from milk. Some cheeses have a strong flavour.

cheetah **cheetahs**
NOUN A **cheetah** is a large wild animal of the cat family, with black spots.

chemist **chemists**
NOUN 1 A **chemist** is a person who makes up medicine.
NOUN 2 The **chemist** is a shop where you can buy medicine and things like soap and toothpaste.

NOUN 3 A **chemist** can be a scientist trained in chemistry.

chemistry
NOUN **Chemistry** is the scientific study of how substances are made up and how they work together.

cheque **cheques**
NOUN A **cheque** is a piece of paper that people use to pay for things.

cherry **cherries**
NOUN A **cherry** is a small round red or black fruit with a hard seed called a stone in the middle.
See *Fruit* on page 257.

chess
NOUN **Chess** is a game for two people. It is played on a board marked in black and white squares.

chest **chests**
NOUN 1 Your **chest** is the top part of the front of your body, between your neck and your waist.
NOUN 2 A **chest** is a large heavy box, usually made of wood.

chestnut **chestnuts**
NOUN 1 A **chestnut** is a large tree.
NOUN 2 A **chestnut** is also a shiny brown nut that grows on a chestnut tree.

chew **chews, chewing, chewed**
VERB When you **chew** food, you bite it several times.

chick **chicks**
NOUN A **chick** is a baby bird.
See *Young animals* on page 260.

chicken **chickens**
NOUN A **chicken** is a bird kept on a farm for its eggs and meat.

chickenpox
NOUN **Chickenpox** is an illness that gives you itchy spots.

chief chiefs

NOUN A **chief** is a person in charge of other people.

child children

NOUN A **child** is a young boy or girl.

childhood

NOUN A person's **childhood** is the time of life when they are a child.

childish

ADJECTIVE You call a person **childish** if they are not acting in an adult way.

children

PLURAL NOUN **Children** is the plural of **child**.

chilly chillier, chilliest

ADJECTIVE If you feel **chilly**, you are not quite warm enough to be comfortable.

chime chimes

NOUN A **chime** is the musical sound made by a bell or a clock.

chimney chimneys

NOUN A **chimney** is a pipe which takes smoke from a fire up into the air.

chimpanzee chimpanzees

NOUN A **chimpanzee** is a small ape with dark fur that lives in forests in Africa.

chin chins

NOUN Your **chin** is the part of your face below your mouth.

chip chips, chipping, chipped

NOUN **1** A **chip** is a long thin fried piece of potato.

NOUN **2** A silicon **chip** is a tiny piece of special material used in computers.

VERB **3** When you **chip** something, you break a small piece off it.

chisel chisels

NOUN A **chisel** is a tool with a long thin blade and a sharp end, which is used for cutting wood or stone.

chocolate chocolates

NOUN **1** Chocolate is a brown sweet or drink made from cocoa.

NOUN **2** A **chocolate** is a sweet covered with a layer of chocolate.

choice choices

NOUN **1** A **choice** is the different things that you can choose from.

NOUN **2** A **choice** can also be someone or something that you choose. *If you need a captain, Jessica would be a good choice.*

choir choirs

NOUN A **choir** is a group of people who sing together.

choke chokes, choking, choked

VERB If you **choke**, you cannot breathe because not enough air can get to your lungs. *He choked on a chicken bone.*

choose chooses, choosing, chose, chosen

VERB To **choose** something is to decide which thing you want to have or do.

chop chops, chopping, chopped

VERB **1** When someone **chops** something like wood, they cut it with an axe.

NOUN **2** A **chop** is a slice of meat on a bone.

chorus choruses

NOUN A **chorus** is a part of a song which is repeated after each verse.

chose

VERB **Chose** is the past tense of **choose**.

chosen

VERB **Chosen** is the past participle of **choose**.

Christian **Christians**

NOUN A **Christian** is someone who follows the teachings of Jesus Christ.

Christmas **Christmases**

NOUN **Christmas** is a Christian festival held on December 25, when the birth of Jesus Christ is celebrated.

chrysalis **chrysalises**

NOUN A **chrysalis** is a butterfly or moth when it is developing from a caterpillar to a fully grown adult.

chuckle **chuckles, chuckling, chuckled**

VERB When you **chuckle**, you laugh quietly.

church **churches**

NOUN A **church** is a building where Christians worship.

cigarette **cigarettes**

NOUN A **cigarette** is a thin roll of paper with tobacco in, which people smoke.

cinema **cinemas**

NOUN A **cinema** is a place where people watch films.

circle **circles**

NOUN A **circle** is a perfect round shape.
circular ADJECTIVE
See *Colours and flat shapes* on page 271.

circuit **circuits**

NOUN A **circuit** is the complete path that an electric current flows through. You can make a simple circuit with a battery, a bulb and wires.

circumference **circumferences**

NOUN The **circumference** of a circle is the distance around its edge.

circus **circuses**

NOUN A **circus** is a travelling group of people such as clowns and acrobats.

city **cities**

NOUN A **city** is a large busy town.

claim **claims, claiming, claimed**

VERB **1** If someone **claims** something, they ask for it because it is theirs.
VERB **2** If you **claim** something is the case, you say it is the case. *Amy **claims** she was the first to finish.*

clap **claps, clapping, clapped**

VERB When you **clap**, you make a noise by hitting your hands together.

class **classes**

NOUN **1** A **class** is a group of people who are taught together.
NOUN **2** A **class** is also a group of people or things that are alike in some way.

classify **classifies, classifying, classified**

VERB To **classify** things is to arrange them in groups with similar features. *These books are **classified** as non-fiction.*

classroom **classrooms**

NOUN A **classroom** is a room in a school where children have lessons.

clause **clauses**

NOUN In grammar, a **clause** is a group of words with a subject and a verb. It may be a complete sentence or one part of a sentence. For example, "the girl laughed" is a clause because it has a subject (the girl) and a verb (laughed).

claw claws

NOUN The **claws** of a bird or animal are the hard curved nails at the end of its feet.

clay

NOUN **Clay** is a type of sticky earth that goes hard when it is dry. It is used to make bricks and pots.

clean cleaner, cleanest

ADJECTIVE If something is **clean**, it is free from dirt.

clear clearer, clearest; clears, clearing, cleared

ADJECTIVE **1** If a thing is **clear**, you can see through it.

ADJECTIVE **2** If something you say or write is **clear**, it is easy to understand.

VERB **3** If you **clear** an area, you move things that are not wanted out of the way.

clench clenches, clenching, clenched

VERB When you **clench** your fist or teeth, you close them tightly.

clever cleverer, cleverest

ADJECTIVE Someone who is **clever** is able to learn and understand things easily.

click clicks, clicking, clicked

VERB When you **click** something, it makes a short snapping sound.

cliff cliffs

NOUN A **cliff** is a steep hill by the sea.

climate climates

NOUN The **climate** of a place is the sort of weather it usually has.

climb climbs, climbing, climbed

VERB When you **climb** something, you move upwards using your hands and feet.

cling clings, clinging, clung

VERB If you **cling** to someone or something, you hold onto them tightly.

clinic clinics

NOUN A **clinic** is where people go to get help from a doctor or nurse.

clip clips, clipping, clipped

NOUN **1** A **clip** is something small and springy which holds things in place.

VERB **2** If you **clip** something like a hedge, you cut small pieces off it.

cloak cloaks

NOUN A **cloak** is a loose coat without sleeves that fastens at the neck.

cloakroom cloakrooms

NOUN A **cloakroom** is a room where coats can be left.

clock clocks

NOUN A **clock** is an instrument that measures and shows the time.

clockwise

ADVERB If something goes **clockwise**, it moves in the same direction as the hands on a clock.

clockwork

ADJECTIVE **Clockwork** toys move when they are wound up with a key.

close closer, closest; closes, closing, closed

(*rhymes with* **dose**) ADJECTIVE **1** If something is **close**, it is very near.

(*rhymes with* **doze**) VERB **2** When you **close** something like a door, you shut it.

a
b
Cc
d
e
f
g
h
i
j
k
l
m
n
o
p
q
r
s
t
u
v
w
x
y
z

closed
ADJECTIVE If something is **closed**, it is not open.

cloth **cloths**
NOUN **1** Cloth is material made from something like cotton or wool.
NOUN **2** A **cloth** is a piece of cloth used for cleaning.

clothes
PLURAL NOUN **Clothes** are the things people wear, such as shirts, trousers and dresses.

cloud **clouds**
NOUN **1** A **cloud** is a patch of white or grey mist that floats in the sky.
NOUN **2** You can use **cloud** to describe a lot of smoke, steam or dust.
cloudy ADJECTIVE

clover
NOUN **Clover** is a small wild plant. It has white or purple flowers, and leaves divided into three parts.

clown **clowns**
NOUN A **clown** is someone in a circus who wears funny clothes and does silly things to make people laugh.

club **clubs**
NOUN A **club** is an organization joined by people who are interested in the same thing, such as chess or riding.

clue **clues**
NOUN A **clue** is something that helps to solve a problem or mystery.

clump **clumps**
NOUN A **clump** is a small group of plants growing together.

clumsy **clumsier, clumsiest**
ADJECTIVE Someone who is **clumsy** moves awkwardly and carelessly.
clumsily ADVERB

clung
VERB **Clung** is the past tense of **cling**.

cluster **clusters**
NOUN A **cluster** is a number of things close together in a small group.

clutch **clutches, clutching, clutched**
VERB **1** If you **clutch** something, you hold it tightly with your hand.
NOUN **2** A **clutch** is a group of eggs laid by a bird.
See **Collective nouns** on page 262.

clutter
NOUN **Clutter** is an untidy mess.

co-
PREFIX Co- means together. For example, "coeducation" is boys and girls being taught together.
See **Prefixes** on page 264.

coach **coaches**
NOUN **1** A **coach** is a long motor vehicle used for taking passengers on long journeys.
NOUN **2** A **coach** is also a section of a train that carries passengers.
NOUN **3** A **coach** is someone who trains you for a sport or gives you extra lessons.

coal
NOUN **Coal** is a hard black rock which is dug out of the ground and burned to give heat.

coarse **coarser, coarsest**
ADJECTIVE Anything that is **coarse** looks and feels rough.

coast **coasts**
NOUN The **coast** is the place where the land meets the sea.

coat **coats**
NOUN **1** A **coat** is a piece of clothing with long sleeves, that you wear over other clothes when you go out.
NOUN **2** An animal's **coat** is its fur.
NOUN **3** A layer of paint is called a **coat**.

cobweb **cobwebs**
NOUN A **cobweb** is a net made by a spider to trap insects.

cock **cocks**

NOUN A **cock** is any male bird.

cocoa

NOUN **Cocoa** is a brown powder made from the seeds of the cacao tree, and also a hot drink made from this powder.

coconut **coconuts**

NOUN A **coconut** is a large nut with white flesh, milky juice, and a hard hairy shell.

cocoon **cocoons**

NOUN A **cocoon** is a covering of silky threads that some young insects make for themselves before they grow into adults.

cod

NOUN A **cod** is a large sea fish which is caught for food.

code **codes**

NOUN 1 A **code** is a system of changing letters in a message for other letters or symbols, so that only people who know the code can read it.
NOUN 2 A **code** is also a group of letters and numbers that identify something. *Do you know the telephone **code** for York?*
NOUN 3 A **code** is also a set of rules.

coffee

NOUN **Coffee** is a coarse powder made by grinding roasted coffee beans, and also a hot drink made from this powder.

cog **cogs**

NOUN A **cog** is a wheel with teeth which turns another part of a machine.

coil **coils**

NOUN A **coil** is a series of loops into which something has been wound.

coin **coins**

NOUN A **coin** is a small piece of metal used as money.

cold **colder, coldest; colds**

ADJECTIVE 1 If the weather is **cold**, the temperature outside is low.
NOUN 2 A **cold** is a common illness. You sneeze and your nose feels blocked.

collage **collages**

NOUN A **collage** is a picture made by sticking pieces of paper or cloth onto a surface.

collapse **collapses, collapsing, collapsed**

VERB If someone or something **collapses**, they suddenly fall down.

collar **collars**

NOUN 1 The **collar** of a shirt or jacket is the part that fits round your neck.
NOUN 2 A **collar** is also a leather band round the neck of a dog or cat.

collect **collects, collecting, collected**

VERB 1 If you **collect** a number of things, you bring them together for a special reason. *She **collected** sticks for firewood.*
VERB 2 If you **collect** someone or something from a place, you call there and take them away. *We had to **collect** her from school.*

collection **collections**

NOUN A **collection** is a group of things brought together over a period of time. *My dad's got a huge stamp **collection**.*

collective noun **collective nouns**

NOUN In grammar, a **collective noun** refers to a group of things. For example, a group of sheep is called a "flock". *See Collective nouns on page 262.*

college **colleges**

NOUN A **college** is where people go to study after they have left school.

collide **collides, colliding, collided**
VERB If a moving object **collides** with something, it hits it.
collision NOUN

colon **colons**
NOUN The punctuation mark : is a **colon**. You can use it in several ways, for example in front of a list of things. See *Punctuation* on page 264.

colour **colours**
NOUN The **colour** of something is the way it looks in daylight. *The colour of grass is green.*
See *Colours* on page 271.

colt **colts**
NOUN A **colt** is a young male horse.

column **columns**
NOUN **1** A **column** is a tall stone post which supports part of a building.

NOUN **2** A **column** is also a vertical strip of print in a newspaper or magazine.
NOUN **3** If numbers are arranged in vertical lists, these are called **columns**.

comb **combs**
NOUN A **comb** is a flat piece of plastic or metal with narrow teeth on one edge. You use it to tidy your hair.

come **comes, coming, came, come**
VERB **1** To **come** to a place is to move there or arrive there.
VERB **2** If you **come** from a place, you were born there, or it is your home.

comedy **comedies**
NOUN A **comedy** is a play or film that makes people laugh.

comet **comets**
NOUN A **comet** is an object which travels around the sun, leaving a long bright trail behind it.

comfort **comforts, comforting, comforted**
VERB If you **comfort** someone, you make them feel less worried or unhappy.

comfortable
ADJECTIVE If something is **comfortable**, it is easy to wear or use.

comic **comics**
NOUN A **comic** is a magazine that tells stories in pictures.

comma **commas**
NOUN A **comma** is a punctuation mark (,) which is used to separate parts of a sentence or items on a list.
See *Punctuation* on page 264.

command **commands, commanding, commanded**
VERB If you **command** someone to do something, you order them to do it.

commercial **commercials**
NOUN A **commercial** is an advertisement on television or radio.

common
ADJECTIVE If something is **common**, you often see it or it often happens.

common noun **common nouns**
NOUN **Common nouns** name things in general. For example, "boy", "dog" and "computer" are all common nouns.
See *Noun* on page 262.

common sense
NOUN If you have **common sense**, you usually act sensibly and do the right thing.

commotion

NOUN A **commotion** is a lot of noise, confusion and excitement.

communicate communicates, communicating, communicated

VERB If you **communicate** with someone, you give them information by talking or writing to them.

compact disc compact discs

NOUN A **compact disc** is a round flat silver-coloured object which can store information. It is called a **CD** for short.

company companies

NOUN **1 Company** is being with others so you are not lonely.

NOUN **2** A **company** is a group of people who work together to make or sell things.

comparative comparatives

NOUN In grammar, the **comparative** is the form of an adjective which has "more" of that adjective. For example, "happier" is the comparative of "happy".

See *Adjective* on page 263.

compare compares, comparing, compared

VERB When you **compare** two or more things, you look at them to see in what ways they are the same or different.

compass compasses

NOUN **1** A **compass** is an instrument with a needle that always points to north.

NOUN **2** A **pair of compasses** is an instrument used for drawing circles.

compass point compass points

NOUN The main **compass points** are north, south, east and west.

competition competitions

NOUN A **competition** is an event to find out who is best at doing something.

complain complains, complaining, complained

VERB If you **complain**, you say that you are not happy about something.

complete

ADJECTIVE **1** If something is **complete**, it has been finished.

ADJECTIVE **2** If you talk about a **complete** thing, you mean all of it. *I need a* **complete** *change of clothes.*

complicated

ADJECTIVE Something **complicated** is made up of so many parts that it is difficult to understand or deal with.

compose composes, composing, composed

VERB If you **compose** something, like a poem or a piece of music, you write it.

compound compounds

NOUN In language, a **compound** is a word that is made up of two or more words. "Playground", "armchair" and "toothache" are all compounds.

computer computers

NOUN A **computer** is a machine that stores information and works things out according to instructions in a program.

concave

ADJECTIVE A **concave** surface curves inwards.

conceal conceals, concealing, concealed

VERB If you **conceal** something, you hide it carefully.

concentrate concentrates, concentrating, concentrated

VERB If you **concentrate** on something, you give it all your attention.

concerned

ADJECTIVE If you are **concerned** about something, it worries you.

concert **concerts**

NOUN A **concert** is a performance by musicians, usually in a big hall.

conclusion **conclusions**

NOUN **1** A **conclusion** is something you decide is true after you have thought carefully.

NOUN **2** The **conclusion** of something is its ending.

concrete

NOUN **Concrete** is a building material made of cement, sand and water, which goes hard when it is set.

condition **conditions**

NOUN **1** The **condition** of something is the state it is in.

NOUN **2** A **condition** is a rule you must agree to before you are allowed to do something. *You can go out on one **condition** – you must be home by five.*

conductor **conductors**

NOUN A **conductor** is someone who controls the way musicians play together.

cone **cones**

NOUN A **cone** is a solid curved shape with a flat circular base and a pointed top.

See Solid shapes on page 271.

confess **confesses, confessing, confessed**

VERB If you **confess**, you say that you have done something wrong.

confident

ADJECTIVE **1** If you are **confident** about something, you are sure about it.

ADJECTIVE **2** People who are **confident** know that they can do something well.

confuse **confuses, confusing, confused**

VERB **1** To **confuse** someone means to make them unsure what to do. *The new road layout **confused** everyone.*

VERB **2** If you **confuse** two things, you mix them up by mistake. *I always **confuse** the twins because they are so alike.*

congratulate **congratulates, congratulating, congratulated**

VERB If you **congratulate** someone, you say you are pleased that something special has happened to them.

conjunction **conjunctions**

NOUN In grammar, a **conjunction** is a word that joins two other words or parts of a sentence. "And", "but", "while" and "although" are all conjunctions.

conker **conkers**

NOUN **Conkers** are hard brown nuts from a horse chestnut tree.

connect **connects, connecting, connected**

VERB If you **connect** two things, you join them together.

connective **connectives**

NOUN In grammar, a **connective** is a word or phrase that joins parts of a text. For example, "and", "at last" and "because" are connectives.

conquer **conquers, conquering, conquered**

VERB To **conquer** people is to take control of their country by force.

conscious

ADJECTIVE If you are **conscious**, you are awake and know what is happening.

consecutive

ADJECTIVE If things are **consecutive**, they happen one after the other. *October, November and December are **consecutive** months.*

consider considers, considering, considered
VERB If you **consider** something, you think about it carefully.

consist consists, consisting, consisted
VERB Something that **consists** of particular things is made up of them.

consonant consonants
NOUN A **consonant** is any letter of the alphabet except a, e, i, o and u. See **vowel**.

constant
ADJECTIVE Something that is **constant** happens all the time. *She complained of a constant headache.*

construct constructs, constructing, constructed
VERB If you **construct** something, you build it or make it.

consume consumes, consuming, consumed
VERB If you **consume** something, you eat or drink it, or use it up.

contain contains, containing, contained
VERB The things that something **contains** are the things in it.

container containers
NOUN A **container** is something you put things in.

content
ADJECTIVE If you are **content**, you are happy and satisfied with your life.

contents
PLURAL NOUN The **contents** of something like a box or cake are the things in it. The **contents page** of a book tells you what is in it.

contest contests
NOUN A **contest** is a competition or game which you try to win.

continent continents
NOUN A **continent** is a very large area of land, such as Africa or Asia.

continue continues, continuing, continued
VERB If you **continue** to do something, you go on doing it.

continuous
ADJECTIVE Something that is **continuous** goes on without stopping.

contraction contractions
NOUN A **contraction** is a shortened form of word or words. For example, "I'm" is a contraction of "I am".

contradict contradicts, contradicting, contradicted
VERB If you **contradict** someone, you say the opposite of what they have just said.

control controls, controlling, controlled
VERB **1** If you **control** something, you make it behave exactly as you want it to.
NOUN **2** The **controls** on a machine are knobs or other things used to work it.

convenient
ADJECTIVE If something is **convenient**, it is easy to use or do.

conversation conversations
NOUN If you have a **conversation** with someone, you talk to each other.

convex
ADJECTIVE A **convex** surface curves outwards.

convince convinces, convincing, convinced
VERB If someone or something **convinces** you, they make you believe that something is true.

cook cooks, cooking, cooked
VERB When you **cook** food, you prepare it for eating by heating it.

cooker cookers
NOUN A **cooker** is a piece of equipment for cooking food.

cool cooler, coolest
ADJECTIVE If something is **cool**, its temperature is low but it is not cold.

coordinates
NOUN **Coordinates** are two numbers or letters which help you find the exact position of something. They are often used on maps, graphs and charts.

cope copes, coping, coped
VERB If you **cope** with a task or problem, you deal with it successfully.

copper
NOUN **Copper** is a reddish-brown metal.

copy copies, copying, copied
NOUN **1** A **copy** is something made to look exactly like something else.
VERB **2** If you **copy** something, you make a copy of it.
VERB **3** If you **copy** what someone does, you do the same thing.

coral corals
NOUN **Coral** is a hard substance that forms in the sea from the skeletons of tiny animals called corals.

cord cords
NOUN **Cord** is thick, strong string.

core cores
NOUN The **core** of a fruit is the hard part in the middle that contains seeds.

cork corks
NOUN **1** **Cork** is the light bark of the cork oak tree.
NOUN **2** A **cork** is a piece of cork used to block the open end of a bottle.

corn
NOUN **Corn** is a cereal crop, such as wheat or sweet corn.

corner corners
NOUN A **corner** is the place where two edges or roads join.

correct corrects, correcting, corrected
ADJECTIVE **1** Something that is **correct** is true and has no mistakes.
VERB **2** If you **correct** your work, you put right any mistakes you made.

corridor corridors
NOUN A **corridor** is a long passage in a building or train.

cost costs, costing, cost
VERB If something **costs** an amount of money, you can buy it for that amount.

costume costumes
NOUN A **costume** is the clothes worn by an actor, or that people wear for special events.

cosy cosier, cosiest
ADJECTIVE A house or room that is **cosy** is comfortable and warm, and not too big.

cot cots
NOUN A **cot** is a bed with high sides for a baby or a young child.

cottage cottages
NOUN A **cottage** is a small house, usually in the country.

cotton
NOUN **1 Cotton** is cloth made from the soft fibres of the cotton plant.
NOUN **2 Cotton** is also a thread used for sewing.
NOUN **3 Cotton wool** is soft fluffy cotton, often used for cleaning the skin.

cough coughs
NOUN A **cough** is a noise made by someone forcing air out of their throat.

could
VERB **1 Could** is part of the verb **can**. You use **could** to say that something might happen. *It could rain tomorrow.*
VERB **2** You also say **could** when you are asking for something politely. *Could you please tell me the way to the station?*

council councils
NOUN The **council** is a group of people who look after the affairs of a town, district or county.

count counts, counting, counted
VERB **1** When you **count**, you say numbers in order. *Count up to a hundred.*
VERB **2** If you **count** a number of things, you are finding out how many there are.

counter counters
NOUN **1** A **counter** is a long narrow table in a shop, where things are sold.
NOUN **2** A **counter** is also a small round flat object, usually made of plastic, that is used in board games.

country countries
NOUN **1** A **country** is a land that has its own government and language.
NOUN **2** The **country** is land away from towns and cities.

couple couples
NOUN **1** A **couple** of things or people means two of them. *It should only take a couple of days.*
NOUN **2** Two people are sometimes called a **couple**, especially if they are married or having a relationship.

coupon coupons
NOUN A **coupon** is a piece of printed paper that allows you to pay less than usual for something.

courage
NOUN **Courage** is not showing that you are afraid of something.

course courses
NOUN **1** A **course** is a series of lessons.
NOUN **2** A **course** can also be one part of a meal.
of course PHRASE You use **of course** to make something you are saying stronger. *Of course I still want to go.*

court courts
NOUN **1** A **court** is an area marked out for a game like tennis or badminton.
NOUN **2** A **court** is also a place where things to do with the law are decided.
NOUN **3** The **court** of a king or queen is where they live with their family.

courtyard courtyards
NOUN A **courtyard** is an open flat area of ground with walls all round it.

cousin cousins
NOUN Your **cousin** is a child of your uncle or aunt.

cover covers, covering, covered
VERB **1** If you **cover** something, you put something over it to protect or hide it.
NOUN **2** The **covers** on a bed are the blankets or duvet that you have over you to keep you warm.
NOUN **3** The **cover** of a book or magazine is the outside of it.

a
b
Cc
d
e
f
g
h
i
j
k
l
m
n
o
p
q
r
s
t
u
v
w
x
y
z

a
b
Cc
d
e
f
g
h
i
j
k
l
m
n
o
p
q
r
s
t
u
v
w
x
y
z

cow cows
NOUN A **cow** is a large farm animal that gives milk.

coward cowards
NOUN A **coward** is someone who avoids anything dangerous, painful or difficult.

cowboy cowboys
NOUN A **cowboy** is a man whose job is to look after cattle.

crab crabs
NOUN A **crab** is a sea animal. It has four pairs of legs, two pincers, and a flat round body covered by a shell.

crack cracks, cracking, cracked
VERB **1** If you **crack** something, or it cracks, it has a small split in it but does not quite break.
NOUN **2** A **crack** is the line on something that shows it is nearly broken.
NOUN **3** A **crack** is also a sudden loud noise.

cracker crackers
NOUN **1** A **cracker** is a thin crisp biscuit, often slightly salty.
NOUN **2** A **cracker** can be a cardboard tube covered in coloured paper, that people have at parties. It makes a sharp sound when you pull the ends apart.

cradle cradles
NOUN A **cradle** is a small box-shaped bed for a baby.

crane cranes
NOUN **1** A **crane** is a machine that moves heavy things by lifting them.

crane
NOUN **2** A **crane** is also a large water bird with long legs and a long neck.

crash crashes, crashing, crashed
NOUN **1** A **crash** is a traffic accident.
NOUN **2** A **crash** is also a sudden loud noise like something breaking.
VERB **3** If something **crashes**, it hits something else and makes a loud noise.

crate crates
NOUN A **crate** is a large box used for transporting or storing things.

crawl crawls, crawling, crawled
VERB When you **crawl**, you move forward on your hands and knees.

crayon crayons
NOUN A **crayon** is a coloured pencil.

craze crazes
NOUN A **craze** is something that is very popular for a short time.

crazy crazier, craziest
ADJECTIVE **1** Someone or something **crazy** is very strange or foolish.
ADJECTIVE **2** If you are **crazy** about something, you are very keen on it.

creak creaks, creaking, creaked
VERB If something **creaks**, it makes an odd squeaking sound.

cream
ADJECTIVE **1** Something that is **cream** in colour is yellowish-white.
NOUN **2** **Cream** is the pale yellow liquid taken from the top of milk.

crease creases, creasing, creased
NOUN **1** A **crease** is a line made by folding or wrinkling something.
VERB **2** If you **crease** something, you make lines appear on it.

create creates, creating, created
VERB To **create** something means to cause it to happen, or exist.

creature creatures
NOUN A **creature** is any animal, such as a bird, fish or insect.

creep creeps, creeping, crept
VERB If you **creep** somewhere, you move quietly and slowly.

crescent crescents
NOUN A **crescent** is a curved shape that is wider in the middle than at the ends, like a new moon.

crew crews
NOUN A **crew** is the people who work on a ship, aircraft or spaceship.

cricket crickets
NOUN **1** Cricket is an outdoor game between two teams of eleven players.
NOUN **2** A **cricket** is a small jumping insect that makes a chirping sound by rubbing its wings together.

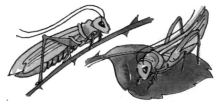

cried
VERB **Cried** is the past tense of **cry**.

cries
VERB **Cries** is a present tense form of **cry**.

crime crimes
NOUN A **crime** is something which is against the law.

criminal criminals
NOUN A **criminal** is someone who has done something that is against the law.

crimson
ADJECTIVE **Crimson** is dark red.

crinkle crinkles, crinkling, crinkled
VERB When something **crinkles**, it becomes slightly creased.

crisp crisper, crispest; crisps
ADJECTIVE **1** Things like fruit and biscuits that are **crisp** are fresh and firm.
NOUN **2** A **crisp** is a crunchy, thinly sliced piece of fried potato.

criticize criticizes, criticizing, criticized; also spelt criticise
VERB If you **criticize** someone, you say what you think is wrong with them.

crocodile crocodiles
NOUN A **crocodile** is a large reptile, about five metres long.
See *Reptiles* on page 259.

crocus crocuses
NOUN **Crocuses** are small yellow, purple or white spring flowers.

crooked
ADJECTIVE Something that is **crooked** is bent or twisted.

crop crops
NOUN A **crop** is plants grown for food.

cross crosser, crossest; crosses, crossing, crossed
ADJECTIVE **1** Someone who is **cross** is angry about something.
NOUN **2** A **cross** is a mark like + or ×.
VERB **3** If you **cross** something like a road, you go from one side to the other.

crossing crossings
NOUN A **crossing** is a place where you can cross the road safely.

crouch crouches, crouching, crouched
VERB If you **crouch** down, you bend your legs under you so that you are close to the ground.

a
b
Cc
d
e
f
g
h
i
j
k
l
m
n
o
p
q
r
s
t
u
v
w
x
y
z

crow crows
NOUN A **crow** is a large black bird.

crowd crowds
NOUN A **crowd** is a large number of people together in one place.

crowded
ADJECTIVE A place that is **crowded** is full of people.

crown crowns
NOUN A **crown** is an ornament that kings and queens sometimes wear on their heads.

cruel crueller, cruellest
ADJECTIVE Someone who is **cruel** hurts people or animals without caring.

cruise cruises
NOUN A **cruise** is a holiday on a ship that travels to different places.

crumb crumbs
NOUN A **crumb** is a very small piece of dry food such as bread or biscuit.

crumble crumbles, crumbling, crumbled
VERB If you **crumble** something that is soft, it breaks into lots of little pieces.

crumple crumples, crumpling, crumpled
VERB If you **crumple** paper or cloth, you squash it so that it is full of creases.

crunch crunches, crunching, crunched
VERB If you **crunch** something, you crush it noisily, for example between your teeth or under your feet.

crush crushes, crushing, crushed
VERB To **crush** something is to destroy its shape by squeezing it.

crust crusts
NOUN The **crust** is a hard layer on the outside of something such as bread.

cry cries, crying, cried
VERB **1** When you **cry**, tears come from your eyes.
NOUN **2** A **cry** is a sudden sound that you make when you are surprised or hurt.

crystal crystals
NOUN A **crystal** is a mineral that has formed into a regular shape.

cub cubs
NOUN A **cub** is a young wild animal such as a lion, fox or bear.
See *Young animals* on page 260.

cube cubes
NOUN A **cube** is a solid shape with six square faces all the same size.
See *Solid shapes* on page 271.

cuboid cuboids
NOUN A **cuboid** is a rectangular box shape with six faces. All the faces are rectangles.
See *Solid shapes* on page 271.

cuckoo cuckoos
NOUN A **cuckoo** is a grey bird. Cuckoos lay their eggs in other birds' nests.

cucumber cucumbers
NOUN A **cucumber** is a long, thin, dark green vegetable, eaten raw.
See *Vegetables* on page 256.

cuddle cuddles, cuddling, cuddled
VERB When you **cuddle** someone, you put your arms round them.

culprit culprits
NOUN A **culprit** is someone who has done something harmful or wrong.

cunning
ADJECTIVE Someone who is **cunning** plans to get what they want, often by tricking other people.

cup cups
NOUN **1** A **cup** is a small container with a handle, which you drink out of.
NOUN **2** A **cup** is also a prize for the winner of a game or competition.

cupboard cupboards
NOUN A **cupboard** is a piece of furniture with doors and shelves.

cure cures, curing, cured
NOUN **1** A **cure** is something that makes people better when they have been ill.
VERB **2** If someone or something **cures** a person, they make them well again.

curiosity
NOUN **Curiosity** is wanting to know about things.

curious
ADJECTIVE **1** Someone who is **curious** wants to know more about something.
ADJECTIVE **2** Something that is **curious** is unusual and hard to explain.

curl curls, curling, curled
VERB **1** If an animal **curls** up, it makes itself into a rounded shape.
NOUN **2** **Curls** are pieces of hair shaped in curves and circles.
curly ADJECTIVE

currant currants
NOUN **Currants** are small dried grapes.

current currents
NOUN **1** A **current** is a steady movement of water or air.
NOUN **2** A **current** is also the movement of electricity through a wire.

curriculum curriculums or curricula
NOUN A **curriculum** is the different courses taught at a school or college.

curry curries
NOUN **Curry** is an Indian dish made with spices.

cursor cursors
NOUN A **cursor** is a small sign on a computer screen that shows where the next letter or number will appear.

curtain curtains
NOUN A **curtain** is a large piece of material that you pull across a window to cover it.

curve curves
NOUN A **curve** is a smooth, gradually bending line.
curved ADJECTIVE

cushion cushions
NOUN A **cushion** is a soft object put on a seat to make it more comfortable.

custom customs
NOUN A **custom** is something that people usually do. *It's his **custom** to take the dog for a walk after supper.*

customer customers
NOUN A **customer** is a person who buys something, especially from a shop.

cut cuts, cutting, cut
VERB **1** If you **cut** yourself, you hurt yourself by accident on something sharp.
VERB **2** If you **cut** something, you use a knife or scissors to remove parts of it.

cutlery
NOUN **Cutlery** is the knives, forks and spoons that you eat your food with.

cycle cycles, cycling, cycled
NOUN **1** A **cycle** is a bicycle.
VERB **2** If you **cycle**, you ride a bicycle.
cyclist NOUN

cygnet cygnets
NOUN A **cygnet** is a young swan.
*See **Young animals** on page 260.*

cylinder cylinders
NOUN A **cylinder** is a three-dimensional shape like a tube with flat circular ends.
cylindrical ADJECTIVE
*See **Solid shapes** on page 271.*

a
b
Cc
d
e
f
g
h
i
j
k
l
m
n
o
p
q
r
s
t
u
v
w
x
y
z

Dd

a
b
c
Dd
e
f
g
h
i
j
k
l
m
n
o
p
q
r
s
t
u
v
w
x
y
z

dad dads
NOUN Your **dad** is your father.

daffodil daffodils
NOUN A **daffodil** is a yellow trumpet-shaped flower that blooms in the spring.

dagger daggers
NOUN A **dagger** is a weapon like a knife.

daily
ADJECTIVE Something that is **daily** happens every day.

dairy dairies
NOUN A **dairy** is a shop or company that sells milk and food made from milk, such as butter and cheese.

daisy daisies
NOUN A **daisy** is a small wild flower with white petals and a yellow centre.

dam dams
NOUN A **dam** is a wall built across a river or stream to hold back water.

damage damages, damaging, damaged
VERB To **damage** something means to harm or spoil it.

damp damper, dampest
ADJECTIVE Something that is **damp** is slightly wet.

dance dances, dancing, danced
VERB When you **dance**, you move your body in time to music.

dandelion dandelions
NOUN A **dandelion** is a wild plant with bright yellow flowers.

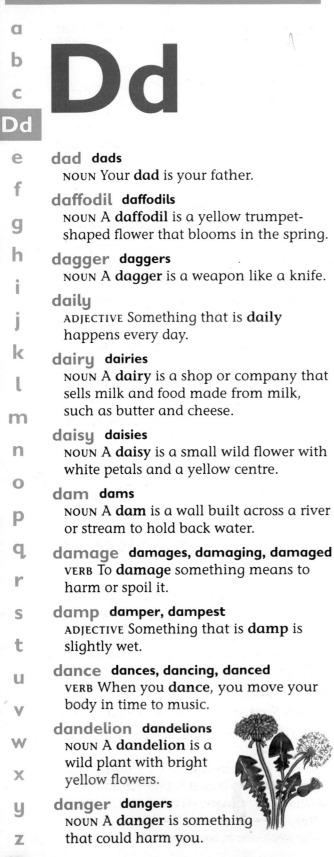

danger dangers
NOUN A **danger** is something that could harm you.

dangerous
ADJECTIVE If something is **dangerous**, it is likely to harm you.

dare dares, daring, dared
VERB If you **dare** to do something, you are brave enough to do it.

dark darker, darkest
ADJECTIVE When it is **dark**, there is not enough light to see properly.
darkness NOUN

dart darts, darting, darted
VERB 1 If a person or animal **darts**, they move suddenly and quickly.
NOUN 2 A **dart** is a short arrow that you throw in the game of darts.

dash dashes, dashing, dashed
VERB 1 If you **dash** somewhere, you run or go there quickly.
NOUN 2 A **dash** is the punctuation mark (–) which shows a change of subject, or which may be used instead of brackets.
See *Punctuation* on page 264.

data
NOUN **Data** is information, usually in the form of facts or figures.

database databases
NOUN A **database** is a collection of information, often stored in a computer.

date dates
NOUN 1 If someone asks you the **date**, you tell them the day and the month.
NOUN 2 A **date** is a small brown sticky fruit which grows on palm trees.

daughter daughters
NOUN A girl is the **daughter** of her parents.

dawdle dawdles, dawdling, dawdled
VERB If you **dawdle**, you walk slowly, taking more time than you should.

dawn

NOUN **Dawn** is the time of day when it first begins to get light.

day **days**

NOUN A **day** is the 24 hours between one midnight and the next.

daylight

NOUN **Daylight** is the light that there is during the day before it gets dark.

dazzle **dazzles, dazzling, dazzled**

VERB If a light **dazzles** you, it is so bright that you cannot really see for a while.

de-

PREFIX When **de-** is added to a noun or verb, it means to remove. For example, "deforest" means to take away the forest.
See *Prefixes* on page 264.

dead

ADJECTIVE A person, animal or plant that is **dead** is no longer living.

deaf **deafer, deafest**

ADJECTIVE Someone who is **deaf** cannot hear very well, or cannot hear at all.

deal **deals, dealing, dealt**

VERB 1 When you **deal** in a card game, you give cards to the players.

VERB 2 If you **deal with** something, you do what needs to be done with it.

dear **dearer, dearest**

ADJECTIVE 1 You use **Dear** at the beginning of a letter before the name of the person you are writing to.

ADJECTIVE 2 If something is **dear**, it costs a lot of money.

death

NOUN **Death** is the end of life, when an animal or person dies.

decade **decades**

NOUN A **decade** is a period of ten years.

decay **decays, decaying, decayed**

VERB When something like a plant or piece of meat **decays**, it becomes rotten.

deceive **deceives, deceiving, deceived**

VERB If someone **deceives** you, they make you believe something untrue.

December

NOUN **December** is the 12th month of the year. It has 31 days.

decide **decides, deciding, decided**

VERB If you **decide** to do something, you make up your mind to do it.

decimal **decimals**

ADJECTIVE 1 A **decimal** system involves counting in units of ten.

NOUN 2 A **decimal** or **decimal fraction** is written with a dot followed by numbers, such as 0·2, 8·35. The numbers after the dot represent tenths, hundredths and so on.

NOUN 3 A **decimal point** is the dot that comes between whole numbers and fractions.

NOUN 4 A **decimal place** is the position of a number after a decimal point.

decision **decisions**

NOUN A **decision** is a choice you make about what you think should be done.

deck **decks**

NOUN A **deck** is a floor on a ship or bus.

decorate **decorates, decorating, decorated**

VERB 1 If you **decorate** something, you add things to make it more attractive.

VERB 2 If someone **decorates** a room, they paper it or paint it.

decorations PLURAL NOUN

decrease

decrease decreases, decreasing, decreased
VERB If something **decreases**, or if you decrease it, it becomes less.

deep deeper, deepest
ADJECTIVE If something is **deep**, it goes a long way down. *The river is very **deep**.*

deer
NOUN A **deer** is a large hoofed animal. Male deer have horns called antlers.

defeat defeats, defeating, defeated
VERB If you **defeat** someone, you beat them in a game or battle.

defend defends, defending, defended
VERB If you **defend** someone or something, you do something to protect them against danger.
defence NOUN

define defines, defining, defined
VERB If you **define** something, you say what it is or what it means.

definite
ADJECTIVE **1** Something that is **definite** is unlikely to be changed. *We have a **definite** date for the outing.*
ADJECTIVE **2 Definite** can also mean certain or true. *Lots of stories were going round, but they heard nothing **definite**.*
definitely ADVERB

definition definitions
NOUN A **definition** explains the meaning of a word.

degree degrees
NOUN **1** A **degree** is a unit of measurement of temperature, for example, 20°C.
NOUN **2** In maths, a **degree** is a unit of measurement of angles. For example, a right angle is 90°.

delay delays, delaying, delayed
VERB If something **delays** you, it causes you to slow down or be late.

delete deletes, deleting, deleted
VERB If you **delete** some writing, you cross it out or remove it.

deliberate
ADJECTIVE If you do something that is **deliberate**, you do it on purpose.
deliberately ADVERB

delicate
ADJECTIVE **1** Something that is **delicate** is small and graceful.
ADJECTIVE **2** Someone who is **delicate** becomes ill easily.

delicious
ADJECTIVE Food that is **delicious** tastes or smells very nice.

delight delights, delighting, delighted
VERB If something **delights** you, it gives you a lot of pleasure.
delighted ADJECTIVE

deliver delivers, delivering, delivered
VERB If you **deliver** something, you take it to someone and hand it to them.

demand demands, demanding, demanded
VERB If you **demand** something, you say strongly that is what you want.

demonstrate **demonstrates, demonstrating, demonstrated**
VERB **1** If someone **demonstrates** something, they show you how to do it.
VERB **2** If people **demonstrate**, they hold a public meeting or march to show they are strongly for or against something.
demonstration NOUN

den **dens**
NOUN A **den** is the home of some wild animals such as lions or foxes.

dense **denser, densest**
ADJECTIVE Something **dense** is hard to see through. *They were in a **dense** forest.*

dent **dents, denting, dented**
VERB If somebody **dents** something, they make a dip in it by hitting it.

dentist **dentists**
NOUN A **dentist** is someone who looks after people's teeth.

deny **denies, denying, denied**
VERB If you **deny** something, you say that it is untrue.

depart **departs, departing, departed**
VERB When someone or something **departs** from a place, they leave it.
departure NOUN

depend **depends, depending, depended**
VERB **1** If you **depend** on someone, you need them.
VERB **2** If you can **depend** on someone, you know you can trust them.

depth
NOUN The **depth** of something is how deep it is.

descend **descends, descending, descended**
VERB To **descend** means to go down.

descending
ADJECTIVE When things are in **descending** order, each thing is lower than the one before it. *The numbers 10, 9, 8 and 7 are in **descending** order.*

describe **describes, describing, described**
VERB If you **describe** a person or thing, you say what they are like.
description NOUN

desert **deserts**
NOUN A **desert** is very dry land with very little plant life.

deserted
ADJECTIVE If a place is **deserted**, there are no people there.

deserve **deserves, deserving, deserved**
VERB If you **deserve** something, you have earned it by what you have done.

design **designs, designing, designed**
NOUN **1** A **design** is a pattern that is used to decorate something.
VERB **2** If you **design** something, you plan it and make a drawing of it.

desk **desks**
NOUN A **desk** is a special table that you use for writing or reading.

dessert **desserts**
NOUN A **dessert** is a sweet food served after the main course of a meal.

destroy **destroys, destroying, destroyed**
VERB To **destroy** something means to damage it so much it cannot be mended.

detail **details**
NOUN A **detail** is a small part or thing that you notice when you look at something carefully.

a
b
c
Dd
e
f
g
h
i
j
k
l
m
n
o
p
q
r
s
t
u
v
w
x
y
z

a
b
Dd
e
f
g
h
i
j
k
l
m
n
o
p
q
r
s
t
u
v
w
x
y
z

detective detectives

NOUN A **detective** is a person whose job is to find out who did a crime.

determined

ADJECTIVE If you are **determined** to do something, nothing will stop you.

develop develops, developing, developed

VERB When something **develops**, it grows or becomes more advanced.

dew

NOUN **Dew** is the small drops of water that form on surfaces outdoors at night.

diagonal

ADJECTIVE A **diagonal** line slants from one corner of something to the opposite corner.

diagram diagrams

NOUN A **diagram** is a drawing that explains something.

dial dials

NOUN A **dial** is a numbered disc on an instrument like a clock.

dialogue dialogues

NOUN In a story, play or film, **dialogue** is conversation.

diameter diameters

NOUN A **diameter** is a straight line drawn right through the centre of a circle.

diamond diamonds

NOUN **1** A **diamond** is a very hard, clear jewel which sparkles.

NOUN **2** A **diamond** is also a shape with four straight sides, like a square but slightly flattened.

See *Colours and flat shapes* on page 271.

diary diaries

NOUN A **diary** is a book in which to write about what you have done.

dice

NOUN **Dice** are small cubes with spots on each of their six sides.

dictionary dictionaries

NOUN A **dictionary** is a book in which words are listed alphabetically and explained.

did

VERB **Did** is the past tense of **do**.

didn't

VERB **Didn't** is a contraction of **did not**.

die dies, dying, died

VERB When a person, animal or plant **dies**, they stop living.

diesel diesels

NOUN A **diesel** is a kind of engine that burns a special oil instead of petrol.

diet diets

NOUN **1** A **diet** is the food that a person or animal normally eats.

NOUN **2** A **diet** is also a special range of foods that a doctor tells someone to eat if they have a health or weight problem.

difference differences

NOUN **1** The **difference** between two things is the way in which they are unlike each other.

NOUN **2** In maths, you can work out the **difference** between two numbers by taking the smaller number away from the larger number.

different

ADJECTIVE Something that is **different** from something else is not like it in one or more ways.

difficult

ADJECTIVE Something that is **difficult** is not easy to do or understand.

difficulty NOUN

dig **digs, digging, dug**
VERB When people **dig**, they break up soil or sand with a spade or garden fork.

digest **digests, digesting, digested**
VERB When you **digest** food, your body breaks it down so that it can be used.
digestion NOUN

digit **digits**
NOUN A **digit** is a written symbol for any of the numbers from 0 to 9. For example, 384 is a three-digit number.

digital
ADJECTIVE **1 Digital** instruments such as watches have changing numbers instead of a dial with hands. See **analogue**.
NOUN **2 Digital television** is television in which the picture is sent in digital form.

dim **dimmer, dimmest**
ADJECTIVE If the light is **dim**, it is rather dark and it is hard to see things.

din
NOUN A **din** is a loud, annoying noise.

dinghy **dinghies**
NOUN A **dinghy** is a small open boat that you sail or row.

dining room **dining rooms**
NOUN A **dining room** is the room where people have their meals.

dinner **dinners**
NOUN **Dinner** is the main meal of the day.

dinosaur **dinosaurs**
NOUN A **dinosaur** was a large reptile which lived and became extinct in prehistoric times.

Triceratops

Stegosaurus

dip **dips, dipping, dipped**
VERB If you **dip** something into a liquid, you put it in quickly.

direct **directs, directing, directed**
VERB **1** If you **direct** someone, you show them the way to go.
VERB **2** A person who **directs** something, like a film, is in charge of it.
ADJECTIVE **3 Direct** means in a straight line without stopping, for example on a journey. *Is there a **direct** flight to Paris?*

direction **directions**
NOUN **1** A **direction** is the way in which someone or something is moving or pointing.
NOUN **2 Directions** are instructions that tell you what to do or which way to go.

dirt
NOUN **Dirt** is dust, mud or stains on a surface or fabric.

dirty **dirtier, dirtiest**
ADJECTIVE Something that is **dirty** is marked or covered with mud or stains.

dis-
PREFIX **Dis-** is added to the beginning of words to form a word that means the opposite, for example "agree" → "disagree".
See *Prefixes* on page 264.

disabled
ADJECTIVE A **disabled** person has a condition or injury that makes it hard or impossible to do some things.
disability NOUN

disagree **disagrees, disagreeing, disagreed**
VERB If you **disagree** with someone, you think what they are saying is wrong.

disappear **disappears, disappearing, disappeared**
VERB If someone **disappears**, they go out of sight.

disappoint **disappoints, disappointing, disappointed**
VERB If something **disappoints** you, it is not as good as you thought it would be.
disappointment NOUN

a
b
c
Dd
e
f
g
h
i
j
k
l
m
n
o
p
q
r
s
t
u
v
w
x
y
z

disapprove

disapprove

VERB If you **disapprove** of something, you think it is wrong or bad.

disaster disasters

NOUN A **disaster** is something very bad that happens, such as an air crash.
disastrous ADJECTIVE

disc discs

NOUN A **disc** is a flat round object.

disco discos

NOUN A **disco** is a place where people go to dance to pop music.

discover discovers, discovering, discovered

VERB When you **discover** something, you find it or find out about it.
discovery NOUN

discuss discusses, discussing, discussed

VERB When you **discuss** something, you talk about it with someone else.
discussion NOUN

disease diseases

NOUN A **disease** is an illness in people, animals or plants.

disguise disguises

NOUN A **disguise** is something that changes the way you look, so that people do not recognize you.

disgust

NOUN **Disgust** is a feeling of strong dislike for someone or something.

dish dishes

NOUN A **dish** is a shallow container for cooking or serving meals in.

dishonest

ADJECTIVE If someone is **dishonest**, they are not to be trusted.

dishwasher dishwashers

NOUN A **dishwasher** is a machine that washes things like plates.

disk disks

NOUN A **disk** is used for storing information in a computer.

dislike dislikes, disliking, disliked

VERB If you **dislike** someone or something, you do not like them.

dismiss dismisses, dismissing, dismissed

VERB When someone in authority **dismisses** you, they tell you to leave.

display displays

NOUN A **display** is an arrangement of things which is done to show to people.

dissolve dissolves, dissolving, dissolved

VERB If something **dissolves** in a liquid, it becomes mixed in with it. See **solution**.

distance distances

NOUN The **distance** between two things is the amount of space between them.

distant

ADJECTIVE **Distant** means far away.

distinct

ADJECTIVE If something is **distinct**, you can hear or see it clearly.

distribute distributes, distributing, distributed

VERB If you **distribute** things like leaflets, you hand them out to several people.

district districts

NOUN A **district** is the area around a place. *He's the only doctor in this **district**.*

disturb disturbs, disturbing, disturbed

VERB If you **disturb** someone, you interrupt them or spoil their peace and quiet.

disturbance disturbances

NOUN A **disturbance** is something that spoils people's peace and quiet.

ditch ditches

NOUN A **ditch** is a channel dug at the side of a road or field, to drain water.

dive dives, diving, dived

VERB To **dive** is to jump head first into water with your arms above your head.
diver NOUN

divide divides, dividing, divided

VERB **1** When something is **divided**, it is separated into smaller parts.
VERB **2** When you **divide** numbers, you share them into equal groups. For example, 15 can be divided into 3 groups of 5, or 5 groups of 3.
$15 \div 3 = 5$ or $15 \div 5 = 3$

divisible

ADJECTIVE A number that is **divisible** can be divided by another number without leaving a remainder. 27 is divisible by 3.

division divisions

NOUN **1** Division is separating something into two or more parts.
NOUN **2** In maths, **division** is the process of dividing one number by another. The sign $\div$ is used for division.

divorce divorces

NOUN A **divorce** is the legal ending of a marriage.

Diwali

NOUN **Diwali** is a Hindu festival of light that is celebrated in the autumn.

dizzy dizzier, dizziest

ADJECTIVE If you feel **dizzy**, your head feels funny, as if you are going to fall over.

do does, doing, did, done

VERB **1** If you **do** something, you get on and finish it. *Have you done your work?*
VERB **2** Do can be used with other verbs. *Do you want some more?*

doctor doctors

NOUN A **doctor** is a person who treats people when they are ill.

document documents

NOUN **1** A **document** is a piece of paper which is an official record of something.
NOUN **2** A **document** is also a piece of text stored as a file in a computer.

dodge dodges, dodging, dodged

VERB If you **dodge**, you move suddenly out of the way.

does

VERB **Does** is a present tense form of **do**.

doesn't

VERB **Doesn't** is a contraction of **does not**.

dog dogs

NOUN A **dog** is an animal. Dogs bark and are often kept as pets, or used to guard things.

doll dolls

NOUN A **doll** is a child's toy that looks like a baby or a small person.

dollar dollars

NOUN A **dollar** is a unit of money in countries such as the USA and Australia.

dolphin dolphins

NOUN A **dolphin** is a mammal which lives in the sea.

a
b
c
Dd
e
f
g
h
i
j
k
l
m
n
o
p
q
r
s
t
u
v
w
x
y
z

dome

dome **domes**
NOUN A **dome** is a round roof.

domino **dominoes**
NOUN A **domino** is a small black rectangular block, marked with spots. Dominoes are used for playing games.

done
VERB Done is the past participle of **do**.

donkey **donkeys**
NOUN A **donkey** is an animal like a small horse, with longer ears.

don't
VERB **Don't** is a contraction of **do not**.

door **doors**
NOUN A **door** swings or slides to open and close the entrance to something.

dose **doses**
NOUN A **dose** is the amount of a medicine that you have to take.

dot **dots**
NOUN A **dot** is a small round mark.

double
ADJECTIVE If something is **double** the size or amount of something else, it is twice as big.

doubt **doubts**
NOUN If you have a **doubt** about something, you are not sure about it.

doubtful
ADJECTIVE **1** If you are **doubtful** about something, you are not sure about it.
ADJECTIVE **2** Something that is **doubtful** seems unlikely or uncertain.

dough
NOUN **Dough** is the floury mixture used to make things like pastry or bread.

doughnut **doughnuts**
NOUN A **doughnut** is a ring of sweet dough cooked in hot fat.

dove **doves**
NOUN A **dove** is a bird like a small pigeon.

down
PREPOSITION **1** If you go **down** a hill, you go to a lower level.
ADVERB **2** If you put something **down**, you put it on a surface.
ADVERB **3** If an amount of something goes **down**, it gets less. *My pocket money's gone down.*
NOUN **4** Down is soft feathers.

downstairs
ADVERB If you go **downstairs**, you go towards the ground floor.

doze **dozes, dozing, dozed**
VERB When you **doze**, you sleep lightly.

dozen **dozens**
NOUN If you have a **dozen** things, you have 12 of them.

draft **drafts**
NOUN A **draft** is an early rough version of something you are writing.

drag **drags, dragging, dragged**
VERB If you **drag** a heavy object, you pull it along the ground.

dragon **dragons**
NOUN In stories, a **dragon** is a fierce animal like a big lizard. It has wings and claws and breathes fire.

dragonfly **dragonflies**
NOUN A **dragonfly** is a brightly-coloured insect, usually found near water.

See *Insects* on page 259.

drain **drains, draining, drained**
NOUN **1** A **drain** is a pipe that carries water away.
VERB **2** If a liquid **drains** away, it flows slowly to somewhere else.

drake drakes

NOUN A **drake** is a male duck.

drama dramas

NOUN **1** A **drama** is a serious play for the theatre, television or radio.

NOUN **2 Drama** is exciting and interesting things that happen.

dramatic

ADJECTIVE Something **dramatic** is very exciting and interesting.

dramatically ADVERB

drank

VERB **Drank** is the past tense of **drink**.

draught draughts

NOUN **1** A **draught** is a current of cold air coming into a room or vehicle.

PLURAL NOUN **2 Draughts** is a game played with round pieces on a board.

draw draws, drawing, drew, drawn

VERB **1** When you **draw**, you use something like a pencil or crayon to make a picture or a pattern.

VERB **2** When you **draw** the curtains, you pull them across a window.

NOUN **3** A **draw** is the result in a game or competition in which nobody wins.

drawbridge drawbridges

NOUN A **drawbridge** is a bridge that can be pulled up to stop people getting into a castle.

drawer drawers

NOUN A **drawer** is a box that slides in and out of a piece of furniture.

drawing drawings

NOUN A **drawing** is a picture made with a pencil, pen or crayon.

dread dreads, dreading, dreaded

VERB If you **dread** something, you feel worried and frightened about it.

dreadful

ADJECTIVE Something that is **dreadful** is very bad or unpleasant.

dream dreams, dreaming, dreamed or dreamt

VERB **1** When you **dream**, you see events in your mind while you are asleep.

VERB **2** If you **dream** while you are awake, you think about things you would like to happen.

dream NOUN

dress dresses, dressing, dressed

VERB **1** When you **dress**, you put on your clothes.

NOUN **2** A **dress** is a piece of clothing for women or girls made up of a skirt and top joined together.

drew

VERB **Drew** is the past tense of **draw**.

dribble dribbles, dribbling, dribbled

VERB **1** When babies **dribble**, water trickles from their mouth.

VERB **2** When players **dribble** the ball in a game like football, they kick it several times quickly to keep it moving.

drift drifts, drifting, drifted

VERB **1** When something **drifts**, it is carried along slowly by wind or water.

NOUN **2** A **drift** is a pile of snow heaped up by the wind.

drill drills

NOUN A **drill** is a tool for making holes.

drink drinks, drinking, drank, drunk

VERB **1** When you **drink**, you take liquid into your mouth and swallow it.

NOUN **2** A **drink** is a liquid which you swallow to stop you being thirsty.

a
b
c
Dd
e
f
g
h
i
j
k
l
m
n
o
p
q
r
s
t
u
v
w
x
y
z

drip drips, dripping, dripped
VERB When something **drips**, drops of liquid fall from it one after the other.

drive drives, driving, drove, driven
VERB If someone **drives** a vehicle, they make it move and control it.

drizzle
NOUN **Drizzle** is light rain.

drop drops, dropping, dropped
VERB **1** If you **drop** something, you let it fall.
NOUN **2** A **drop** is a tiny amount of liquid.

drought droughts
NOUN A **drought** is a long period of time when no rain falls.

drove
VERB **Drove** is the past tense of **drive**.

drown drowns, drowning, drowned
VERB If someone **drowns**, they die because they have gone under water and cannot breathe.

drug drugs
NOUN A **drug** is a substance that is used to treat or prevent disease, or stop pain. Some drugs can be dangerous.

drum drums
NOUN A **drum** is a musical instrument which you hit to make a noise. It has skin stretched tightly over the end.

drunk
VERB **Drunk** is the past participle of **drink**.

dry drier or dryer, driest
ADJECTIVE Something that is **dry** has no water in it at all.
dry VERB

duck ducks
NOUN A **duck** is a common water bird with short legs and webbed feet.

due
ADJECTIVE If something is **due** at a particular time, it should happen then.

dug
VERB **Dug** is the past tense of **dig**.

dull duller, dullest
ADJECTIVE **1** Something that is **dull** is not interesting.
ADJECTIVE **2** **Dull** means not bright.
ADJECTIVE **3** A **dull** pain is not sharp.

dumb
ADJECTIVE Someone who is **dumb** is unable to speak.

dungeon dungeons
NOUN A **dungeon** is a dark underground prison in a castle.

during
PREPOSITION Something that happens **during** a period of time happens in that period. *I worked **during** the holidays.*

dusk
NOUN **Dusk** is the part of the day when it is beginning to get dark.

dust
NOUN **Dust** is dry fine powdery material such as particles of earth, dirt or pollen.
dusty ADJECTIVE

dustbin dustbins
NOUN A **dustbin** is a large container with a lid, for rubbish.

duty duties
NOUN A **duty** is something you feel you should do. *He only went to see his aunt because he felt it was his **duty**.*

duvet duvets
NOUN A **duvet** is a bed cover filled with feathers or other light material.

dye dyes, dyeing, dyed
VERB If you **dye** something such as hair or cloth, you change its colour by soaking it in a special liquid.

dying
VERB See **die**.

Ee

each

ADJECTIVE **Each** means every one taken separately. *She gave **each** child a pencil.*

eager

ADJECTIVE If you are **eager**, you very much want to do or have something.

eagle eagles

NOUN An **eagle** is a large strong bird with a sharp curved beak and claws.

ear ears

NOUN Your **ears** are the parts of your body that you use for hearing.

early earlier, earliest

ADJECTIVE OR ADVERB **1 Early** means near the beginning of a period of time. *We took the **early** train to school.*

ADJECTIVE OR ADVERB **2** You also use **early** to mean sooner than expected. *I arrived at the party **early**.*

earn earns, earning, earned

VERB If you **earn** something, such as money, you get it by working for it.

earring earrings

NOUN An **earring** is a piece of jewellery that is fixed to the ear for decoration.

earth

NOUN **1** The **Earth** is the planet we live on.

NOUN **2** The soil that plants grow in is also called **earth**.

earthquake earthquakes

NOUN An **earthquake** is when the ground shakes because of movement beneath the surface.

east

NOUN **East** is one of the four main points of the compass. It is the direction in which the sun rises. See **compass point**.

eastern ADJECTIVE

Easter

NOUN **Easter** is a Christian festival that celebrates Christ's return to life.

easy easier, easiest

ADJECTIVE Something that is **easy** can be done without difficulty.

easily ADVERB

eat eats, eating, ate, eaten

VERB When you **eat**, you chew and swallow food.

echo echoes

NOUN An **echo** is a sound that bounces back from something like the walls of a cave or building.

eclipse eclipses

NOUN An **eclipse** of the Sun is when the Moon comes in front of the Sun and hides it for a short time.

edge edges

NOUN **1** An **edge** is the end or side of something.

NOUN **2** An **edge** is where two faces of a three-dimensional shape meet. For example, a cuboid has 12 edges.

edible

ADJECTIVE Something that is **edible** is safe to eat.

edit edits, editing, edited

VERB **1** If you **edit** a piece of writing, you correct it so that it is ready for printing.

VERB **2** When someone **edits** a film or television programme, they select different parts and arrange them in a particular order.

educate educates, educating, educated

VERB To **educate** someone means to teach them over a long period, so that they learn about many different things.

a
b
c
d
Ee
f
g
h
i
j
k
l
m
n
o
p
q
r
s
t
u
v
w
x
y
z

education
NOUN **Education** is the teaching you receive at school, college or university.

eel eels
NOUN An **eel** is a long thin fish that looks like a snake.

effect effects
NOUN An **effect** is a change made by something. *I'm still suffering from the effects of my cold.*

effort efforts
NOUN **Effort** is the physical or mental energy needed to do something.

egg eggs
NOUN **1** An **egg** is an oval object laid by female birds. Reptiles, fish and insects also lay eggs. A baby animal develops inside the egg until it is ready to be born.

NOUN **2** In a female mammal, an **egg** is a cell produced in its body which can develop into a baby.

elastic
ADJECTIVE **1** Something **elastic** is able to stretch easily.
NOUN **2** **Elastic** is a material, like rubber, which stretches and can then return to its original size.

elbow elbows
NOUN Your **elbow** is the joint in the middle of your arm where it bends.

electric
ADJECTIVE A machine or other object that is **electric** works by using electricity.
electrical ADJECTIVE

electricity
NOUN **Electricity** is a form of energy that is used for heating and lighting, and to work machines. It comes along wires.

electronic
ADJECTIVE Something **electronic** has transistors or silicon chips which control an electric current.
electronically ADVERB

elephant elephants
NOUN An **elephant** is a large four-legged mammal with a long trunk, large ears, and ivory tusks.

elf elves
NOUN In fairy stories, an **elf** is a tiny boy who can do magic things.

else
ADVERB You can use **else** to mean other than this or more than this. *Can you think of anything else?*

e-mail or email
NOUN **E-mail** is the sending of messages from one computer to another.

embarrass embarrasses, embarrassing, embarrassed
VERB To **embarrass** someone means to make them feel shy, ashamed or guilty about something.

embryo embryos
NOUN An **embryo** is a human being or animal which has just begun to develop inside its mother's body.

emerald emeralds
NOUN An **emerald** is a bright green precious stone.

emerge emerges, emerging, emerged
VERB If someone **emerges** from a place, they come out so that they can be seen.

emergency emergencies
NOUN An **emergency** is an unexpected and serious event which needs immediate action to deal with it.

emotion emotions
NOUN **Emotion** is a strong feeling, such a love or fear.

employ employs, employing, employed

VERB If someone **employs** you, they pay you to work for them.

employer employers

NOUN **Employers** are people who pay other people to work for them.

empty emptier, emptiest; empties, emptying, emptied

ADJECTIVE **1** Something that is **empty** has no people or things in it.

VERB **2** If you **empty** a container, you pour or take everything out of it.

enchanted

ADJECTIVE In stories, something that is **enchanted** is under a magic spell.

encourage encourages, encouraging, encouraged

VERB If you **encourage** someone, you tell them that what they are doing is good and they should go on doing it.

encyclopedia encyclopedias

NOUN An **encyclopedia** is a book or set of books giving information about many different subjects.

end ends, ending, ended

NOUN **1** The **end** of a period of time or an event is the last part.

NOUN **2** The **end** of something is the farthest point of it. *The bathroom is at the end of the passage.*

VERB **3** If something **ends**, it finishes.

ending endings

NOUN An **ending** is the last part of a word, story, play or film.

enemy enemies

NOUN Your **enemy** is someone who fights or works against you.

energetic

ADJECTIVE Someone who is **energetic** is active and lively.

energetically ADVERB

energy

NOUN **1 Energy** is the strength you need to do things. You get energy from food.

NOUN **2 Energy** is also the power that makes things heat up, make a sound, give light or move. Electricity is one kind of energy.

engine engines

NOUN **1** An **engine** is a machine that makes things move.

NOUN **2** An **engine** is also a large vehicle that pulls a railway train.

engineer engineers

NOUN An **engineer** is a person who designs or builds things such as machinery, instruments or bridges.

enjoy enjoys, enjoying, enjoyed

VERB If you **enjoy** doing something, you like doing it very much.

enjoyable ADJECTIVE   **enjoyment** NOUN

enormous

ADJECTIVE Something that is **enormous** is extremely large.

enough

ADJECTIVE **Enough** means as much as you need. *Have you had **enough** to eat?*

enter enters, entering, entered

VERB **1** If you **enter** a place, you go into it.

VERB **2** If you **enter** a competition or examination, you take part in it.

entertain entertains, entertaining, entertained

VERB If you **entertain** somebody, you do something that they enjoy and find amusing.

entertainment

NOUN **Entertainment** is things that people watch for pleasure, such as shows and films.

enthusiastic

ADJECTIVE If you are **enthusiastic** about something, you are very interested in it, or excited about it.

entire

ADJECTIVE **Entire** means the whole of something. *The entire class came to my party.*

entrance **entrances**

NOUN An **entrance** is the way into a place.

envelope **envelopes**

NOUN An **envelope** is a folded paper cover for a letter or card.

envious

ADJECTIVE If you are **envious** of somebody, you wish you could have the same things that they have.

environment **environments**

NOUN The **environment** is the natural world around us.

envy **envies, envying, envied**

VERB If you **envy** somebody, you wish you could have the same things that they have.

episode **episodes**

NOUN An **episode** is one of several parts of a story or drama.

equal

ADJECTIVE If two things are **equal**, they are the same as each other in size, number or amount.

equals

VERB In maths, the symbol = stands for **equals**. The numbers on each side of it have the same value: $2 + 2 = 4$

equation **equations**

NOUN **Equations** are sometimes called number sentences. The numbers on the left equal the numbers on the right. For example, $3 + 3 = 2 \times 3$ is an equation.

equator

NOUN The **equator** is an imaginary line drawn round the centre of the earth, lying halfway between the North and South Poles.

equipment

NOUN **Equipment** is the things that you need to do something. *We need some new kitchen equipment – especially a fridge.*

erupt **erupts, erupting, erupted**

VERB When a volcano **erupts**, it throws out hot molten lava, ash and steam.

escape **escapes, escaping, escaped**

VERB If a person or animal **escapes**, they get away from somebody or something.

especially

ADVERB You say **especially** to mean most of all. *I like cats, especially black ones.*

essay **essays**

NOUN An **essay** is a short piece of writing on a particular subject.

essential

ADJECTIVE Something that is **essential** is absolutely necessary.

estate **estates**

NOUN **1** An **estate** is a large area of land in the country, belonging to one person or group.

NOUN **2** An **estate** is also an area of land with lots of houses on it.

estimate estimates, estimating, estimated

VERB If you **estimate** something, you guess the size or amount of it.

evaporate evaporates, evaporating, evaporated

VERB When a liquid **evaporates**, it becomes less because it is changing from a liquid into a gas.

evaporation NOUN

even

ADVERB **1** You say **even** when something is rather surprising. *I like to play outside even when it is raining.*

ADJECTIVE **2** If something like a path is **even**, it is smooth and flat.

ADJECTIVE **3** An **even** number can be divided by two, with no remainder. *2, 18 and 36 are all even numbers.*

evening evenings

NOUN The **evening** is the part of the day between late afternoon and the time you usually go to bed.

event events

NOUN An **event** is something important that happens.

eventually

ADVERB **Eventually** means in the end, after a lot of delays or problems.

ever

ADVERB **Ever** means at any time in the past or future. *Have you ever seen such a big dog?*

evergreen evergreens

NOUN An **evergreen** is a tree or other plant which keeps its leaves all year round.

every

ADJECTIVE **Every** means each one. *I spoke to every child in that class.*

every other PHRASE **Every other** means one in every two. *I see my friend every other week.*

everybody

PRONOUN **Everybody** means every person. *Everybody has to eat.*

everyone

PRONOUN You can use **everyone** instead of **everybody**.

everything

PRONOUN **Everything** means all of something.

everywhere

ADVERB **Everywhere** means in all places. *Children everywhere love stories.*

evidence

NOUN **Evidence** is anything you see, read or are told which gives you reason to believe something.

evil

ADJECTIVE An **evil** person is extremely wicked.

ewe ewes

NOUN A **ewe** is a female sheep.

ex-

PREFIX **Ex-** means former, for example "husband" → "ex-husband".
See *Prefixes* on page 264.

exact

ADJECTIVE Something that is **exact** is accurate in every detail.

exactly

ADVERB You say **exactly** when you mean no more and no less. *My father is exactly two metres tall.*

exaggerate exaggerates, exaggerating, exaggerated

VERB If you **exaggerate**, you say something is better or worse than it really is.

a
b
c
d
Ee
f
g
h
i
j
k
l
m
n
o
p
q
r
s
t
u
v
w
x
y
z

examination examinations

NOUN **1** An **examination**, called an **exam** for short, is a test people take to find out how much they have learned.

NOUN **2** A doctor makes a medical **examination** to find out how healthy you are.

examine examines, examining, examined

VERB If you **examine** something, you look at it carefully or closely.

example examples

NOUN An **example** is one thing which shows what the rest of a set is like. *This is an **example** of my work.*

excellent

ADJECTIVE Something that is **excellent** is extremely good.

except

PREPOSITION **Except** means apart from. *Everyone went outside **except** David.*

exception exceptions

NOUN An **exception** is something that does not fit in with a general rule. *With the **exception** of bats, mammals cannot fly.*

exchange exchanges, exchanging, exchanged

VERB If you **exchange** something, you change it for something else.

excite excites, exciting, excited

VERB If something **excites** you, it makes you feel happy and interested.

exciting ADJECTIVE   **excitement** NOUN

excited

ADJECTIVE If you feel **excited**, you feel happy and unable to rest.

exclaim exclaims, exclaiming, exclaimed

VERB When you **exclaim**, you speak suddenly or loudly, because you are excited or angry.

exclamation NOUN

exclamation mark exclamation marks

NOUN An **exclamation mark** is a punctuation mark (!) used in writing to express a strong feeling.
See *Punctuation* on page 264.

excuse excuses

NOUN An **excuse** is a reason you give for doing something, or not doing it.

exercise exercises

NOUN **1** **Exercise** is regular movements you make to keep fit.

NOUN **2** An **exercise** is a piece of work that you do to help you learn something.

exhausted

ADJECTIVE When you are **exhausted**, you are so tired you have no energy left.

exhibition exhibitions

NOUN An **exhibition** is a collection of pictures or other things in a public place where people can come to see them.

exist exists, existing, existed

VERB Things that **exist** are present in the world or universe now.
existence NOUN

exit exits

NOUN An **exit** is the way out of a place.

expand expands, expanding, expanded

VERB When something **expands**, it gets bigger.

expect expects, expecting, expected

VERB If you **expect** something, you think it will happen.

expedition expeditions

NOUN An **expedition** is a journey made for a special reason.

expel **expels, expelling, expelled**
VERB If someone is **expelled** from school, they are told not to come back because their behaviour has been so bad.

expensive
ADJECTIVE Something that is **expensive** costs a lot of money.

experience **experiences**
NOUN **1** An **experience** is something that happens to you.
NOUN **2** Experience is knowing about something because you have been doing it for a long time.

experiment **experiments**
NOUN An **experiment** is the testing of something, either to find out its effect or to prove something.

expert **experts**
NOUN An **expert** is someone who is very skilled at doing something or who knows a lot about something.

explain **explains, explaining, explained**
VERB **1** To **explain** means to say things to help people understand.
VERB **2** When you **explain**, you give reasons for something that happened.

explanation **explanations**
NOUN **1** An **explanation** is something that helps people understand something. *She gave us a clear explanation of the way the machine works.*
NOUN **2** An **explanation** is something that tells you why something happened.

explode **explodes, exploding, exploded**
VERB If something such as a firework **explodes**, it bursts with a loud bang.
explosion NOUN

explore **explores, exploring, explored**
VERB If you **explore** a place, you travel in it to find out what it is like.
exploration NOUN   **explorer** NOUN

explosive **explosives**
NOUN An **explosive** is a substance that can explode.

express **expresses, expressing, expressed**
VERB If you **express** an idea or feeling, you put it into words or show it by the way you act. *He could only express the way he felt by bursting into tears.*

expression **expressions**
NOUN Your **expression** is the look on your face that lets people know what you are thinking or feeling.

extinct
ADJECTIVE If an animal or plant family is **extinct**, it no longer has any living members. *The dodo has been extinct for more than 300 years.*

extra
ADJECTIVE You use **extra** to mean more than usual. *You'd better take an extra jumper – it's going to be cold.*

extraordinary
ADJECTIVE Someone or something that is **extraordinary** is very special or unusual.

extreme
ADJECTIVE **Extreme** means very great. *Extreme cold can cause many problems.*
extremely ADVERB

eye **eyes**
NOUN **1** Your **eyes** are the part of your body that you use for seeing.
NOUN **2** The **eye** of a needle is the small hole at one end.

eyesight
NOUN **Eyesight** is the ability to see.

Ff

a
b
c
d
e
Ff
g
h
i
j
k
l
m
n
o
p
q
r
s
t
u
v
w
x
y
z

fable fables
NOUN A **fable** is a story that is meant to teach you something. Fables often have animals as the main characters.

fabric fabrics
NOUN **Fabric** is material made in some way such as by weaving or knitting.

face faces, facing, faced
NOUN **1** Your **face** is the front part of your head from your chin to your forehead. See *Your face* on page 258.
VERB **2** If you **face** something, you have your face towards it.
NOUN **3** The **face** of a clock or watch is the part with the numbers on it that show the time.
NOUN **4** A **face** is a surface of a three-dimensional shape.

fact facts
NOUN A **fact** is something that is true.
factual ADJECTIVE

factor factors
NOUN A **factor** is a whole number which will divide exactly into another whole number. For example, 3 is a factor of 12.

factory factories
NOUN A **factory** is a large building where a lot of things are made.

fade fades, fading, faded
VERB **1** If a colour **fades**, it gets paler.
VERB **2** If the light **fades**, it gets darker.

fail fails, failing, failed
VERB **1** If someone **fails** when they try to do something, they cannot do it.
VERB **2** If something **fails**, it stops working. *The brakes failed, and the car hit a wall.*

failure failures
NOUN If something is a **failure**, it does not work as planned. *The picnic was a failure because it rained all day.*

faint faints, fainting, fainted; fainter, faintest
VERB **1** If someone **faints**, they become unconscious for a short time.
ADJECTIVE **2** Something like a sound or mark that is **faint** is not easy to hear or see.

fair fairer, fairest; fairs
ADJECTIVE **1** Something that is **fair** seems reasonable to most people.
ADJECTIVE **2** People who are **fair** have light-coloured hair.
NOUN **3** A **fair** is a form of entertainment that takes place outside with stalls, sideshows, and machines to ride on.

fairly
ADVERB **Fairly** means quite or rather.

fairy fairies
NOUN In stories, **fairies** are tiny people with wings, who have magical powers.

fairy tale fairy tales
NOUN A **fairy tale** is a story in which magical things happen.

faithful
ADJECTIVE If you are **faithful** to someone, you can be trusted and relied on.

fake fakes
NOUN A **fake** is a copy of something made to trick people into thinking that it is genuine.

fall **falls, falling, fell, fallen**
VERB **1** When someone or something **falls**, they drop towards the ground.
VERB **2** If someone's face **falls**, they suddenly look upset or disappointed.

false
ADJECTIVE **1** If something is **false**, it is not the real thing. *My uncle has a false tooth.*
ADJECTIVE **2** If something you say is **false**, it is not true.

familiar
ADJECTIVE Something **familiar** is well-known or easy to recognize. *It was good to see a familiar face.*

family **families**
NOUN **1** A **family** is a group of people made up of parents and their children.
NOUN **2** A **family** is also a group of animals or plants of the same kind. *Lions and tigers belong to the cat family.*

famine **famines**
NOUN A **famine** is a shortage of food which may cause many people to die.

famous
ADJECTIVE Someone or something **famous** is very well known.

fan **fans**
NOUN **1** A **fan** is an object which creates a draught of cool air when it moves.

NOUN **2** If you are a **fan** of something or of someone famous, you are very interested in them.

fantastic
ADJECTIVE Something **fantastic** is wonderful and very pleasing.

fantasy **fantasies**
NOUN **1** A **fantasy** is a story about things that do not exist in the real world.
NOUN **2** **Fantasy** is imagining things.

far **farther** or **further; farthest** or **furthest**
ADVERB **1** **Far** means a long way away. *Are you going far?*
ADVERB **2** You use **far** to ask questions about distance. *How far is the town?*

fare **fares**
NOUN A **fare** is the money that you pay to go on something like a plane or a bus.

farm **farms**
NOUN A **farm** is a large area of land together with buildings, used for growing crops or keeping animals.

farmer **farmers**
NOUN A **farmer** is a person who owns or manages a farm.

fascinate **fascinates, fascinating, fascinated**
VERB If something **fascinates** you, it interests you very much.

fashion **fashions**
NOUN A **fashion** is the style of things like clothes that are popular for a time.
fashionable ADJECTIVE

fast **faster, fastest; fasts, fasting, fasted**
ADJECTIVE **1** Someone or something that is **fast** can move very quickly.
ADJECTIVE **2** If a clock is **fast**, it shows a time that is later than the real time.
VERB **3** If someone **fasts**, they eat no food for a period of time.

fasten **fastens, fastening, fastened**
VERB When you **fasten** something, you close it or do it up. *Remember to fasten your seat belt.*

fat **fatter, fattest; fats**
ADJECTIVE **1** A **fat** person or animal has a heavy body.
NOUN **2** **Fat** is a solid or liquid substance used in cooking. It comes from animals or vegetables.

father **fathers**

NOUN Your **father** is your male parent.

fault **faults**

NOUN **1** If people say something is your **fault**, they are blaming you for something bad that has happened.

NOUN **2** A **fault** is something wrong with the way something was made.

faulty ADJECTIVE

favour **favours**

NOUN A **favour** is something helpful you do for someone.

favourite **favourites**

NOUN Your **favourite** person or thing is the one you like better than all the others. *This teddy is my* ***favourite*** *toy.*

fax **faxes**

NOUN A **fax** is a copy of a document that can be sent along a telephone line.

fear **fears, fearing, feared**

NOUN **1** Fear is the nasty feeling you have when you think you are in danger.

VERB **2** If you **fear** someone or something, you are frightened of them.

feast **feasts**

NOUN A **feast** is a large and special meal for many people.

feat **feats**

NOUN A **feat** is a brave or impressive act.

feather **feathers**

NOUN A **feather** is one of the very light pieces that make up a bird's coat.

February

NOUN **February** is the second month of the year. It has 28 days except in a leap year, when it has 29.

fed

VERB Fed is the past tense of **feed**.

feed **feeds, feeding, fed**

VERB If you **feed** a person or animal, you give them food.

feel **feels, feeling, felt**

VERB **1** If you **feel** something, like happy or sad, that is how you are at that time.

VERB **2** If you **feel** an object, you touch it to find out what it is like.

feeling **feelings**

NOUN A **feeling** is something you feel, like anger or happiness.

feet

PLURAL NOUN **Feet** is the plural of **foot**.

felt

VERB **1** Felt is the past tense of **feel**.

NOUN **2** Felt is a thick cloth made by pressing short threads together.

female **females**

NOUN A **female** is a person or animal that belongs to the sex that can have babies or young.

female ADJECTIVE

feminine

ADJECTIVE Someone who is **feminine** has the qualities generally expected of a woman, such as gentleness.

fence **fences**

NOUN A **fence** is a wooden or wire barrier between two areas of land.

ferocious

ADJECTIVE A **ferocious** animal or person is violent and fierce.

ferry **ferries**

NOUN A **ferry** is a boat that takes passengers and sometimes vehicles across a short stretch of water.

festival **festivals**

NOUN **1** A **festival** is an organized series of events and performances.

NOUN **2** A **festival** can also be a special day or period of religious celebration.

fetch fetches, fetching, fetched
VERB If you **fetch** something, you go and get it and bring it back.

fete fetes
NOUN A **fete** is an outdoor event with competitions and stalls which sell things.

fever fevers
NOUN If you have a **fever** when you are ill, you have a high temperature.

few fewer, fewest
ADJECTIVE **Few** means a small number of things. *I saw him a **few** minutes ago.*

fibre fibres
NOUN A **fibre** is a thin thread of something such as wool or cotton.

fiction
NOUN **Fiction** is books or stories about people and events which are made up by the author. See **non-fiction**.

fidget fidgets, fidgeting, fidgeted
VERB If you **fidget**, you keep moving about because you are nervous or bored.

field fields
NOUN A **field** is a piece of land with a fence around, used to grow crops or keep animals in.

fierce fiercer, fiercest
ADJECTIVE An animal that is **fierce** is dangerous.

fight fights, fighting, fought
VERB If you **fight** someone, you try to hurt them.

figure figures
NOUN **1** A **figure** is any of the numbers from 0 to 9. See **digit**.
NOUN **2** A **figure** is also the shape of a person. *It was just getting dark when I saw a small **figure** coming towards me.*

file files
NOUN **1** A **file** is a box or folded piece of card that you keep papers in.
NOUN **2** A **file** is also a set of data in a computer, which is stored under a name.
NOUN **3** A **file** is also a metal tool with rough surfaces which is used to smooth things like wood or metal.

fill fills, filling, filled
VERB If you **fill** something, you put so much into it there is no room for any more.

film films
NOUN **1** A **film** is moving pictures shown on a screen.
NOUN **2** **Film** is a long narrow piece of plastic that is used in a camera to take photographs.

filthy filthier, filthiest
ADJECTIVE Something **filthy** is very dirty.

fin fins
NOUN A fish's **fins** are like small wings that stick out of its body. They help the fish to swim and to keep its balance.

final
ADJECTIVE In a series of any kind, the **final** one is the last one.
finally ADVERB

find finds, finding, found
VERB When you **find** someone or something, you see the person or thing you have been looking for.

fine

a
b
c
d
e

Ff

g
h
i
j
k
l
m
n
o
p
q
r
s
t
u
v
w
x
y
z

fine finer, finest; fines

ADJECTIVE **1** Something that is **fine** is extremely good.

ADJECTIVE **2** Something like a thread or nib that is **fine** is very thin.

ADJECTIVE **3** If you say you are **fine**, you mean you are well and happy.

ADJECTIVE **4** When the weather is **fine**, it is dry and sunny.

NOUN **5** A **fine** is money that is paid as a punishment.

finger fingers

NOUN Your **fingers** are the four long jointed parts at the end of your hand.

fingernail fingernails

NOUN Your **fingernails** are the thin hard areas that cover the ends of your fingers.

fingerprint fingerprints

NOUN A **fingerprint** is a mark that shows the skin pattern at the tip of a finger.

finish finishes, finishing, finished

VERB When you **finish** something, like a meal or a book, you reach the end of it.

fir firs

NOUN A **fir** is a tall pointed evergreen tree with cones, and leaves like needles.

fire fires, firing, fired

NOUN **1** Fire is the flames produced when something burns.

NOUN **2** A **fire** is also something powered by coal, gas or electricity that gives out heat.

VERB **3** If someone **fires** a gun, a bullet is sent from the gun they are using.

fire engine fire engines

NOUN A **fire engine** is a large vehicle that carries firefighters and equipment for putting out fires.

firefighter firefighters

NOUN A **firefighter** is a person whose job is to put out fires and rescue trapped people and animals.

fireplace fireplaces

NOUN A **fireplace** is the opening beneath a chimney where a fire can be lit.

firework fireworks

NOUN A **firework** is a thing that burns with coloured sparks when you light it. Some fireworks make a loud noise.

firm firmer, firmest

ADJECTIVE **1** Something that is **firm** does not move easily when you press or push it. *This pear isn't ripe – it is too firm!*

ADJECTIVE **2** If someone is **firm** with you about something, you know they will not change their mind.

first

ADJECTIVE OR ADVERB If something is **first** or happens first, it is number one and comes before anything else.

first aid

NOUN **First aid** is simple treatment given as soon as possible to a person who is injured or who suddenly becomes ill.

first person

NOUN The **first person** refers to yourself when you are speaking or writing. It is expressed as "I" or "we".

fish fishes, fishing, fished

NOUN **1** A **fish** is an animal that lives in water. It has gills, fins and a scaly skin.

VERB **2** To **fish** is to try and catch fish for food or sport.

fisherman fishermen

NOUN A **fisherman** is a person who catches fish as a job or for sport.

fist fists

NOUN You make a **fist** by tucking your fingers into the palm of your hand.

fit fitter, fittest; fits, fitting, fitted

ADJECTIVE **1** Someone who is **fit** is healthy.
VERB **2** If something such as clothing **fits** you, it is the right size for you.
VERB **3** If something **fits** something else, it is the right size to go with it. *This is the lid that **fits** that box.*

fix fixes, fixing, fixed

VERB **1** If you **fix** something that has broken, you make it work again.
VERB **2** If you **fix** something somewhere, you put it there firmly so that it cannot be moved. *She **fixed** a lamp to the wall.*

fizzy fizzier, fizziest

ADJECTIVE A **fizzy** drink is full of little bubbles of gas.

flag flags

NOUN A **flag** is a piece of cloth that can be fixed to a pole as a symbol of a nation, or as a signal.

flake flakes

NOUN A **flake** is a small thin piece of something.

flame flames

NOUN A **flame** is a flickering tongue or blaze of fire.

flamingo flamingos

NOUN A **flamingo** is a long-legged wading bird with pink feathers.

flannel flannels

NOUN A **flannel** is a small square of towelling, used for washing yourself.

flap flaps, flapping, flapped

NOUN **1** A **flap** is something flat that is fixed along one edge so that the rest of it can move freely.
VERB **2** When a bird **flaps** its wings, it moves them up and down quickly.

flash flashes, flashing, flashed

NOUN **1** A **flash** is a bright light which comes suddenly and only lasts a moment, like lightning in a storm.
VERB **2** If something **flashes** past, it moves so fast that you cannot see it properly.

flask flasks

NOUN A **flask** is a bottle for carrying drinks. It keeps hot drinks hot and cold drinks cold.

flat flats; flatter, flattest

NOUN **1** A **flat** is a set of rooms, usually on one level, for living in.
ADJECTIVE **2** Something that is **flat** is level and smooth.
ADJECTIVE **3** A battery that is **flat** has lost its electrical power.
ADJECTIVE **4** A **flat** shape is one like a circle, that is two-dimensional.
See *Colours and flat shapes* on page 271.

flavour flavours

NOUN The **flavour** of food is its taste.

flea fleas

NOUN A **flea** is a small jumping insect that feeds on blood.

fleece fleeces

NOUN **1** A sheep's **fleece** is its woollen coat.
NOUN **2** A **fleece** is a kind of warm jacket or pullover.

flesh

NOUN **1** Flesh is the soft part of your body.
NOUN **2** The **flesh** of a fruit or vegetable is the soft inner part that you eat.

flew

VERB **Flew** is the past tense of **fly**.

flick flicks, flicking, flicked

VERB If you **flick** something, you move it sharply with your finger.

flies

a b c d e **Ff** g h i j k l m n o p q r s t u v w x y z

flies

VERB **Flies** is a present tense form of **fly**.

NOUN **Flies** is also the plural of **fly**.

flight flights

NOUN **1** A **flight** is a journey through the air by a bird or an aircraft.

NOUN **2** A **flight** of stairs is a set that leads from one level to another without changing direction.

flimsy flimsier, flimsiest

ADJECTIVE Something that is **flimsy** is made of something very thin or weak.

flip flips, flipping, flipped

VERB If you **flip** something, you turn or move it quickly. *He **flipped** a coin.*

flipper flippers

NOUN **1** A **flipper** is one of the broad flat limbs of sea animals, for example seals, that are used for swimming.

NOUN **2** Flippers are broad flat pieces of rubber that you can wear on your feet to help you swim.

float floats, floating, floated

VERB **1** Something that **floats** is supported by water and does not sink.

VERB **2** Something that **floats** through the air moves along gently, supported by the air.

flock flocks

NOUN A **flock** is a group of birds, sheep or goats.

See *Collective nouns* on page 262.

flood floods

NOUN A **flood** is a large amount of water covering an area that is usually dry.

floor floors

NOUN **1** The **floor** of a room is the flat part that you walk on.

NOUN **2** A **floor** of a building is all the rooms on that level. *Our flat is on the third **floor**.*

flop flops, flopping, flopped

VERB If someone or something **flops**, they fall loosely and rather heavily.

floppy disk floppy disks

NOUN A **floppy disk** is a small magnetic disk on which computer data is stored.

flour

NOUN **Flour** is a powder made by grinding grain such as wheat. It is used to make things like bread and cakes.

flow flows, flowing, flowed

VERB If liquid **flows** in a certain direction, it moves there steadily.

flow chart flow charts

NOUN A **flow chart** is a diagram which shows how one action follows on from another. This flow chart shows how to make a cup of tea.

flower flowers

NOUN A **flower** is the part of a plant that has coloured petals. When the petals fade, fruit or seeds develop.

flown

VERB **Flown** is the past participle of **fly**.

flu

NOUN **Flu** is an illness that gives you a fever and makes you ache all over. Flu is an abbreviation of **influenza**.

fluffy fluffier, fluffiest

ADJECTIVE Something that is **fluffy** is very soft and light.

fluid fluids

NOUN **Fluid** is another word for liquid.

flute flutes

NOUN A **flute** is a musical wind instrument consisting of a long tube with holes and keys.

flutter flutters, fluttering, fluttered

VERB If something **flutters**, it flaps or waves with small quick movements.

fly flies, flying, flew, flown

NOUN **1** A **fly** is a small insect with two wings.
See Insects on page 259.
VERB **2** When a bird, insect or aircraft **flies**, it moves through the air.

foal foals

NOUN A **foal** is a young horse.
See Young animals on page 260.

foam

NOUN **Foam** is a mass of tiny bubbles.

focus focuses, focusing, focused

VERB If you **focus** something like a camera or a telescope, you adjust it so that you can see through it clearly.

fog fogs

NOUN **Fog** is a thick mist of water droplets in the air.
foggy ADJECTIVE

fold folds, folding, folded

NOUN **1** **Folds** in material are the curves in it when it does not hang flat. *The curtains hung in soft folds.*
VERB **2** If you **fold** something, you bend it so that one part lies over another.

folder folders

NOUN A **folder** is a piece of folded cardboard for keeping papers in.

folk folks

NOUN **Folk** or folks are people.

follow follows, following, followed

VERB **1** If you **follow** someone who is moving, you move along behind them.
VERB **2** If one thing **follows** another, it happens after it.
VERB **3** If you **follow** instructions or advice, you do what you are told.

fond fonder, fondest

ADJECTIVE If you are **fond** of someone, you like them very much.

font fonts

NOUN In printing, a **font** is a complete set of type of one style and size.

food

NOUN **Food** is what people and animals eat to stay alive.

food chain food chains

NOUN A **food chain** is a series of living things that are linked because each one feeds on the next. For example, a plant may be eaten by a rabbit that may be eaten by a fox.

grass → rabbit → fox

foolish

ADJECTIVE Something or somebody **foolish** is silly or unwise.

foot feet

NOUN **1** Your **feet** are the parts of your body that touch the ground when you stand or walk.
NOUN **2** A **foot** is a measure of length, equal to about 30 centimetres.

football footballs

NOUN **1** Football is a game between two teams who try to kick a ball into each other's goal.
NOUN **2** A **football** is a large ball used in games of football.

footprint footprints

NOUN A **footprint** is a mark in the shape of a foot that a person or animal leaves on a surface.

footstep footsteps

NOUN A **footstep** is the sound made by someone walking.

forbid forbids, forbidding, forbade, forbidden

VERB If someone **forbids** you to do something, they order you not to do it.

force forces, forcing, forced

VERB **1** If you **force** someone or something, you use your power or strength to make them do what you want. *Dad forced me to save half my pocket money.*

NOUN **2** A **force** is a push or a pull.

NOUN **3** The **force** of something is also the powerful effect it has. *The force of the storm damaged many trees.*

forecast forecasts, forecasting, forecast

VERB **1** If someone **forecasts** something, they say what they think is going to happen in the future.

NOUN **2** A weather **forecast** tells you what sort of weather to expect.

forehead foreheads

NOUN Your **forehead** is the front of your head, between your hair and eyebrows.

foreign

ADJECTIVE Something that is **foreign** is to do with a country that is not your own.

forest forests

NOUN A **forest** is a large area where trees grow close together.

forgave

VERB **Forgave** is the past tense of **forgive**.

forget forgets, forgetting, forgot, forgotten

VERB If you **forget** something, you do not remember or think about it.

forgive forgives, forgiving, forgave, forgiven

VERB If you **forgive** someone who has done something bad, you stop being cross with them.

fork forks

NOUN **1** A **fork** is a tool with three or four prongs on the end of a handle. You use a small fork for eating and a large fork for digging in the garden.

NOUN **2** A **fork** in a road or tree is the point where it divides into two.

form forms, forming, formed

NOUN **1** A **form** is a piece of paper with questions on it and spaces where you should write the answers.

NOUN **2** A **form** is also a class in school.

VERB **3** When something **forms**, it takes shape.

formal

ADJECTIVE Something **formal** is correct and serious.

fortnight fortnights

NOUN A **fortnight** is two weeks.

fortress fortresses

NOUN A **fortress** is a castle or other strong place that is built with defences to keep enemies out.

fortunate

ADJECTIVE **1** Someone who is **fortunate** has good luck.

ADJECTIVE **2** Something that is **fortunate** brings you success or gives you an advantage.

fortune fortunes

NOUN **1** **Fortune** is good or bad luck.

NOUN **2** A **fortune** is a lot of money.

forward

ADVERB If you move **forward** or **forwards**, you move the way you are facing.

look forward PHRASE If you **look forward** to something, you want it to happen.

fossil **fossils**

NOUN A **fossil** is the hardened remains of a prehistoric animal or plant that are found inside a rock.

fought

VERB **Fought** is the past tense of **fight**.

foul **fouler, foulest**

ADJECTIVE If something is **foul**, it is extremely unpleasant.

found

VERB **Found** is the past tense of **find**.

foundation **foundations**

NOUN The **foundations** of a building are the solid layers of material put below the ground to support it.

fountain **fountains**

NOUN A **fountain** is a jet or spray of water forced up into the air by a pump.

fox **foxes**

NOUN A **fox** is a wild animal like a dog, with reddish-brown fur and a thick tail.

fraction **fractions**

NOUN **1** In maths, a **fraction** is a part of a whole number, for example $\frac{1}{4}$.
See *Fractions* on page 272.
NOUN **2** A **fraction** is also a tiny part of something.

fracture **fractures**

NOUN A **fracture** is a crack or break in something, especially a bone.

fragile

ADJECTIVE Something that is **fragile** is easily broken or damaged.

fragment **fragments**

NOUN A **fragment** of something is a small piece or part of it.

frame **frames**

NOUN A **frame** is the part surrounding something like a window or picture, or the lenses of a pair of glasses.

freckle **freckles**

NOUN **Freckles** are small, light brown spots on someone's skin.

free

ADJECTIVE **1** If a person or animal is **free**, they can go where they want.
Tom opened the cage and set the bird free.
ADJECTIVE **2** If something is **free**, it does not cost anything.
freedom NOUN

freeze **freezes, freezing, froze, frozen**

VERB **1** If a liquid **freezes**, it becomes solid because the temperature is low.
VERB **2** If you **freeze** something, you store it at a very low temperature.

freezer **freezers**

NOUN A **freezer** is a refrigerator for freezing and storing food.

frequent

ADJECTIVE If something is **frequent**, it happens often.
frequency NOUN **frequently** ADVERB

a
b
c
d
e
Ff
g
h
i
j
k
l
m
n
o
p
q
r
s
t
u
v
w
x
y
z

fresh

fresh **fresher, freshest**
ADJECTIVE **1** If food is **fresh**, it has been picked or made recently.
ADJECTIVE **2** Fresh water is water that is not salty.
ADJECTIVE **3** If you feel **fresh**, you feel rested and full of energy.
ADJECTIVE **4** Fresh air is the air outside.

friction
NOUN **Friction** is the force which is produced when two surfaces rub against each other.

Friday **Fridays**
NOUN **Friday** is the day between Thursday and Saturday.

fridge **fridges**
NOUN A **fridge** is a large metal container. It is kept cool so that the food in it stays fresh longer. Fridge is an abbreviation of **refrigerator**.

friend **friends**
NOUN A **friend** is someone you know well and like very much.

friendly **friendlier, friendliest**
ADJECTIVE If you are **friendly** to someone, you behave in a kind and pleasant way to them.

fright
NOUN **Fright** is a sudden feeling of fear.

frighten **frightens, frightening, frightened**
VERB If something **frightens** you, it makes you afraid.

frightening
ADJECTIVE Something that is **frightening** makes you feel afraid.

frog **frogs**
NOUN A **frog** is a small amphibious animal with smooth skin, big eyes, and long back legs which it uses for jumping. See *Amphibians* on page 259.

front **fronts**
NOUN **1** The **front** of something is the part that faces forward.
ADJECTIVE **2** A **front** room or garden is on the side of a building that faces the street.
in front PHRASE **In front** means ahead or further forward.
in front of PHRASE If you do something **in front of** someone, you do it while they are there.

frost **frosts**
NOUN When there is a **frost**, the weather is very cold and the ground becomes covered with tiny ice crystals.

frown **frowns, frowning, frowned**
VERB If you **frown**, your eyebrows are drawn together. People frown when they are angry, worried, or thinking hard.

froze
VERB **Froze** is the past tense of **freeze**.

frozen
VERB **1** Frozen is the past participle of **freeze**.
ADJECTIVE **2** If something like a lake or river is **frozen**, its surface has turned to ice.
ADJECTIVE **3** If you say you are **frozen**, you mean you are very cold.

fruit **fruits**
NOUN A **fruit** is the part of a plant that develops from the flower and contains the seeds. Many fruits are good to eat. See *Fruit* on page 257.

fry **fries, frying, fried**
VERB When you **fry** food, you cook it in a pan that contains hot fat or oil.

fuel fuels

NOUN **Fuel** is something like petrol or coal, that is burned to provide heat or power.

full fuller, fullest

ADJECTIVE If something is **full**, there is no room for anything more.

full stop full stops

NOUN A **full stop** is the punctuation mark (.) which you use at the end of a sentence.
See *Punctuation* on page 264.

fun

NOUN **Fun** is something enjoyable that makes you feel happy.

funeral funerals

NOUN A **funeral** is a ceremony held when a person has died. The body is buried or burned.

fungus fungi or funguses

NOUN A **fungus** is a plant such as a mushroom or mould that does not have flowers or leaves.

funnel funnels

NOUN **1** A **funnel** is an open cone which narrows to a tube. You use a funnel to pour liquid into containers.
NOUN **2** A **funnel** is also a metal chimney on a ship or steam engine.

funny funnier, funniest

ADJECTIVE **1** **Funny** people or things make you laugh.
ADJECTIVE **2** Something that is **funny** is rather strange or surprising.
funnily ADVERB

fur

NOUN **Fur** is the soft thick body hair of many animals.
furry ADJECTIVE

furious

ADJECTIVE Someone who is **furious** is extremely angry.

furniture

NOUN **Furniture** is large objects such as tables, beds and chairs, that people have in rooms.

further furthest

ADJECTIVE **1** **Further** is a comparative form of **far**.
ADJECTIVE **2** **Further** can mean more. *Write for **further** details.*
ADVERB **3** If someone goes **further** than someone else, they travel a longer way.

fury

NOUN **Fury** is violent or extreme anger.

fuss fusses, fussing, fussed

NOUN **1** A **fuss** is worried or anxious behaviour that is unnecessary and often not welcome. *I don't know why you're making such a **fuss** about it.*
VERB **2** If someone **fusses**, they worry about unimportant things.

future futures

NOUN **1** The **future** is the time that is to come.
ADJECTIVE **2** **Future** is to do with time that is to come. *We need to look after the environment for **future** generations.*
NOUN **3** The **future tense** of a verb is the form used to talk about something that will happen in the future. For example, the sentence "Ben will be at school tomorrow" is in the future tense.

a b c d e **Ff** g h i j k l m n o p q r s t u v w x y z

Gg

gain gains, gaining, gained
NOUN **1** A **gain** is an increase in the amount of something.
VERB **2** If you **gain** from something, you get something good out of it.
VERB **3** If a clock or watch **gains**, it moves too fast.

galaxy galaxies
NOUN **1** A **galaxy** is a large group of stars and planets in space.
NOUN **2** The **galaxy** is the group of stars and planets that the earth belongs to.
galactic ADJECTIVE

gale gales
NOUN A **gale** is a strong wind.

galleon galleons
NOUN A **galleon** is a large sailing ship used hundreds of years ago.

gallery galleries
NOUN **1** A **gallery** is a place that shows paintings or sculptures.
NOUN **2** In a hall or theatre, a **gallery** is a raised area at the back where people can sit and get a good view of what is happening.

gallon gallons
NOUN A **gallon** is a measure of volume equal to about four and a half litres.

gallop gallops, galloping, galloped
VERB When a horse **gallops**, it runs fast.

game games
NOUN A **game** is a something you play for sport or fun. Most games have rules.

gander ganders
NOUN A **gander** is a male goose.

gang gangs
NOUN A **gang** is a group of people who do things together.

gaol gaols
Gaol is another spelling of **jail**.

gap gaps
NOUN A **gap** is a space between two things, or a hole in something solid.

garage garages
NOUN **1** A **garage** is a building in which someone can keep a car.
NOUN **2** A **garage** is also a place that sells petrol or repairs cars.

garden gardens
NOUN A **garden** is land next to a house where people can grow things like trees, flowers or grass.

garlic
NOUN **Garlic** is the small white bulb of an onion-like plant which has a strong taste and smell. It is used in cooking.

garment garments
NOUN A **garment** is a piece of clothing.

gas gases
NOUN Gas is a substance that is not liquid or solid. Air is a mixture of gases. Another type of gas is used as a fuel for cookers and central heating.

gasp gasps, gasping, gasped
VERB When you **gasp**, you take a short quick breath through your mouth, especially when you are surprised or in pain.

gate gates

NOUN A **gate** is a type of door that is used at the entrance to a garden or field.

gather gathers, gathering, gathered

VERB **1** If people or animals **gather**, they come together in a group.

VERB **2** If you **gather** things, you collect them from different places. *Early people used to **gather** berries for food.*

gave

VERB **Gave** is the past tense of **give**.

gaze gazes, gazing, gazed

VERB If you **gaze** at something, you look steadily at it for a long time.

general generals

ADJECTIVE **1** You use **general** when you are talking about most of the people in a group. *There was a **general** rush for the door when the bell rang.*

NOUN **2** A **general** is an army officer of very high rank.

generally ADVERB

generous

ADJECTIVE Someone who is **generous** is kind and willing to help others by giving them money or time.

gentle gentler, gentlest

ADJECTIVE Someone who is **gentle** is kind, calm and sensitive.

gently ADVERB

gentleman gentlemen

NOUN A **gentleman** is a polite name for a man.

genuine

ADJECTIVE Something **genuine** is real and not false or pretend.

geography

NOUN **Geography** is the study of the countries of the world, and of things like their rivers, mountains and people.

geographical ADJECTIVE

gerbil gerbils

NOUN A **gerbil** is a small furry animal with long back legs, often kept as a pet.

germ germs

NOUN A **germ** is a tiny living thing that can make people ill. You cannot see germs without using a microscope.

get gets, getting, got

VERB **1** Get often means the same as become. *It **gets** dark earlier in winter.*

VERB **2** If you **get** into a particular situation, you put yourself in that situation. *We **got** into a muddle.*

VERB **3** If you **get** something done, you do it or you persuade someone to do it.

VERB **4** If you **get** something, you fetch it or are given it. *I'll **get** us all a cup of tea.*

VERB **5** If you **get** a train, bus or plane, you travel on it.

ghost ghosts

NOUN A **ghost** is a shadowy figure of someone no longer living that some people believe they see.

giant giants

NOUN **1** In fairy stories, a **giant** is someone who is huge and strong.

ADJECTIVE **2** Anything that is much larger than usual can be called **giant**. *A **giant** wave was coming towards us.*

giddy giddier, giddiest

ADJECTIVE If you feel **giddy**, you feel dizzy.

a b c d e f **Gg** h i j k l m n o p q r s t u v w x y z

gift gifts
NOUN A **gift** is a present.

gigantic
ADJECTIVE Something **gigantic** is extremely large.

giggle giggles, giggling, giggled
VERB If you **giggle**, you make quiet little laughing noises.

gill gills
NOUN The **gills** of a fish are the organs on its sides which it uses for breathing.

ginger
NOUN **Ginger** is a plant root with a hot spicy flavour, used in cooking.

giraffe giraffes
NOUN A **giraffe** is a large African mammal with a very long neck.

girl girls
NOUN A **girl** is a female child.

give gives, giving, gave, given
VERB If you **give** someone something, you hand it to them or provide it for them. *Dad **gave** me a job cleaning the car.*
give way PHRASE If something **gives way**, it collapses.

glacier glaciers
NOUN A **glacier** is a huge frozen river of slow-moving ice.

glad gladder, gladdest
ADJECTIVE If you are **glad**, you are happy and pleased.

glance glances, glancing, glanced
VERB 1 If you **glance** at something, you look at it quickly.
NOUN 2 A **glance** is a quick look.

glare glares, glaring, glared
VERB 1 If you **glare** at someone, you look at them angrily.
VERB 2 If the sun or a light **glares**, it shines with a very bright light.

glass glasses
NOUN 1 Glass is a hard transparent material that is easily broken. It is used to make windows and bottles.
NOUN 2 A **glass** is a container that you can drink from, made of glass.

glasses
PLURAL NOUN Glasses are two lenses in a frame, which some people wear over their eyes to help them see better.

gleam gleams, gleaming, gleamed
VERB If something **gleams**, it shines and reflects light.

glide glides, gliding, glided
VERB When something **glides**, it moves silently and smoothly.

glider gliders
NOUN A **glider** is an aircraft that does not have an engine, but flies by floating on air currents.

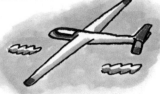

glimpse glimpses, glimpsing, glimpsed
VERB If you **glimpse** something, you see it very briefly.

glisten glistens, glistening, glistened
VERB If something **glistens**, it shines or sparkles. *Her eyes **glistened** with tears.*

glitter glitters, glittering, glittered
VERB If something **glitters**, it shines in a sparkling way. *Her diamond necklace **glittered** under the lights.*

gloat gloats, gloating, gloated
VERB If you **gloat**, you show great pleasure in your own success or in other people's failure.

globe globes
NOUN A **globe** is a round model of the Earth with a map of the world drawn on it.

gloomy gloomier, gloomiest
ADJECTIVE 1 If a place is **gloomy**, it is dark and dull.
ADJECTIVE 2 If people are **gloomy**, they are unhappy and not at all hopeful.
gloomily ADVERB

glossary glossaries
NOUN A **glossary** is a list of explanations of special words, usually found at the back of a book.

glossy glossier, glossiest
ADJECTIVE Something that is **glossy** is smooth and shiny.

glove gloves
NOUN A **glove** is a piece of clothing which covers your hand, with separate places for each finger.

glow glows, glowing, glowed
VERB If something **glows**, it shines with a steady dull light.

glue
NOUN **Glue** is a thick sticky liquid used for joining things together.

gnarled
ADJECTIVE Something that is **gnarled** is old, twisted and rough. *The old gardener's hands were **gnarled**.*

gnat gnats
NOUN A **gnat** is a very small flying insect that bites people.

gnaw gnaws, gnawing, gnawed
VERB If people or animals **gnaw** something hard, they keep biting on it.

gnome gnomes
NOUN In fairy stories, a **gnome** is a tiny old man.

go goes, going, went, gone
VERB 1 If you **go** somewhere, you move or travel there.
VERB 2 If something **goes** well, it is successful.
VERB 3 If you are **going** to do something, you will do it.
VERB 4 If a clock or watch **goes**, it works.

goal goals
NOUN 1 A **goal** in games such as football or hockey is the space into which players try to get the ball so that they can score.
NOUN 2 It is also called a **goal** when a player gets the ball into the goal.
NOUN 3 If something is your **goal**, you hope to succeed in doing it one day.

goat goats
NOUN A **goat** is an animal with short coarse hair, horns, and a short tail.

goblin goblins
NOUN In fairy stories, a **goblin** is a small ugly creature who likes to make trouble.

god gods
NOUN 1 A **god** is a person or thing that people worship.
NOUN 2 The name **God** is given to the god who is worshipped by some people, such as Christians or Jews.

goddess goddesses
NOUN A **goddess** is a female god.

a
b
c
d
e
f
Gg
h
i
j
k
l
m
n
o
p
q
r
s
t
u
v
w
x
y
z

goggles

goggles

PLURAL NOUN **Goggles** are special glasses that fit closely round your eyes to protect them.

go-kart **go-karts**

A **go-kart** is a very small motor vehicle with four wheels, used for racing.

gold

NOUN **1 Gold** is a valuable, yellow-coloured metal that is used for making things like jewellery.
ADJECTIVE **2** Something that is **gold** in colour is warm yellow.

golden

ADJECTIVE Something that is **golden** is made of gold or is a gold colour.

goldfish

NOUN A **goldfish** is a gold or orange-coloured fish which is often kept as a pet.

golf

NOUN **Golf** is a game in which players use long sticks called clubs to hit a small ball into special holes.

gone

VERB **Gone** is the past participle of **go**.

good **better, best**

ADJECTIVE **1** Someone who is **good** is kind and caring, and can be trusted.
ADJECTIVE **2** A child or animal that is **good** is well-behaved and obedient.
ADJECTIVE **3** If something like a film or book is **good**, people like it.
ADJECTIVE **4** Someone who is **good** at something is skilful and successful at it.

goodbye

You say **goodbye** to someone when you or they are leaving.

good night

You say **good night** to someone when you or they are going to bed.

goods

PLURAL NOUN **Goods** are things that can be bought or sold.

goose **geese**

NOUN A **goose** is a large bird with a long neck and webbed feet. Its cry is a loud honking noise.

gorilla **gorillas**

NOUN The **gorilla** is the largest of the apes. It lives in African forests.

got

VERB **1 Got** is the past tense of **get**.
VERB **2** You can use **have got** instead of **have**. *We have got a map.*
VERB **3** You can use **have got to** instead of **have to**, when talking about something you must do. *We have got to win.*

government **governments**

NOUN A **government** is the group of people who run a country and decide about important things such as medical care and old age pensions.

grab **grabs, grabbing, grabbed**

VERB If you **grab** something, you take hold of it suddenly and roughly.

graceful

ADJECTIVE Someone or something that is **graceful** moves in a smooth way which is pleasant to watch.

gradual

ADJECTIVE Something that is **gradual** happens slowly.
gradually ADVERB

graffiti

NOUN **Graffiti** is words or pictures that are scribbled on walls in public places.

grain grains

NOUN **1** Grain is the seeds of plants like wheat or corn, that we use for food.

NOUN **2** A **grain** of something such as sand or salt is a tiny hard piece of it.

gram grams

NOUN A **gram** (g) is a small unit of mass and weight. One sheet of paper weighs about four grams. There are 1000 grams in a kilogram.

grammar

NOUN **Grammar** is the rules of a language.

grand grander, grandest

ADJECTIVE Buildings that are **grand** are large and look important.

grandad grandads

NOUN Your **grandad** is your grandfather.

grandchild grandchildren

NOUN Someone's **grandchild** is the child of their son or daughter.

grandfather grandfathers

NOUN Your **grandfather** is the father of one of your parents.

grandmother grandmothers

NOUN Your **grandmother** is the mother of one of your parents.

grandparent grandparents

NOUN Your **grandparents** are your parents' parents.

granny grannies

NOUN; INFORMAL Your **granny** is your grandmother.

grape grapes

NOUN A **grape** is a small green or purple fruit. Grapes grow in bunches on vines. They can be eaten raw, used for making wine, or dried to make raisins, sultanas or currants.
See Fruit on page 257.

grapefruit grapefruits

NOUN A **grapefruit** is a large round fruit. It is like an orange but it is larger and has a pale yellow skin.
See Fruit on page 257.

graph graphs

NOUN A **graph** is a diagram which shows how two sets of information are related.

This week's rain

level of water in rain barrel — days

grasp grasps, grasping, grasped

VERB **1** If you **grasp** something, you hold it firmly.

VERB **2** If you **grasp** an idea, you understand it.

grass grasses

NOUN **Grass** is a common green plant with long thin leaves. It grows on lawns and in parks.

grasshopper grasshoppers

NOUN A **grasshopper** is an insect. It has long back legs and can jump well. The male makes a chirping sound by rubbing its back legs against its wings.
See Insects on page 259.

grate grates, grating, grated

NOUN **1** A **grate** is a framework of metal bars in a fireplace.

VERB **2** If you **grate** food, you shred it into small pieces.

grateful

ADJECTIVE If you are **grateful** for something nice that someone has done, you have warm feelings towards them and want to thank them.

grave graver, gravest; graves

ADJECTIVE **1** Something that is **grave** is important, serious and worrying.

NOUN **2** A **grave** is a place where a dead person is buried.

a
b
c
d
e
f
Gg
h
i
j
k
l
m
n
o
p
q
r
s
t
u
v
w
x
y
z

a
b
c
d
e
f

Gg

h
i
j
k
l
m
n
o
p
q
r
s
t
u
v
w
x
y
z

gravel

NOUN **Gravel** is small stones used for making roads and paths.

gravity

NOUN **Gravity** is the force that makes things fall when you drop them.

gravy

NOUN **Gravy** is a brown sauce made from meat juices.

graze **grazes, grazing, grazed**

VERB **1** When animals **graze**, they eat grass.

VERB **2** If you **graze** your skin, you scrape it against something and hurt yourself.

grease

NOUN **1** Grease is a thick oil which is put on the moving parts of cars and other machines to make them work smoothly.

NOUN **2** Grease is also an oily substance produced by your skin and found in your hair.

greasy ADJECTIVE

great **greater, greatest**

ADJECTIVE **1** You say something is **great** when it is large in size, number or amount. *The waves threw a **great** shower of pebbles onto the seafront.*

ADJECTIVE **2** Great also means important. *I like to hear about **great** scientists.*

ADJECTIVE **3** INFORMAL Great can mean wonderful. *Paul had a **great** time.*

greedy **greedier, greediest**

ADJECTIVE Someone who is **greedy** wants more than they need of something.

greedily ADVERB

green **greener, greenest**

ADJECTIVE **1** Something that is **green** is the colour of grass.

See *Colours* on page 271.

ADJECTIVE **2** Green is used to describe people who are interested in protecting the environment.

greengrocer **greengrocers**

NOUN A **greengrocer** is a shopkeeper who sells fruit and vegetables.

greenhouse **greenhouses**

NOUN A **greenhouse** is a building which has glass walls and a glass roof. It is used to grow plants in.

greet **greets, greeting, greeted**

VERB When you **greet** someone, you look pleased to see them, and say something friendly.

greeting **greetings**

NOUN A **greeting** is something friendly that you say or do when you meet someone.

grew

VERB **Grew** is the past tense of **grow**.

grey **greyer, greyest**

ADJECTIVE Something that is **grey** is the colour of clouds on a rainy day.

See *Colours* on page 271.

grid **grids**

NOUN A **grid** is a pattern of lines crossing each other to form squares.

grief

NOUN Someone who feels **grief** is very sad, often because a person or animal they love has died.

grill **grills, grilling, grilled**

VERB If you **grill** food, you cook it on metal bars under or over heat.

grim **grimmer, grimmest**

ADJECTIVE **1** If a situation or piece of news is **grim**, it is unpleasant and worrying.

ADJECTIVE **2** If someone looks **grim**, they are serious because they are worried or angry about something.

grin grins, grinning, grinned
VERB If you **grin**, you give a broad smile.

grind grinds, grinding, ground
VERB **1** If you **grind** something, such as pepper, you crush it into a fine powder.
VERB **2** If you **grind** your teeth, you rub your upper and lower teeth together.

grip grips, gripping, gripped
VERB **1** If you **grip** something, you take hold of it firmly.
VERB **2** If something **grips** you, you find it very interesting.

groan groans, groaning, groaned
VERB If you **groan**, you make a long low sound of pain or unhappiness.

groceries
PLURAL NOUN **Groceries** are foods such as flour, sugar and tinned foods.

groove grooves
NOUN A **groove** is a deep line cut into a surface.

ground grounds
NOUN **1** The **ground** is the surface of the earth or the floor of a room.
NOUN **2** A **ground** is an area of land where people play sports such as football or cricket.
PLURAL NOUN **3** The **grounds** of a large house are the land around it which belongs to it.
VERB **4** **Ground** is the past tense of **grind**.

group groups
NOUN **1** A **group** of things or people is a number of them that are linked together in some way.
NOUN **2** A **group** is also a number of musicians who perform music together.

grow grows, growing, grew, grown
VERB **1** When a person **grows**, they get bigger. All living things can grow.
VERB **2** If you **grow** plants, you put seeds or young plants in the ground and look after them.
VERB **3** When someone **grows up**, they gradually change from being a child into being an adult.

growl growls, growling, growled
VERB When an animal **growls**, it makes a low rumbling sound, usually because it is angry.

grown
VERB **Grown** is the past participle of **grow**.

grown-up grown-ups
NOUN; INFORMAL A **grown-up** is an adult.

growth
NOUN **Growth** means getting bigger.

grub grubs
NOUN A **grub** is a wormlike insect that has just hatched from its egg.

grumble grumbles, grumbling, grumbled
VERB If you **grumble**, you complain in a bad-tempered way.

grunt grunts, grunting, grunted
VERB When a pig **grunts**, it makes a low rough noise.

guarantee guarantees, guaranteeing, guaranteed
VERB **1** If someone or something **guarantees** something, they make certain that it will happen.
NOUN **2** A **guarantee** is a written promise that if something you have bought goes wrong it will be replaced or mended free.

guard

guard guards, guarding, guarded
VERB **1** If you **guard** a person or object, you stay near to them to keep them safe or to make sure they do not escape.
NOUN **2** A **guard** is a person who guards something or somewhere.

guess guesses, guessing, guessed
VERB If you **guess** something, you give an answer without knowing if it is right.

guest guests
NOUN A **guest** is someone who stays at your home or who goes to an event because they have been invited.

guide guides, guiding, guided
VERB **1** If you **guide** someone, you show them where to go or what to do.
NOUN **2** A **guide** is someone who shows you round places.

guidebook guidebooks
NOUN A **guidebook** is a book that gives information about a place.

guilty guiltier, guiltiest
ADJECTIVE **1** If you are **guilty** of doing something wrong, you did it.
ADJECTIVE **2** If you feel **guilty**, you are unhappy because you have done something wrong.

guinea pig guinea pigs
NOUN A **guinea pig** is a small furry animal without a tail, often kept as a pet.

guitar guitars
NOUN A **guitar** is a musical instrument with strings that you play with your fingers.

gulf gulfs
NOUN A **gulf** is a large area of sea which stretches a long way into the land.

gulp gulps, gulping, gulped
VERB **1** If you **gulp** food or drink, you swallow large amounts of it.
VERB **2** If you **gulp**, you swallow air because you are nervous.

gum gums
NOUN **1** Your **gums** are the firm flesh your teeth are set in.
NOUN **2** Gum is a soft sweet that people chew but do not swallow.
NOUN **3** Gum is also glue for sticking paper.

gumboot gumboots
NOUN Gumboots are long rubber boots that you wear to keep your feet dry.

gun guns
NOUN A **gun** is a weapon which fires bullets or shells.

gunpowder
NOUN Gunpowder is a powder that explodes when it is lit. It is used for making things such as fireworks.

gust gusts
NOUN A **gust** is a sudden rush of wind.

gutter gutters
NOUN **1** A **gutter** is the edge of a road next to the pavement, where rain collects and flows away.
NOUN **2** A **gutter** is also an open pipe at the edge of a roof, where rain collects and flows away.

gym gyms
NOUN **1** Gym is physical exercises, especially ones using equipment such as bars and ropes. Gym is an abbreviation of **gymnastics**.

NOUN **2** A **gym** is a room with special equipment for physical exercises. Gym here is an abbreviation of **gymnasium**.

Hh

habit habits

NOUN A **habit** is something that you do often or regularly, sometimes without thinking about it.

habitat habitats

NOUN The **habitat** of an animal or plant is its natural home.

had

VERB **Had** is the past tense of **have**.

haddock

NOUN A **haddock** is an edible sea fish.

haiku

NOUN **Haiku** is a Japanese poem of 17 syllables in three lines.

hail hails, hailing, hailed

NOUN **1 Hail** is frozen rain. It falls in small balls of ice called hailstones.
VERB **2** When it is **hailing**, frozen rain is falling.

hair hairs

NOUN Your **hair** is made up of a large number of fine threads that grow on your head. Hair also grows on other parts of the body and on the bodies of some other animals.

hairdresser hair̶d̶r̶e̶s̶s̶e̶r̶s̶

NOUN A **haird**̶r̶e̶s̶s̶e̶r̶ ̶i̶s̶ ̶t̶r̶a̶i̶ned to cut and style peop̶l̶e̶

hairy ha̶i̶r̶i̶e̶r̶,̶ ̶h̶a̶i̶r̶i̶e̶s̶t̶

ADJECTI̶V̶E̶ ̶S̶o̶m̶e̶thing that is **hairy** i̶s̶ ̶c̶o̶v̶e̶r̶e̶d̶ ̶i̶n̶ ̶h̶a̶i̶r̶.̶

hajj

NOUN Th̶e̶ ̶h̶a̶j̶j̶ ̶i̶s̶ ̶a̶ ̶p̶i̶l̶g̶r̶i̶m̶a̶g̶e̶ to Mecca that eve̶r̶y̶ ̶M̶u̶s̶l̶i̶m̶ ̶s̶h̶o̶u̶l̶d̶ ̶m̶a̶ke at least once in̶ ̶t̶h̶e̶i̶r̶ ̶l̶i̶f̶e̶ ̶i̶f̶ ̶h̶ealthy and wealth̶y̶

half halves

NOUN **1** A **half** is one of two equal parts of something.
See *Fractions* on page 272.

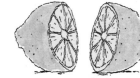

ADVERB **2** When you are talking about time, you can use **half** to mean 30 minutes after a particular hour. *She was home by **half** past three.*

halfway

ADVERB **Halfway** is the middle of the distance between two points. *He stopped* **halfway** *down the stairs.*

hall halls

NOUN **1** A **hall** is the room just inside the front door of a home which leads into other rooms.
NOUN **2** A **hall** is also a large room or building used for public events.

Halloween

NOUN **Halloween** is October 31. Children celebrate it by dressing up, often as ghosts and witches.

halve halves, halving, halved

VERB If you **halve** something, you divide it into two equal parts.

ham

NOUN **Ham** is meat from the back leg of a pig. It is specially treated so that it can be kept for a long time.

hamburger hamburgers

NOUN A **hamburger** is a piece of minced meat shaped into a flat disc. Hamburgers are often eaten in a bread roll.

hammer

hammer hammers

NOUN A **hammer** is a tool that is used for hitting things, such as nails into wood.

hammock hammocks

NOUN A **hammock** is a piece of strong cloth or netting which is hung between two supports and used as a bed.

hamster hamsters

NOUN A **hamster** is a small furry rodent which is often kept as a pet. Hamsters have very short tails, and large cheek pouches for carrying food.

hand hands, handing, handed

NOUN 1 Your **hand** is the part of your body which is at the end of your arm. It has four fingers and a thumb.

NOUN 2 The **hands** of a clock point to the numbers to tell you the time.

VERB 3 When you **hand** something to someone, you pass it to them.

handbag handbags

NOUN A **handbag** is a small bag that women use to carry things such as money and keys.

handkerchief handkerchiefs

NOUN A **handkerchief** is a small square of fabric that you use for wiping your nose.

handle handles, handling, handled

NOUN 1 The **handle** of an object is the part you hold to pick it up and carry it.

NOUN 2 The **handle** of a door or window is the knob or lever that is used for opening or closing it.

VERB 3 If you **handle** something, you touch or feel it with your hands.

handlebar handlebars

NOUN **Handlebars** are the bar and handles at the front of a bicycle, for steering.

handsome

ADJECTIVE A **handsome** man has a very attractive face.

handwriting

NOUN Someone's **handwriting** is the way in which they write with a pen or pencil.

handy handier, handiest

ADJECTIVE 1 If something is **handy**, it is near. *I like to keep my glasses* **handy**.

ADJECTIVE 2 If an object is **handy**, it is easy to handle or use.

hang hangs, hanging, hung

VERB If you **hang** something up, you fix it there so that it does not touch the ground. ***Hang** your coat on the hook.*

hangar hangars

NOUN A **hangar** is a large building where aircraft are kept.

hanger hangers

NOUN A **hanger** is a curved piece of metal, wood or plastic that you hang clothes on.

hang-glider hang-gliders

NOUN A **hang-glider** is an aircraft without an engine. The pilot hangs in a harness from the frame.

Hanukkah or **Chanukah**

NOUN **Hanukkah** is the eight-day Jewish festival of lights.

happen happens, happening, happened

VERB 1 If something **happens**, it takes place. *What happens if I press this button?*

VERB 2 ... en to do something, ... happened to be

dresser
dresser is trai...
's hair.

...rier, hairiest
... Someone or some... covered with hair.

...e **hajj** *is the journey ...*
...ry Muslim must mak...
their life if they are h...
...y enough to do so.

... great

... eel
... s
... s are the

harbour harbours

NOUN A **harbour** is an area of deep water where boats can stay safely.

hard harder, hardest

ADJECTIVE **1** An object that is **hard** is very firm and stiff.

ADJECTIVE **2** If something is **hard** to do, you can only do it with a lot of effort.

hard disk hard disks

NOUN A **hard disk** is a permanent part of a computer. It is used to store large amounts of data.

harden hardens, hardening, hardened

VERB If something **hardens**, it becomes hard or gets harder.

hardly

ADVERB If you can **hardly** do something, you can only just do it. *The box was so heavy I could **hardly** lift it.*

hardware

NOUN **1** Hardware is tools and equipment made of metal.

NOUN **2** Hardware is also computer machinery.

hare hares

NOUN A **hare** is an animal like a large rabbit, but with longer ears and legs. It does not live in a burrow but rests in grass or in a ploughed field.

harm

NOUN **Harm** is injury to a person or animal.

harmful ADJECTIVE   **harmless** ADJECTIVE

harness harnesses

NOUN **1** A **harness** is a set of straps which fit round a person's body to hold the person firmly in place.

NOUN **2** A horse's **harness** is a set of straps fastened round its head or body.

harsh harsher, harshest

ADJECTIVE **1** A person who is **harsh** is unkind.

ADJECTIVE **2** Weather that is **harsh** is cold and unpleasant.

ADJECTIVE **3** A voice or other sound that is **harsh** sounds rough and unpleasant.

harvest harvests

NOUN **Harvest** is the time when farmers cut and gather their ripe crop.

has

VERB **Has** is a present tense form of **have**.

hat hats

NOUN A **hat** is a head covering for wearing outside.

hatch hatches, hatching, hatched

VERB When a baby bird, insect or other animal **hatches**, it comes out of its egg by breaking the shell.

hate hates, hating, hated

VERB If you **hate** something, you have a strong feeling of dislike for it.

haul hauls, hauling, hauled

VERB To **haul** something means to move it with a long steady pull.

haunted

ADJECTIVE A place that is **haunted** is often visited by a ghost.

have has, having, had

VERB **1** Have can be used with other verbs to form the past tense. *I **have** already seen that film.*

VERB **2** If you **have** something, you own or possess it. *We **have** two tickets for the football match.*

VERB **3** If you **have** to do something, you must do it.

haven't

haven't

VERB **Haven't** is a contraction of **have not.**

hawk **hawks**

NOUN A **hawk** is a large bird of prey that eats small animals.

hay

NOUN **Hay** is grass which has been cut and dried to feed animals.

head **heads, heading, headed**

NOUN **1** Your **head** is the part of your body which has your brain, eyes and mouth in it.

NOUN **2** The **head** of something is the top, start or most important end. *Our teacher sat at the **head** of the table.*

NOUN **3** The **head** of a group or organization is the person in charge.

VERB **4** If you **head** in a particular direction, you move that way.

VERB **5** To **head** a ball means to hit it with your head.

headache **headaches**

NOUN A **headache** is a pain in your head.

heading **headings**

NOUN A **heading** is a title at the top of a piece of writing.

headlight **headlights**

NOUN The **headlights** on a motor vehicle are the large powerful lights at the front.

headline **headlines**

NOUN **1** A **headline** is the title of a newspaper article printed in large type.

NOUN **2** The **headlines** are the main points of the radio or television news.

headphones

PLURAL NOUN **Headphones** are a pair of small speakers that you wear over or in your ears to listen to a recording without other people hearing.

headquarters

NOUN The **headquarters** of an organization is the place where the leaders of the organization work.

head teacher **head teachers**

NOUN The **head teacher** is the teacher who is in charge of a school.

heal **heals, healing, healed**

VERB If something **heals**, it becomes healthy or normal again.

health

NOUN A person's **health** is how their body is, and whether they are well or ill.

healthy **healthier, healthiest**

ADJECTIVE **1** Someone who is **healthy** is well and not suffering from any illness.

ADJECTIVE **2** Something that is **healthy** is good for your health.

heap **heaps**

NOUN A **heap** is a lot of things piled up, usually rather untidily.

hear **hears, hearing, heard**

VERB When you **hear** sounds, you notice them by using your ears.

hearing

NOUN **Hearing** is the sense which makes it possible for you to be aware of sounds.

heart **hearts**

NOUN **1** Your **heart** is the organ that pumps the blood round inside your body.

NOUN **2** A **heart** is a shape like a heart, used especially as a symbol of love.

heat **heats, heating, heated**

NOUN **1 Heat** is warmth.

VERB **2** To **heat** something means to raise its temperature.

heather

NOUN **Heather** is a plant with small purple or white flowers that grows wild on hills and moorland.

heaven

NOUN **Heaven** is a place of happiness where God is believed to live.

heavy heavier, heaviest

ADJECTIVE Something that is **heavy** weighs a lot or weighs more than usual.

Hebrew

NOUN **Hebrew** is an ancient language now spoken in Israel, where it is the official language.

hedge hedges

NOUN A **hedge** is a row of bushes growing close together.

hedgehog hedgehogs

NOUN A **hedgehog** is a small animal with sharp spikes all over its back. It defends itself by rolling up into a ball.

heel heels

NOUN **1** Your **heel** is the back part of your foot.
NOUN **2** The **heel** of a shoe is the raised part underneath, at the back.

height heights

NOUN **1** The **height** of a person is how tall they are.
NOUN **2** The **height** of an object is its measurement from bottom to top.

held

VERB **Held** is the past tense of **hold**.

helicopter helicopters

NOUN A **helicopter** is an aircraft with large blades which turn very quickly. It can take off vertically, hover and fly.

helmet helmets

NOUN A **helmet** is a hard hat that you wear to protect your head.

help helps, helping, helped

VERB **1** To **help** someone means to make something better or easier for them.
VERB **2** If you **help yourself** to something, you take it. *Help yourself to sandwiches.*
VERB **3** If you can't **help** something, you cannot control it or change it. *I can't help feeling sorry for him.*
helpful ADJECTIVE

helping helpings

NOUN A **helping** of food is the amount of it that you get in a single serving.

helpless

ADJECTIVE Someone who is **helpless** cannot cope on their own.

hem hems

NOUN The **hem** of a piece of material is the part that is folded over and sewn.

hemisphere hemispheres

NOUN A **hemisphere** is one half of a sphere. It can also be half of the Earth.
See *Solid shapes* on page 271.

hen hens

NOUN **1** A **hen** is a female chicken.
NOUN **2** A **hen** can also be any female bird.

heptagon heptagons

NOUN A **heptagon** is a flat shape with seven straight sides.
See *Colours and flat shapes* on page 271.

her

PRONOUN **1** You use **her** to refer to a woman, girl or any female animal that has already been mentioned. *I like Katherine. I often play with her.*
ADJECTIVE **2** You also use **her** to show that something belongs to a particular female. *My dog Fluff won't eat her food.*

herd herds

NOUN A **herd** is a large group of animals of one kind that live together.
See *Collective nouns* on page 262.

here

here
ADVERB You say **here** to mean the place where you are. *I'll stand here and wait.*

here and there PHRASE **Here and there** means in various places. *Bits of paper were lying here and there on the floor.*

hero **heroes**
NOUN **1** A **hero** is a man or boy who has done something brave and good.
NOUN **2** The **hero** of a story is the man or boy that the story is about. See **heroine**.

heroine **heroines**
NOUN **1** A **heroine** is a woman or girl who has done something brave and good.
NOUN **2** The **heroine** of a story is the woman or girl that the story is about. See **hero**.

heron **herons**
NOUN A **heron** is a bird that lives near water and eats fish.

herring **herrings**
NOUN A **herring** is a silvery fish that lives in large shoals in northern seas.

herself
PRONOUN If a girl or woman does something **herself**, no one else does it. *The baby pulled herself up.*

hesitate **hesitates, hesitating, hesitated**
VERB If you **hesitate**, you pause while you are doing something, or just before you do it.

hexagon **hexagons**
NOUN A **hexagon** is a flat shape with six straight sides.
hexagonal ADJECTIVE
See *Colours and flat shapes* on page 271.

hibernate **hibernates, hibernating, hibernated**
VERB When certain animals, such as bears, **hibernate**, they spend the winter in a sleep-like state.

hide **hides, hiding, hid, hidden**
VERB **1** If you **hide** somewhere, you go where you cannot be seen.
VERB **2** If you **hide** something, you put it in a place where it cannot be seen.
hidden ADJECTIVE

high **higher, highest**
ADJECTIVE **1** Something that is **high** is a long way from the bottom to the top. *The wall round the garden is quite high.*
ADJECTIVE OR ADVERB **2** If something is **high**, it is a long way up. *There was an aeroplane high above her.*

hill **hills**
NOUN A **hill** is a rounded area of land which is higher than the land surrounding it.

him
PRONOUN You use **him** to refer to a man, boy or any male animal that has already been mentioned. *James asked me to ring him back.*

himself
PRONOUN If a boy or man does something **himself**, no one else does it. *Ben hurt himself quite badly.*

Hindu Hindus

NOUN A **Hindu** is a person who believes in Hinduism, an Indian religion which has many gods. Hindus believe that people have another life on earth after death.

hinge hinges

NOUN **Hinges** are pieces of metal, wood or plastic that are used to hold a door or lid so that it can swing freely.

hint hints, hinting, hinted

NOUN **1** A **hint** is a suggestion, clue or helpful piece of advice.
VERB **2** If you **hint**, or **hint at** something, you suggest it in a way that is not obvious. *I **hinted** that I would like a bicycle for my birthday.*

hip hips

NOUN Your **hips** are the two parts at the sides of your body between your waist and your upper legs.

hippopotamus hippopotamuses or hippopotami

NOUN A **hippopotamus** is a large African animal with thick skin and short legs. It lives in herds on the banks of large rivers, and spends a lot of time in the water. It is often called a **hippo** for short.

hire hires, hiring, hired

VERB If you **hire** something, you pay money so that you can use it for a time.

his

ADJECTIVE OR PRONOUN You use **his** to show that something belongs to a man, boy or any male animal. *Robert combed **his** hair.*

hiss hisses, hissing, hissed

VERB To **hiss** means to make a long "sss" sound.

historical

ADJECTIVE **Historical** stories are stories about things that happened in the past.

history histories

NOUN **History** is a study or record of the past.

hit hits, hitting, hit

VERB If you **hit** something, you touch it quickly and hard.

hive hives

NOUN A **hive** is a house for bees, made so that the beekeeper can collect the honey. See **beehive**.

hoard hoards, hoarding, hoarded

VERB **1** If you **hoard** things, you save or store them even though they may no longer be useful.
NOUN **2** A **hoard** is a store of things that has been saved or hidden.

hoarse hoarser, hoarsest

ADJECTIVE A **hoarse** voice sounds rough.

hobby hobbies

NOUN A **hobby** is something you enjoy doing in your spare time, such as collecting stamps or bird-watching.

hockey

NOUN **Hockey** is a game in which two teams use long sticks with curved ends to try and hit a small ball into the other team's goal.

hold holds, holding, held

VERB **1** When you **hold** something, you keep it in your hand or arms.
VERB **2** If something **holds** a particular amount of something, it can contain that amount. *This jug **holds** one litre.*

a
b
c
d
e
f
g
Hh
i
j
k
l
m
n
o
p
q
r
s
t
u
v
w
x
y
z

hole

hole **holes**
NOUN A **hole** is an opening or space in something. *The dog buried his bone in a **hole** in the garden.*

holiday **holidays**
NOUN A **holiday** is time away from school or work.

hollow
ADJECTIVE Something that is **hollow** has a space inside it. *The owl lived in a **hollow** tree trunk.*

holly
NOUN **Holly** is an evergreen tree with prickly leaves. It often has bright red berries in winter.

home **homes**
NOUN Your **home** is the place where you live and feel you belong.

homesick
ADJECTIVE If you are **homesick**, you are sad because you are away from home.

homework
NOUN **Homework** is school work that children do at home.

homograph **homographs**
NOUN **Homographs** are words which are spelt the same but have different meanings, for example "calf" (part of your leg) and "calf" (a young cow).

homonym **homonyms**
NOUN **Homonyms** are words which are pronounced or spelt in the same way but which mean different things. Homographs and homophones are homonyms.

homophone **homophones**
NOUN **Homophones** are words which sound the same but have different meanings or spellings, for example "right" and "write".

honest
ADJECTIVE Someone who is **honest** tells the truth and can be trusted.

honey
NOUN **Honey** is a sweet sticky food that is made by bees.

hood **hoods**
NOUN A **hood** is a part of a coat or jacket that you can pull over your head.

hoof **hooves** or **hoofs**
NOUN The **hoof** of an animal such as a horse is the hard bony part of its foot.

hook **hooks**
NOUN A **hook** is a curved piece of metal or plastic that is used for catching, holding or hanging things, for example a picture hook.

hoop **hoops**
NOUN A **hoop** is a large ring, often used as a toy.

hoot **hoots, hooting, hooted**
VERB 1 To **hoot** means to make a long "oo" sound like an owl.
VERB 2 If a car horn **hoots**, it makes a loud honking noise.

hop **hops, hopping, hopped**
VERB 1 If you **hop**, you jump on one foot.
VERB 2 When animals or birds **hop**, they jump with two feet together.

hope **hopes, hoping, hoped**
VERB If you **hope** that something will happen, you want it to happen.

hopeful
ADJECTIVE If you are **hopeful**, you are fairly sure that something you want to happen will happen.

hopeless
ADJECTIVE 1 You say a situation is **hopeless** when it is very bad and you do not think it will get better.
ADJECTIVE 2 If somebody is **hopeless** at doing something, they cannot do it well. *I'm **hopeless** at arithmetic.*

horizon **horizons**

NOUN The **horizon** is the line in the far distance where the sky seems to touch the land or the sea.

horizontal

ADJECTIVE Something that is **horizontal** is level, like the horizon. See **vertical**.

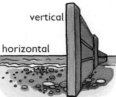

horn **horns**

NOUN **1** Horns are the hard pointed growths on the heads of animals such as goats.

NOUN **2** A **horn** is a musical instrument made of brass.

NOUN **3** On vehicles, a **horn** makes a loud noise as a warning.

horrible

ADJECTIVE Someone or something that is **horrible** is awful or very unpleasant.

horribly ADVERB

horror

NOUN **Horror** is a strong feeling of fear or disgust.

horse **horses**

NOUN A **horse** is a large animal which people can ride. Horses are also used for pulling things like carts.

horseshoe **horseshoes**

NOUN A **horseshoe** is a piece of metal shaped like a U. It is fixed under a horse's hoof, to protect it.

hose **hoses**

NOUN A **hose** is a long tube that sprays water.

hospital **hospitals**

NOUN A **hospital** is a place where sick and injured people are cared for.

hot **hotter, hottest**

ADJECTIVE **1** Something that is **hot** has a high temperature.

ADJECTIVE **2** If you feel **hot**, you feel too warm to be comfortable.

ADJECTIVE **3** You say food is **hot** if it has a strong taste caused by spices. *This curry is too **hot** for me.*

hotel **hotels**

NOUN A **hotel** is a building where people pay to stay, usually for a few nights.

hour **hours**

NOUN An **hour** is a period of 60 minutes. There are 24 hours in a day.

house **houses**

NOUN A **house** is a building where people live.

hover **hovers, hovering, hovered**

VERB When a bird or aircraft **hovers**, it stays in the same place in the air.

hovercraft **hovercraft** or **hovercrafts**

NOUN A **hovercraft** is a vehicle that travels over water or land on a cushion of air.

how

ADVERB **1** You can use **how** in questions to ask about the way something is done or known. *How did you know that?*

ADVERB **2** How can also be used to ask about a measurement or quantity. *How much is the fare to Brighton?*

ADVERB **3** How is often used in greetings. *How are you?*

however

ADVERB You use **however** when you are adding a comment that is surprising after what you have just said. *I was sure I was going to win the race.* **However**, *a younger girl came first.*

howl howls, howling, howled

VERB To **howl** means to make a long, loud cry. *The dog* **howls** *when I sing.*

hug hugs, hugging, hugged

VERB If you **hug** someone, you put your arms round them and hold them close.

huge

ADJECTIVE Something that is **huge** is extremely big.

hum hums, humming, hummed

VERB If you **hum**, you sing with your lips closed.

human humans

NOUN A **human** is a person.

hump humps

NOUN A **hump** is a large lump on the back of an animal such as a camel, which is used for storing fat and water.

hundred hundreds

A **hundred** is the number 100.

hung

VERB **Hung** is the past tense of **hang**.

hungry hungrier, hungriest

ADJECTIVE When you are **hungry**, you want to eat.
hungrily ADVERB

hunt hunts, hunting, hunted

VERB 1 To **hunt** means to chase wild animals to kill them for food or sport.
VERB 2 If you **hunt** for something, you look for it.

hurricane hurricanes

NOUN A **hurricane** is a storm with very high winds.

hurry hurries, hurrying, hurried

VERB If you **hurry** somewhere, you go there as quickly as you can.

hurt hurts, hurting, hurt

VERB 1 If part of your body **hurts**, you feel pain.
VERB 2 If you have been **hurt**, you have been injured.
ADJECTIVE 3 If someone feels **hurt**, they feel unhappy because someone has been unkind to them.

husband husbands

NOUN A woman's **husband** is the man she is married to.

hut huts

NOUN A **hut** is a small simple building with one or two rooms.

hutch hutches

NOUN A **hutch** is a cage made of wood and wire netting. Pets such as rabbits are kept in hutches.

hygiene

NOUN **Hygiene** is keeping yourself and your surroundings clean, especially to stop the spread of disease.

hymn hymns

NOUN A **hymn** is a Christian song in praise of God.

hyphen hyphens

NOUN A **hyphen** is a punctuation mark (-) used to join together words or parts of words, for example "left-handed".
See **Punctuation** on page 264.

Ii

ice ices, icing, iced

NOUN **1** Ice is water that has frozen solid.
VERB **2** If you **ice** cakes, you cover them with icing.

iceberg icebergs

NOUN An **iceberg** is a large mass of ice floating in the sea.

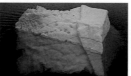

ice cream ice creams

NOUN **Ice cream** is a very cold sweet-tasting creamy food.

ice skate ice skates

NOUN An **ice skate** is a boot with a metal blade fixed underneath. You wear it when you skate on ice.

icicle icicles

NOUN An **icicle** is a pointed piece of ice which hangs from roofs, or wherever water has been dripping and freezing.

icing

NOUN **Icing** is a mixture of powdered sugar and water or egg whites. It is used to cover cakes as a decoration.

icy icier, iciest

ADJECTIVE Something which is **icy** has ice on it, or is very cold. *This wind is icy.*

idea ideas

NOUN **1** If you have an **idea**, you suddenly think of a way of doing something.
NOUN **2** An **idea** is a picture in your mind.

ideal

ADJECTIVE The **ideal** person or thing is the best one possible for the situation.

identical

ADJECTIVE Things that are **identical** are exactly the same in every detail.

idle idler, idlest

ADJECTIVE An **idle** person is someone who does not do very much.

igloo igloos

NOUN An **igloo** is a dome-shaped house built out of blocks of snow.

ignore ignores, ignoring, ignored

VERB If you **ignore** someone, you deliberately take no notice of them.

ill

ADJECTIVE Someone who is **ill** has something wrong with their health.

illness illnesses

NOUN An **illness** is something like a cold or measles that people can suffer from.

illuminations

PLURAL NOUN **Illuminations** are coloured lights put up to decorate a town.

illustrate illustrates, illustrating, illustrated

VERB If you **illustrate** something, you add pictures to it.

illustration illustrations

NOUN An **illustration** is a picture or diagram in a book or magazine.

illustrator illustrators

NOUN An **illustrator** is an artist who draws pictures for books and magazines.

I'm

I'm is a contraction of **I am**.

imaginary

ADJECTIVE Something that is **imaginary** is not real. It is only in your mind. *She has imaginary talks with famous people.*

a
b
c
d
e
f
g
h
Ii
j
k
l
m
n
o
p
q
r
s
t
u
v
w
x
y
z

imagination

a b c d e f g h **li** j k l m n o p q r s t u v w x y z

imagination

NOUN Your **imagination** is your ability to think of ideas, or to form pictures in your mind.

imagine imagines, imagining, imagined

VERB When you **imagine** something, you form a picture of it in your mind.

imitate imitates, imitating, imitated

VERB If you **imitate** someone, you copy the way they speak or behave.

imitation imitations

NOUN An **imitation** is a copy of something else.

immediately

ADVERB If something happens **immediately**, it happens right away.

impatient

ADJECTIVE Someone who is **impatient** does not like to be kept waiting.

important

ADJECTIVE **1** If someone says something is **important**, they mean it matters a lot.

ADJECTIVE **2** Someone who is **important** has a lot of power in a particular group.

impossible

ADJECTIVE Something that is **impossible** cannot be done.

impressive

ADJECTIVE If something is **impressive**, people admire it, usually because it is large or important.

imprison imprisons, imprisoning, imprisoned

VERB If someone is **imprisoned**, they are locked up, usually in a prison.

improve improves, improving, improved

VERB If something **improves**, it gets better.

improvement improvements

NOUN An **improvement** is a change in something that makes it better.

in

PREPOSITION **1** You use **in** to say where something is, or where it is going. *Put it in the box.*

PREPOSITION **2** You also use **in** to say when something should happen. *I'll be home in 20 minutes.*

ADVERB **3** You use **in** to mean at home. *Is anybody in?*

inch inches

NOUN An **inch** is a unit of length equal to about two and a half centimetres. There are 12 inches to a foot.

include includes, including, included

VERB If you **include** something in a whole thing, you make it part of the whole thing. *Batteries are included.*

increase increases, increasing, increased

VERB **1** If something **increases**, it becomes greater.

NOUN **2** An **increase** is a rise in the number, level or amount of something.

index indexes

NOUN An **index** is an alphabetical list at the back of a book that helps you find the things you want to read about.

indignant

ADJECTIVE If you are **indignant**, you feel angry about something that is unfair.

individual

ADJECTIVE **Individual** means to do with one particular person, rather than a whole group.

infant infants

NOUN An **infant** is a baby or young child.

influence influences

NOUN An **influence** is the effect that someone or something has on you, that can change the way you think or behave. *That boy is a bad influence on you.*

informal

ADJECTIVE **1 Informal** means relaxed. You usually speak or behave in this way when you are with people you know well.

ADJECTIVE **2** In a dictionary, a word shown as **informal** is more suitable for everyday talk than it is for writing.

information

NOUN If someone gives you **information** about something, they tell you about it.

infuriate infuriates, infuriating, infuriated

VERB If someone or something **infuriates** you, they make you extremely angry.

ingredient ingredients

NOUN **Ingredients** are the things that are used to make something, especially in cookery.

inhabit inhabits, inhabiting, inhabited

VERB If you **inhabit** a place, you live there.

inhabitant inhabitants

NOUN The **inhabitants** of a place are the people who live there.

initial initials

NOUN An **initial** is the first letter of a name. *David Hunt's **initials** are D.H.*

injection injections

NOUN If a doctor or nurse gives you an **injection**, they put medicine into your body with a special needle.

injure injures, injuring, injured

VERB If something **injures** a person or animal, it damages part of their body.
injury NOUN

ink inks

NOUN **Ink** is the coloured liquid that is used for writing and printing.

inland

ADVERB If you go **inland**, you go away from the coast towards the middle of a country.

inn inns

NOUN An **inn** is a small hotel.

innocent

ADJECTIVE Someone who is **innocent** has not done anything wrong.

insect insects

NOUN An **insect** is a small animal with six legs and usually wings. Ants, flies, butterflies and beetles are all insects.

See *Insects* on page 259.

insert inserts, inserting, inserted

VERB If you **insert** an object into something, you put it into it.
*She **inserted** the key in the lock.*

inside

ADVERB, PREPOSITION OR ADJECTIVE **Inside** means in something. *It was raining so they had to play **inside**... It was very cold **inside** the church... He hid his money in an **inside** pocket.*

insist insists, insisting, insisted

VERB If you **insist** on doing something, you refuse to give in.

inspect inspects, inspecting, inspected

VERB If you **inspect** something, you look at every part of it carefully.

inspire inspires, inspiring, inspired

VERB If something **inspires** you, it gives you new ideas and enthusiasm.

instant

ADJECTIVE Something **instant** happens immediately. *The new pop group were an **instant** success.*

a
b
c
d
e
f
g
h
Ii
j
k
l
m
n
o
p
q
r
s
t
u
v
w
x
y
z

instead

instead
ADVERB **Instead** means in place of. *Take the stairs **instead** of the lift.*

instruction **instructions**
NOUN **1** An **instruction** is something that someone tells you to do.
PLURAL NOUN **2 Instructions** are words that tell you how to do something.

instrument **instruments**
NOUN **1** An **instrument** is a tool that is used to do a particular job.
NOUN **2** An **instrument** is also an object such as a piano or guitar, that you play to make music.

insult **insults, insulting, insulted**
VERB If you **insult** someone, you offend them by being rude to them.

integer **integers**
NOUN An **integer** is any of the whole numbers used for counting.

intelligent
ADJECTIVE A person who is **intelligent** can understand, learn and think things out quickly and well.

intend **intends, intending, intended**
VERB If you **intend** to do something, you have decided to do it or plan to do it.

interest **interests**
NOUN If you have an **interest** in something, you want to learn or hear more about it.

interesting
ADJECTIVE If something is **interesting**, it attracts or keeps your attention.

interfere **interferes, interfering, interfered**
VERB If something **interferes** with something else, it gets in the way. *Don't let TV **interfere** with your homework.*

interjection **interjections**
NOUN An **interjection** is a word you say suddenly to show surprise, pain or anger, such as "Ouch!" or "Wow!".

Internet
NOUN The **Internet** is a worldwide communication system that people use through computers.

interpret **interprets, interpreting, interpreted**
VERB If you **interpret** what someone says or does, you say what it means.

interrupt **interrupts, interrupting, interrupted**
VERB **1** If you **interrupt** someone, you start talking before they have finished what they were saying.
VERB **2** If you **interrupt** what someone is doing, you make them stop doing it for a while.

interval **intervals**
NOUN An **interval** is a short break during a play or concert.

interview **interviews, interviewing, interviewed**
VERB If you **interview** someone, you ask them questions about themselves.

introduction **introductions**
NOUN An **introduction** is a piece of writing at the beginning of a book, which usually tells you what it is about.

invent **invents, inventing, invented**
VERB **1** If you **invent** a story or an excuse, you make it up.
VERB **2** If someone **invents** something, such as a machine or an instrument, they are the first person to think of it.

invention **inventions**
NOUN An **invention** is something that is a completely new idea.
*She is working on an **invention** that will help people.*

inventor inventors

NOUN An **inventor** is someone who thinks of new ideas and tries them out to see if they will work.

inverse

NOUN If you turn something upside down or back to front, you have its **inverse**. *Subtraction is the **inverse** of addition.*

investigate investigates, investigating, investigated

VERB If you **investigate** something, you try to find out all the facts about it.

invisible

ADJECTIVE If something is **invisible**, it cannot be seen. For example, germs are invisible unless you use a microscope.

invitation invitations

NOUN When you get an **invitation**, someone asks you to come to something such as a party.

invite invites, inviting, invited

VERB If you **invite** someone, you ask them to come to your home, or a party.

involve involves, involving, involved

VERB If a situation **involves** someone or something, it includes or concerns them. *This project will **involve** a lot of work.*

iron irons

NOUN **1** Iron is a hard metal used to make steel, and things like gates.
NOUN **2** An **iron** is an object with a handle and a flat base. You can heat it and use it to smooth clothes.

irritable

ADJECTIVE If you are feeling **irritable**, you could easily become annoyed.

irritate irritates, irritating, irritated

VERB **1** If something **irritates** you, it annoys you.
VERB **2** If something **irritates** part of your body, it makes it sore or itchy.

Islam

NOUN **Islam** is the Muslim religion, which teaches that there is only one God, Allah. Mohammed is his prophet.
Islamic ADJECTIVE

island islands

NOUN An **island** is a piece of land completely surrounded by water.

IT

IT is an abbreviation of **information technology**.

italics

PLURAL NOUN **Italics** are letters printed in a special sloping way. *This sentence is in italics.*

itch itches, itching, itched

VERB When your skin **itches**, it makes you feel that you want to scratch it.

its

ADJECTIVE You use **its** to show that something belongs to something that has already been mentioned. *The lion lifted **its** head.*

it's

It's is a contraction of **it is**.

itself

PRONOUN If an animal does something itself, no one else does it. *The cat washed **itself**.*

ivory

NOUN **Ivory** is the hard smooth creamy material that comes from the tusks of some animals, such as elephants.

ivy

NOUN Ivy is an evergreen plant which creeps along the ground and up walls.

Jj

jacket jackets
NOUN A **jacket** is a short coat.

jagged
ADJECTIVE Something **jagged** has an uneven edge with sharp points on it.

jail jails
NOUN A **jail** is a building where criminals are locked up.

jam jams, jamming, jammed
NOUN **1 Jam** is a food that is made by cooking fruit with a lot of sugar. You usually spread jam on bread.
NOUN **2** A **jam** is when there are so many people or vehicles in a place it is impossible for them to move.
VERB **3** If something **jams**, it becomes fixed and will not move.

January
NOUN **January** is the first month of the year. It has 31 days.

jar jars
NOUN A **jar** is a glass container with a wide top used for storing food.

jaw jaws
NOUN Your **jaw** is the bone in which your teeth are set. Some animals, like crocodiles, have very large jaws.

jealous
ADJECTIVE Someone who is **jealous** feels upset because someone else has what they want.

jeans
PLURAL NOUN **Jeans** are trousers that are usually made with a strong cotton cloth.

jelly jellies
NOUN **Jelly** is a clear sweet food that wobbles when you move it.

jellyfish jellyfishes
NOUN A **jellyfish** is a sea animal with a clear soft body and tentacles which may sting.

jerk jerks, jerking, jerked
VERB If something **jerks**, it moves suddenly and sharply.

jersey jerseys
NOUN A **jersey** is a knitted piece of clothing for the upper part of your body.

jet jets
NOUN **1** A **jet** is a stream of liquid, gas or flame forced out under pressure.
NOUN **2** A **jet** is also a plane that is able to fly very fast.

Jew Jews
NOUN A **Jew** is a person who follows the religion of Judaism.

jewel jewels
NOUN A **jewel** is a precious stone, such as a diamond or a ruby, used to make things like rings and necklaces.

jewellery
NOUN **Jewellery** is the name for ornaments that people can wear, like rings and necklaces. It is often made of valuable metal such as gold or silver and may be decorated with precious stones.

jigsaw jigsaws

NOUN A **jigsaw** is a puzzle consisting of a picture on cardboard. The picture has been cut up into small pieces that have to be put together again.

jingle jingles

NOUN A **jingle** is a short catchy phrase or rhyme set to music and used to advertise something on radio or television.

job jobs

NOUN **1** A **job** is the work that someone does to earn money.

NOUN **2** A **job** can also be anything that has to be done. *There are always plenty of jobs to do when I get home.*

joey

NOUN A **joey** is a young kangaroo. *See Young animals on page 260.*

jog jogs, jogging, jogged

VERB **1** To **jog** means to run slowly, often as a form of exercise.

VERB **2** If you **jog** something, you knock it slightly so that it shakes or moves.

VERB **3** If someone or something **jogs** your memory, they remind you of something.

join joins, joining, joined

VERB **1** When two things **join**, they come together.

VERB **2** If you **join** a club or organization, you become a member of it.

NOUN **3** A **join** is a place where two things are fastened together. *Look! You can't see the join.*

joint joints

NOUN **1** A **joint** is a part of your body, such as your elbow or knee, where two bones meet and are able to move.

NOUN **2** A **joint** can also be any place where two things are fastened together.

NOUN **3** A **joint** is also a large piece of meat for roasting.

joke jokes

NOUN A **joke** is something that you say or do to make people laugh.

jolt jolts, jolting, jolted

VERB **1** To **jolt** something means to move or shake it roughly and violently.

NOUN **2** A **jolt** is a sudden jerky movement.

NOUN **3** A **jolt** is also an unpleasant shock or surprise.

jot jots, jotting, jotted

VERB If you **jot** something down, you write it quickly in the form of a short note.

journal journals

NOUN **1** A **journal** is a diary which someone keeps regularly.

NOUN **2** A **journal** is also a magazine that deals with a particular subject, for example a medical journal.

journey journeys

NOUN If you go on a **journey**, you travel from one place to another.

joy

NOUN **Joy** is a feeling of great happiness. **joyful** ADJECTIVE

joystick joysticks

NOUN **1** On a computer, a **joystick** is a lever that controls movement of the cursor on the screen.

NOUN **2** A **joystick** is a lever in an aircraft which the pilot uses to control height and direction.

Judaism

NOUN **Judaism** is the religion of the Jewish people. It is based on the Old Testament of the Bible, and the Talmud or book of laws and traditions.

a
b
c
d
e
f
g
h
i
Jj
k
l
m
n
o
p
q
r
s
t
u
v
w
x
y
z

judge

judge judges

NOUN **1** In law, a **judge** is a person who has the power to decide how the law should be used.

NOUN **2** The **judge** of a competition is a person who has been asked to choose the winner.

jug jugs

NOUN A **jug** is a container with a lip or spout used for holding or serving liquids.

juggle juggles, juggling, juggled

VERB If you **juggle** with objects, you keep throwing them into the air and catching them one at a time, so that there are several in the air at once.

juggler NOUN

juice

NOUN **Juice** is the liquid that comes from fruit such as oranges when you squeeze them.

juicy juicier, juiciest

ADJECTIVE **Juicy** food has a lot of juice in it.

July

NOUN **July** is the seventh month of the year. It has 31 days.

jumble jumbles, jumbling, jumbled

NOUN **1 Jumble** is an untidy muddle of things.

NOUN **2 Jumble** is also things like clothes and books that people no longer want.

VERB **3** If you **jumble** things, you mix them up untidily.

jumble sale NOUN

jump jumps, jumping, jumped

VERB **1** When you **jump**, you spring off the ground using your leg muscles.

VERB **2** If you **jump** something, you spring off the ground and move over or across it. *He jumped a low wall.*

VERB **3** If something or somebody makes you **jump**, you make a sudden sharp movement of surprise.

jumper jumpers

NOUN A **jumper** is a knitted piece of clothing for the top part of the body.

junction junctions

NOUN A **junction** is a place where roads or railway lines meet or cross.

June

NOUN **June** is the sixth month of the year. It has 30 days.

jungle jungles

NOUN A **jungle** is a dense tropical forest.

junior

ADJECTIVE **Junior** means younger, or less important.

junk junks

NOUN **1 Junk** is old or second-hand articles that are sold cheaply or thrown away.

NOUN **2** A **junk** is a Chinese sailing boat that has a flat bottom and square sails.

just

ADVERB **1** If you say that something has **just** happened, you mean it happened a short time ago.

ADVERB **2** If you say you are **just** going to do something, you mean you will do it very soon.

justice

NOUN **Justice** is fairness in the way that people are treated.

justify justifies, justifying, justified

VERB If you **justify** an action or idea, you explain why it is reasonable or necessary.

Kk

kangaroo **kangaroos**
NOUN A **kangaroo** is a large Australian animal which moves forward by jumping on its back legs.

keen **keener, keenest**
ADJECTIVE Someone who is **keen** to do something wants to do it very much.

keep **keeps, keeping, kept**
VERB **1** If you **keep** something for somebody, you save it for them.
VERB **2** If you **keep** doing something, you do it over and over again.
VERB **3** If something **keeps** you a certain way, you stay that way because of it.
*That dog is **keeping** me awake.*

kennel **kennels**
NOUN A **kennel** is a small house for a dog.

kept
VERB **Kept** is the past tense of **keep**.

kerb **kerbs**
NOUN The **kerb** is the edge of the pavement.

ketchup
NOUN **Ketchup** is a cold tomato sauce.

kettle **kettles**
NOUN A **kettle** is a covered container used to boil water.

key **keys**
NOUN **1** A **key** is a specially shaped piece of metal that fits into a lock.
NOUN **2** The **keys** on something like a computer keyboard or a piano are the buttons that you press to use it.
ADJECTIVE **3 Key** words or sentences are an important part of a piece of text.

keyboard **keyboards**
NOUN A **keyboard** is a row of buttons called keys on a piano or computer.

kick **kicks, kicking, kicked**
VERB If you **kick** something, you hit it with your foot.

kid **kids**
NOUN **1** A **kid** is a young goat.
See *Young animals* on page 260.
NOUN **2** INFORMAL A **kid** is a child.

kidnap **kidnaps, kidnapping, kidnapped**
VERB If someone **kidnaps** another person, they take them away by force.

kill **kills, killing, killed**
VERB To **kill** someone or something means to cause them to die.

kilogram **kilograms**
NOUN A **kilogram** (kg) is a unit of mass and weight. One kilogram, or kilo, is equal to 1000 grams.

kilometre **kilometres**
NOUN A **kilometre** is a unit of distance equal to 1000 metres.

kilt **kilts**
NOUN A **kilt** is a pleated skirt worn by men as part of the national costume of Scotland.

kind **kinds; kinder, kindest**
NOUN **1** If you talk about a **kind** of object, you mean a sort of object.
ADJECTIVE **2** Someone who is **kind** behaves in a gentle, caring way.
kindness NOUN

king **kings**
NOUN A **king** is a man who rules a country. Kings are not chosen by the people, but are born into a royal family.

a
b
c
d
e
f
g
h
i
j
Kk
l
m
n
o
p
q
r
s
t
u
v
w
x
y
z

Kk

kingdom kingdoms
NOUN **1** A **kingdom** is a country or region that is ruled by a king or queen.
NOUN **2** The animal **kingdom** is all the animals in the world. *This creature is the largest in the animal **kingdom**.*

kingfisher kingfishers
NOUN A **kingfisher** is a brightly coloured bird that lives by rivers and eats fish.

kiss kisses, kissing, kissed
VERB If you **kiss** someone, you touch them with your lips.

kit kits
NOUN A **kit** is a set of things that are used for a particular purpose. *Have you seen my first aid **kit**?*

kitchen kitchens
NOUN A **kitchen** is a room that is used for cooking and washing-up.

kite kites
NOUN **1** A **kite** is a frame covered with paper or cloth which you fly in the sky at the end of a piece of string.
NOUN **2** In maths, a **kite** is a flat shape with four sides, with two pairs of the same length and none of the sides parallel to each other.
See Colours and flat shapes on page 271.

kitten kittens
NOUN A **kitten** is a young cat.
See Young animals on page 260.

kiwi kiwis
NOUN A **kiwi** is a type of bird found in New Zealand. Kiwis cannot fly.

kiwi fruit kiwi fruits
NOUN A **kiwi fruit** is a fruit with a brown hairy skin and green flesh.
See Fruit on page 257.

knee knees
NOUN Your **knee** is the joint where your leg bends.

kneel kneels, kneeling, kneeled or knelt
VERB When you **kneel**, you bend your legs until your knees are touching the ground.

knew
VERB **Knew** is the past tense of **know**.

knickers
PLURAL NOUN **Knickers** are pants worn by women and girls.

knife knives
NOUN A **knife** is a sharp metal tool that you use to cut things.

knight knights
NOUN Hundreds of years ago, a **knight** was a man in armour who rode into battle for his king or queen.

knit knits, knitting, knitted
VERB If you **knit**, you make something from wool using two long needles.

knob knobs
NOUN **1** A **knob** is a round handle on a door or a drawer.
NOUN **2** A **knob** is also a round button on a piece of equipment such as a radio.

knock knocks, knocking, knocked
VERB If you **knock** on something, you hit it hard.

knot knots
NOUN A **knot** is a tie in something such as string or cloth.

know knows, knowing, knew
VERB **1** If you **know** a fact, you have it in your mind and do not need to learn it.
VERB **2** If you **know** somebody, you have met them before.

knowledge
NOUN **Knowledge** is all the facts and information that you know.

knuckle knuckles
NOUN Your **knuckles** are the bony parts where your fingers join your hands and where your fingers bend.

koala koalas
NOUN A **koala** is an Australian animal that looks like a small bear with grey fur.

Ll

label **labels**

NOUN A **label** is a small notice that tells you what something is or gives you information. *Read the **label** on the medicine bottle.*

laboratory **laboratories**

NOUN A **laboratory** is a place where scientists work, using special equipment.

labour

NOUN **Labour** is hard work.

lace **laces**

NOUN **1 Lace** is a very fine decorated cloth made with a lot of holes in it.
NOUN **2 Laces** are cords that you use to fasten your shoes.

lack **lacks, lacking, lacked**

VERB If you **lack** something, you do not have it when you need it.

ladder **ladders**

NOUN A **ladder** is a wooden or metal frame used for climbing up things like walls or trees.

ladle **ladles**

NOUN A **ladle** is a big deep spoon with a long handle, which is used to serve soup.
ladle VERB

lady **ladies**

NOUN **Lady** is a polite name for a woman. *I think this **lady** was in front of me.*

ladybird **ladybirds**

NOUN A **ladybird** is a small round flying beetle with spots on its wings.
See *Insects* on page 259.

laid

VERB **Laid** is the past tense of **lay**.

lain

VERB **Lain** is the past participle of **lie**.

lake **lakes**

NOUN A **lake** is a large area of fresh water with land all round it.

lamb **lambs**

NOUN A **lamb** is a young sheep.
See *Young animals* on page 260.

lame

ADJECTIVE An animal which is **lame** cannot walk properly.

lamp **lamps**

NOUN A **lamp** is an object that gives light.

lamppost **lampposts**

NOUN A **lamppost** is a tall column in the street, with a lamp at the top.

land **lands, landing, landed**

NOUN **1 Land** is the part of the world that is solid, dry ground.
VERB **2** When an aircraft **lands**, it comes down from the air on to land or water.

landlady **landladies**

NOUN A **landlady** is a woman who lets rooms to people.

landlord **landlords**

NOUN A **landlord** is a man who lets rooms to people.

landmark **landmarks**

NOUN A **landmark** is a building or a feature of the land that can be used to find out where you are.

landscape **landscapes**

NOUN A **landscape** is everything you can see when you look across an area of land.

lane **lanes**

NOUN **1** A **lane** is a narrow road, especially in the country.
NOUN **2** A **lane** is also part of a main road or motorway. It is marked with lines to guide drivers.

a b c d e f g h i j k **Ll** m n o p q r s t u v w x y z

language

a
b
c
d
e
f
g
h
i
j
k
Ll
m
n
o
p
q
r
s
t
u
v
w
x
y
z

language **languages**

NOUN A **language** is the words that are used by the people of a country when they speak or write to each other.

lantern **lanterns**

NOUN A **lantern** is a lamp in a container. It has sides which the light can shine through but which stop the wind from blowing out the light.

lap **laps, lapping, lapped**

NOUN **1** Your **lap** is the flat area formed by the tops of your legs when you are sitting down.

VERB **2** When an animal **laps** up liquid, it drinks using its tongue to get the liquid into its mouth.

large **larger, largest**

ADJECTIVE Something **large** is big.

larva **larvae**

NOUN A **larva** is an insect at an early stage of its life. It looks likes a short fat worm.

laser **lasers**

NOUN A **laser** is a machine which produces a narrow beam of light. Lasers are used for many different things, including medical operations.

last **lasts, lasting, lasted**

ADJECTIVE **1** The **last** thing or event is the most recent one. *I saw him **last** week.*

ADVERB **2** If something happens **last**, it happens after everything else. *I came **last** in the race.*

VERB **3** If something **lasts**, it continues to exist or happen. *Her speech **lasted** an hour.*

at last PHRASE If something happens **at last**, it happens after a long time.

late **later, latest**

ADJECTIVE OR ADVERB **1** If you are **late** arriving somewhere, you get there after the time you were supposed to.

ADJECTIVE OR ADVERB **2 Late** means near the end of a period of time. *We had a picnic in the **late** afternoon.*

lately

ADVERB If something has happened **lately**, it happened not long ago. *Have you seen your cousin **lately**?*

laugh **laughs, laughing, laughed**

VERB When you **laugh**, you make the sound people make when they are happy or think something is funny.
laughter NOUN

launch **launches, launching, launched**

VERB **1** When a rocket or satellite is **launched**, it is sent into the sky.

VERB **2** To **launch** a ship means to send it into the water for the first time.

launderette **launderettes**

NOUN A **launderette** is a shop where people pay to use washing machines.

lava

NOUN **Lava** is a very hot, liquid rock which comes out of volcanoes.

lavatory **lavatories**

NOUN **1** A **lavatory** is a toilet.

NOUN **2** A **lavatory** is also the room where the lavatory is.

law **laws**

NOUN A **law** is a rule that is made by the government.

lawn **lawns**

NOUN A **lawn** is an area of short grass in a garden or park.

lawnmower **lawnmowers**

NOUN A **lawnmower** is a machine for cutting the grass on lawns.

lawyer lawyers

NOUN A **lawyer** is a person who understands the law and can advise people about it.

lay lays, laying, laid

VERB **1** If you **lay** something somewhere, you put it there carefully.

VERB **2** If you **lay** the table, you put things like knives and forks on the table ready for a meal.

VERB **3** When a bird **lays** an egg, it produces the egg out of its body.

layer layers

NOUN A **layer** is a single thickness of something that lies on top of or underneath something else.

layout layouts

NOUN The **layout** of something is the way it is arranged.

lazy lazier, laziest

ADJECTIVE Someone who is **lazy** does not want to work or do anything hard.
lazily ADVERB

lead leads, leading, led

(*rhymes with* **feed**)

VERB **1** If you **lead** someone to a particular place, you go with them to show them the way.

VERB **2** Someone who **leads** a group of people is in charge of them.

VERB **3** If you are **leading** in a race or game, you are winning at that point.

NOUN **4** A dog's **lead** is a long thin piece of leather or a chain. You fix one end to the collar and hold the other end.

(*rhymes with* **fed**) NOUN **5** Lead is a grey, heavy metal.

(*rhymes with* **fed**) NOUN **6** The **lead** in a pencil is the centre part of it that makes a mark on paper.

leader leaders

NOUN The **leader** of a group of people is the person who is in charge.

leaf leaves

NOUN A **leaf** is one of the flat green parts of a plant. Different sorts of plant have differently shaped leaves.

leaflet leaflets

NOUN A **leaflet** is a piece of paper with information or advertising printed on it.

leak leaks, leaking, leaked

VERB **1** If a pipe or container **leaks**, it has a hole which lets gas or liquid escape.

VERB **2** If liquid or gas **leaks**, it escapes from a pipe or container.

lean leans, leaning, leant or **leaned**; leaner, leanest

VERB **1** When you **lean** somewhere, you bend your body in that direction.

VERB **2** When you **lean** on something, you rest your body against it for support.

ADJECTIVE **3** **Lean** meat has little or no fat.

leap leaps, leaping, leapt or **leaped**

VERB If you **leap** somewhere, you jump over a long distance or high in the air.

leap year leap years

NOUN A **leap year** is a year with 366 days. There is a leap year every four years.

learn learns, learning, learnt or **learned**

VERB When you **learn** something, you get to know it or find out how to do it.

least

NOUN **1** The **least** is the smallest possible amount of something. *That is the **least** of my problems.*

ADJECTIVE OR ADVERB **2** Least is a superlative form of **little**, meaning very small in amount. *We bought the **least** expensive bike... She ate the **least** of all of them.*

leather

NOUN **Leather** is the specially treated skin of animals. It is used for making things like shoes and furniture.

leave leaves, leaving, left

VERB **1** When you **leave** a place, you go away from it.

VERB **2** If you **leave** someone somewhere, they stay behind after you go away.

VERB **3** In maths, when you take one number from another, it **leaves** a third number.

led

VERB **Led** is the past tense of **lead**.

ledge ledges

NOUN A **ledge** is a narrow shelf on the side of a cliff or rock face, or on the outside of a building.

leek leeks

NOUN A **leek** is a long white vegetable with green leaves.
See Vegetables on page 256.

left

VERB **1** Left is the past tense of **leave**.

NOUN **2** The **left** is the side that you begin reading on in English.

ADJECTIVE OR ADVERB **3** Left means on or towards the left side of something.
*Turn **left** at the end of the road.*

leg legs

NOUN **1** Legs are the parts of your body which stretch from the hips to the feet.

NOUN **2** The **legs** of an object such as a table are the parts which rest on the floor and support the object's weight.

legend legends

NOUN A **legend** is an old and popular story which may or may not be true.

lemon lemons

NOUN A **lemon** is a yellow, oval fruit. Lemons are juicy but they taste sour.
See Fruit on page 257.

lemonade

NOUN **Lemonade** is a drink made from lemons, sugar and water.

lend lends, lending, lent

VERB If you **lend** something to someone, you let them have it for a while.

length lengths

NOUN **1** The **length** of something is the distance that it measures from one end to the other.

NOUN **2** The **length** of something like a holiday is the period of time that it lasts.

lens lenses

NOUN A **lens** is a curved piece of glass that makes light go in a certain way. Lenses are used in things like cameras, telescopes and glasses.

lent

VERB **Lent** is the past tense of **lend**.

leopard leopards

NOUN A **leopard** is a large wild cat that lives in the forests of Africa and Asia. It has yellow fur with black spots.

less

ADJECTIVE OR ADVERB **Less** is a comparative form of **little**, meaning not as much.
*A shower uses **less** water than a bath.*

lesson lessons

NOUN A **lesson** is a short period of time when you are taught something.

let lets, letting, let

VERB **1** If you **let** someone do something, you allow them to do it.

VERB **2** If someone **lets** a house or flat that they own, they rent it out.

letter letters

NOUN **1** A **letter** is a written message to someone, usually sent through the post.

NOUN **2** Letters are written symbols which go together to make words.

letter box letter boxes

NOUN **1** A **letter box** is an oblong gap in the front door of a house or flat.

NOUN **2** A **letter box** is also a large metal container where you post letters.

lettuce lettuces

NOUN A **lettuce** is a plant with large green leaves that you eat raw in salads.

See *Vegetables* on page 256.

level levels

ADJECTIVE **1** A surface that is **level** is smooth, flat and parallel to the ground.

ADVERB **2** If you are **level** with someone, you are next to them.

NOUN **3** The **level** of a liquid is the height it comes up to. *After heavy rain the river rose to a dangerous **level**.*

lever levers

NOUN **1** A **lever** is a long bar that you put under a heavy object and press down on to make the object move.

NOUN **2** A **lever** is also a handle on a machine that you pull down to make the machine work.

library libraries

NOUN A **library** is a building where books are kept for people to come and read or borrow.

lick licks, licking, licked

VERB If you **lick** something, you move your tongue across it.

lid lids

NOUN A **lid** is a cover for a box or other container.

lie lies, lying, lay, lain; lied

VERB **1** To **lie** somewhere means to rest there horizontally.

VERB **2** To **lie** means to say something that is not true.

life lives

NOUN The **life** of a person or animal is the time between their birth and death.

lifeboat lifeboats

NOUN A **lifeboat** is a boat that is used to rescue people in danger at sea.

lifetime

NOUN Your **lifetime** is the period of time during which you are alive.

lift lifts, lifting, lifted

VERB **1** If you **lift** something, you move it to a higher position.

NOUN **2** A **lift** is a machine like a small room that carries passengers from one floor to another in a building.

light lights; lighter, lightest; lights, lighting, lighted or lit

NOUN **1** **Light** is the brightness from the sun, moon, fire or lamps, that lets you see things.

NOUN **2** A **light** is a lamp or other object that gives out brightness.

ADJECTIVE **3** A place that is **light** is bright because of the sun or the use of lamps.

ADJECTIVE **4** A **light** colour is pale.

ADJECTIVE **5** A **light** object does not weigh much.

VERB **6** To **light** something means to cause light to shine on it or in it.

VERB **7** To **light** a fire means to make it start burning.

lighthouse lighthouses

NOUN A **lighthouse** is a tower with a powerful flashing light at the top, which is used to guide ships or to warn them of danger.

lightning

NOUN **Lightning** is a bright flash of light in the sky produced by natural electricity during a thunderstorm.

like

like likes, liking, liked
PREPOSITION **1** If one thing is **like** another, it is similar to it.
VERB **2** If you **like** someone or something, you find them pleasant.

likely likelier, likeliest
ADJECTIVE Something that is **likely** will probably happen or is probably true.

limb limbs
NOUN A **limb** is an arm or leg.

limerick limericks
NOUN A **limerick** is a funny nonsense poem of five lines.

limit limits
NOUN A **limit** is a line or a point beyond which something cannot go. *There is a speed **limit** on this road.*

limp limps, limping, limped; limper, limpest
VERB **1** If you **limp**, you walk unevenly because you have hurt your leg or foot.
ADJECTIVE **2** Something that is **limp** is soft and floppy. *This lettuce is a bit **limp**.*

line lines
NOUN **1** A **line** is a long thin mark. Some writing paper has lines on it to show you where to write.
NOUN **2** A **line** of people or things is a number of them in a row.

NOUN **3** In a piece of writing, a **line** is a number of words together. *A limerick has five **lines**.*
NOUN **4** A railway **line** is one of the heavy metal rails that trains run on.

linen
NOUN **Linen** is a kind of cloth made from a plant called flax. It is used for things like sheets and tablecloths.

liner liners
NOUN A **liner** is a large passenger ship that makes long journeys.

link links
NOUN **1** A **link** is one of the rings in a chain.
NOUN **2** A **link** is also a connection between two things. *There's a high speed rail **link** between Brighton and London.*

lion lions
NOUN A **lion** is a large wild cat. Lions live in parts of Africa and Asia, in groups called prides.

lioness lionesses
NOUN A **lioness** is a female lion.

lip lips
NOUN Your **lips** are the top and bottom outer edges of your mouth.

liquid liquids
NOUN A **liquid** is anything which is not a solid or a gas, and which can be poured.

list lists
NOUN A **list** is a set of things that are written one below the other.

listen listens, listening, listened
VERB If you **listen** to a sound that you can hear, you pay attention to it.
listener NOUN

lit
VERB **Lit** is the past tense of **light**.

literacy
NOUN **Literacy** is the ability to read and write.

litre litres
NOUN A **litre** is a unit used to measure volume and capacity. A litre is equal to 1000 millilitres.

litter litters
NOUN **1** Litter is rubbish left lying untidily outside.
NOUN **2** A **litter** is a group of animals born to the same mother at the same time.
*See **Collective nouns** on page 262.*

little less, lesser, least

ADJECTIVE **1** Something or someone that is **little** is small in size.

ADVERB **2** Little can mean not much. *Our lazy cat does very **little**.*

live[1] lives, living, lived

(*rhymes with* **give**)

VERB **1** If you **live** in a place, that is where your home is.

VERB **2** To **live** means to be alive.

live[2]

(*rhymes with* **hive**)

ADJECTIVE **1** A **live** animal is living.

ADJECTIVE **2** Live television or radio is broadcast as it happens.

lively livelier, liveliest

ADJECTIVE Someone who is **lively** is cheerful and full of energy.

liver livers

NOUN Your **liver** is a large organ in your body. Its job is to clean your blood.

living

ADJECTIVE **1** Living things are plants, animals and humans that are alive. All living things need food to grow.

NOUN **2** Someone who earns a **living** earns enough money to buy all the things they need. *She earns a **living** as an artist.*

living room living rooms

NOUN The **living room** in a house is the room where the family spend most of their time.

lizard lizards

NOUN A **lizard** is a small reptile with four short legs and a long tail. It has a rough dry skin. The babies hatch from eggs.

See **Reptiles** on page 259.

llama llamas

NOUN A **llama** is a South American animal of the camel family, with long thick hair.

load loads, loading, loaded

NOUN **1** A **load** is things which are being carried somewhere.

VERB **2** When you **load** a camera, you put film into it so that it is ready to use.

VERB **3** When you **load** a computer, you put information or a program into it.

loaf loaves

NOUN A **loaf** is bread that has been baked into one shape. You cut a loaf into slices.

lobster lobsters

NOUN A **lobster** is a sea animal with a hard shell, two large claws and eight legs.

local

ADJECTIVE Local means belonging to the area where you live or work. *I read about it in the **local** paper.*

locate locates, locating, located

VERB To **locate** someone or something is to find out where they are.

location locations

NOUN A **location** is a place, or the position of something. *The school is being moved to a new **location**.*

loch lochs

NOUN Loch is a Scottish word for **lake**.

lock locks, locking, locked

VERB **1** If you **lock** something, you close it and fasten it with a key.

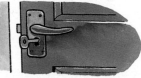

NOUN **2** A **lock** is used to keep something, such as a door or case, closed. You can only open a lock with the right key.

locomotive

locomotive locomotives
NOUN A **locomotive** is the engine which pulls trains along railway tracks.

loft lofts
NOUN A **loft** is the space under the roof of a house, often used for storing things.

log logs
NOUN A **log** is a piece of a thick branch from a tree.

lollipop lollipops
NOUN A **lollipop** is a hard sweet on a stick.

lolly lollies
NOUN **Lolly** is an abbreviation of **lollipop**. A **lolly** is also a piece of flavoured ice or ice cream on a stick.

lonely lonelier, loneliest
ADJECTIVE Someone who is **lonely** is sad because they are on their own, or do not have any friends.

long longer, longest; longs, longing, longed
ADJECTIVE 1 Something **long** takes up more time than usual. *It was a long film.*
ADJECTIVE 2 Something that is **long** is far from one end to the other. *It's a long way from London to New York.*
VERB 3 If you **long** for something, you want it very much.

look looks, looking, looked
VERB 1 If you **look** in a particular direction, you turn your eyes that way.
VERB 2 If you say how someone **looks**, you tell them how they seem to you.
VERB 3 If you **look after** someone, you care for them.
VERB 4 If you **look for** someone or something, you try to find them.
VERB 5 If you are **looking forward** to something, you want it to happen because you think you will enjoy it.

loop loops
NOUN A **loop** is a circular shape in something long and thin. For example, when you tie shoelaces, the bow has two loops in it.

loose looser, loosest
ADJECTIVE 1 Something that is **loose** is not firmly fixed. *I've got a loose tooth.*
ADJECTIVE 2 Things that are **loose** are not fixed together. *She had four loose sheets of paper in her bag.*

lord lords
NOUN Hundreds of years ago, a **lord** was a man who had a lot of power. Now, **Lord** is a title in front of some men's names in Britain.

lorry lorries
NOUN A **lorry** is a large road vehicle that is used to carry loads.

lose loses, losing, lost
VERB 1 If you **lose** something, you cannot find it.
VERB 2 If someone **loses** weight, they become thinner.
VERB 3 If you **lose** something like a game or a race, someone does better than you.

lost
ADJECTIVE 1 If you are **lost**, you cannot find your way or do not know where you are.

VERB 2 **Lost** is the past tense of **lose**.

lot lots
NOUN A **lot** of something, or **lots** of something, is a large amount of it.

lottery lotteries
NOUN A **lottery** is a way of raising money by selling tickets. The winner is chosen by chance.

loud louder, loudest

ADJECTIVE A **loud** sound is one that makes a lot of noise. *The firework went off with a loud bang.*

loudspeaker loudspeakers

NOUN A **loudspeaker** is a piece of equipment that is used so that sounds can be heard. Microphones, radios and CD players all need loudspeakers.

lounge lounges

NOUN A **lounge** in a house or hotel is a room where people sit and relax.

love loves, loving, loved

VERB **1** If you **love** someone, you have strong feelings of affection for them.
VERB **2** If you **love** something, you like it very much. *I love pizza.*

lovely lovelier, loveliest

ADJECTIVE Something that is **lovely** is very pleasing to look at or listen to.

low lower, lowest

ADJECTIVE Something that is **low** measures only a short distance from the ground to the top. *He jumped over the low wall.*

lower lowers, lowering, lowered

VERB **1** If you **lower** something, you move it slowly downwards. *As it was getting dark, she lowered the blind.*
VERB **2** If you **lower** your voice, you speak more quietly.

lower-case

ADJECTIVE **Lower-case** letters are the small letters of the alphabet, such as a, b, c and d. *The letters down the side of this page are lower-case.* See **upper-case**.

loyal

ADJECTIVE If you are **loyal** to someone, you always support them.

luck

NOUN **Luck** is something that seems to happen without any reason. Luck can be good or bad.

lucky luckier, luckiest

ADJECTIVE Someone who is **lucky** seems to have good luck.
luckily ADVERB

luggage

NOUN **Luggage** is all the suitcases, bags and things that you take with you when you are travelling.

lump lumps

NOUN **1** A **lump** is a piece of something solid. *She took a lump of modelling clay.*
NOUN **2** A **lump** on someone's body is a small swelling.

lunar

ADJECTIVE **Lunar** is used to describe something that is to do with the moon.

lunch lunches

NOUN **Lunch** is a meal that you have in the middle of the day.

lung lungs

NOUN Your **lungs** are the two parts of your body inside your chest that fill with air when you breathe.

luxury luxuries

NOUN A **luxury** is something quite expensive to buy, which you like very much but do not need.
luxurious ADJECTIVE

lying

VERB **Lying** is the present participle of **lie**.

Mm

machine machines

NOUN A **machine** is a piece of equipment which does a particular kind of work. It is usually powered by an engine or by electricity.

machinery

NOUN **Machinery** is machines in general.

mad madder, maddest

ADJECTIVE **1** Someone who is **mad** has an illness in their mind.

ADJECTIVE **2** If you describe someone as **mad**, you mean they are foolish or silly.

ADJECTIVE **3** INFORMAL Someone who is **mad** is angry.

ADJECTIVE **4** INFORMAL If you are **mad** about someone or something, you like them very much.

made

VERB **Made** is the past tense of **make**.

magazine magazines

NOUN A **magazine** is a thin book which comes out regularly, usually once a week or once a month. It has articles, stories and pictures.

maggot maggots

NOUN A **maggot** looks like a tiny worm. Maggots change into flies.

magic

NOUN **1** In stories, **magic** is the thing that makes impossible things happen.

ADJECTIVE **2** Magic tricks entertain and puzzle people.

magical ADJECTIVE

magician magicians

NOUN **1** In stories, a **magician** is a man who has magic powers.

NOUN **2** A **magician** is also a real person who can do magic tricks.

magnet magnets

NOUN A **magnet** is a special piece of metal. It pulls or attracts iron or steel towards it. Magnets can also push other magnets away.

magnetic ADJECTIVE

magnificent

ADJECTIVE Something that is **magnificent** is very grand.

magnifying glass magnifying glasses

NOUN A **magnifying glass** is a piece of glass that makes objects appear to be bigger than they really are.

magpie magpies

NOUN A **magpie** is a bird of the crow family. It has black and white markings and a long tail.

mail

NOUN **Mail** is things like letters and parcels that are sent through the post.

main

ADJECTIVE The **main** part of something is the most important part.

maize

NOUN **Maize** is a tall plant that produces sweet corn.

major

ADJECTIVE You use **major** to describe something important. *This is a **major** discovery.*

make makes, making, made

VERB **1** If you **make** something new, you use your skill to shape it or put it together.

VERB **2** To **make** something happen is to cause it. *My new boots made a loud squeak.*

VERB **3** If you **make** a mistake, you do something wrong.

VERB **4** If you **make** someone do something, you force them to do it. *My mum makes me eat vegetables.*

male **males**

NOUN A **male** is a person or animal that belongs to the sex that cannot have babies.

male ADJECTIVE

mammal **mammals**

NOUN A **mammal** is a warm-blooded animal. Female mammals give birth to live babies. They feed their babies with milk from their own bodies.

man **men**

NOUN A **man** is an adult male human being. See **woman**.

manage **manages, managing, managed**

VERB **1** If you **manage** to do something, you succeed in doing it. *He managed to get a seat on the bus.*

VERB **2** Someone who **manages** an organization is in charge of it.

mane **manes**

NOUN The **mane** of an animal such as a horse or a male lion is the long thick hair that grows from its neck.

mango **mangoes** or **mangos**

NOUN A **mango** is a sweet yellowish fruit which grows in tropical countries. See *Fruit* on page 257.

manner **manners**

NOUN **1** The **manner** in which you do something is how you do it.

NOUN **2** Your **manner** is the way in which you behave and talk. *It is good manners to be polite.*

mantelpiece **mantelpieces**

NOUN A **mantelpiece** is a shelf over a fireplace.

manufacture **manufactures, manufacturing, manufactured**

VERB To **manufacture** goods is to make them in a factory.

many

ADJECTIVE **1** If there are **many** people or things, there are a large number of them.

ADJECTIVE **2** You also use **many** to ask how great a quantity is or to give information about it. *How many tickets do you want?*

map **maps**

NOUN A **map** is a drawing of a particular area as it would look from above.

marathon **marathons**

NOUN A **marathon** is a race in which people have to run 26 miles (about 42 kilometres) along roads.

marble **marbles**

NOUN **1** Marble is a very hard stone which shines when it is polished. Statues and parts of buildings are sometimes made of marble.

NOUN **2** Marbles is a children's game played with small coloured glass balls. These balls are also called marbles.

march **marches, marching, marched**

VERB When you **march**, you walk with quick regular steps like a soldier.

March

NOUN **March** is the third month of the year. It has 31 days.

mare **mares**

NOUN A **mare** is an adult female horse.

margarine

margarine
> NOUN **Margarine** is a food that looks like butter but is made from vegetable oil and animal fats. You can spread it on bread and use it for cooking.

margin **margins**
> NOUN The **margin** is the blank space at each side on a written or printed page.

mark **marks**
> NOUN **1** A **mark** is a small stain. *I can't get that **mark** off your shirt.*
> NOUN **2** A **mark** is also something that has been written or drawn. *He made little **marks** on the paper with his pencil.*
> NOUN **3** At school, a **mark** is a letter or number showing how well you have done in homework or in a test.

market **markets**
> NOUN A **market** is a place with many small stalls selling different goods.

marmalade
> NOUN **Marmalade** is a jam made from fruit like oranges or lemons. People often eat it spread on toast for breakfast.

marriage **marriages**
> NOUN **Marriage** is the relationship between a husband and wife.

married
> ADJECTIVE Someone who is **married** has a husband or wife.

marry **marries, marrying, married**
> VERB A man and woman who **marry** become husband and wife.

marsh **marshes**
> NOUN A **marsh** is an area of land which is always very wet and muddy.

marsupial **marsupials**
> NOUN A **marsupial** is a mammal whose babies are carried in a pouch at the front of their mother's body. Kangaroos are marsupials.

marvellous
> ADJECTIVE Something that is **marvellous** is wonderful.

masculine
> ADJECTIVE **Masculine** refers to qualities and things that are typical of men.

mask **masks**
> NOUN A **mask** is something you wear over your face to protect or disguise you.

mass **masses**
> NOUN **1** A **mass** of things is a large number of them grouped together.
> NOUN **2** The **mass** of something is the amount of matter it contains. Mass is measured in grams and kilograms. People often say "weight" when they mean "mass". Mass and weight are different. If you were on the Moon, you would weigh less than on Earth but your mass would not change. See **weight**.
> NOUN **3** In the Roman Catholic church, a **Mass** is a religious service.

massive
> ADJECTIVE Something **massive** is extremely large.

mast **masts**
> NOUN A **mast** is the tall upright pole that supports the sail of a boat.

mat **mats**
> NOUN **1** A **mat** is a small piece of carpet.
> NOUN **2** A **mat** is also something used to protect a table from plates or glasses.

match matches, matching, matched

NOUN **1** A **match** is an organized game of something like tennis or football.

NOUN **2** A **match** is also a thin stick of wood that can make a flame.

VERB **3** If you **match** things, you find a connection between them. *Match the animals with the countries they come from.*

mate mates

NOUN **1** INFORMAL A **mate** is a friend.

NOUN **2** An animal's **mate** is its partner.

material materials

NOUN **1** Material is cloth.

NOUN **2** A **material** is anything that can be used to make something else. Wood, stone, plastic and water are all materials.

mathematics

NOUN **Mathematics** is the study of numbers, quantities and shapes.

maths

NOUN **Maths** is an abbreviation of **mathematics**.

matter matters, mattering, mattered

VERB **1** If something **matters** to you, you care about it and feel it is important.

NOUN **2** A **matter** is something that you have to deal with or think about. *This is a matter for the police.*

mattress mattresses

NOUN A **mattress** is a large flat cushion which is put on a bed to make it comfortable to lie on.

may

VERB If someone says you **may** do something, you are allowed to do it.

May

NOUN **May** is the fifth month of the year. It has 31 days.

maybe

ADVERB You say **maybe** when something is possible but you are not sure about it. *Maybe we could go tomorrow.*

mayor mayors

NOUN The **mayor** of a town or city is the man or woman who has been chosen to be its head.

maze mazes

NOUN A **maze** is a system of paths which is made like a puzzle so that it is difficult to find your way through it.

meadow meadows

NOUN A **meadow** is a field of grass and wild flowers.

meal meals

NOUN A **meal** is food that people eat, usually at set times during the day.

mean means, meaning, meant; meaner, meanest

VERB **1** If you ask what something **means**, you want it explained to you.

VERB **2** If you **mean** what you say, you are serious about it.

VERB **3** If something **means** a lot to you, it is important to you.

VERB **4** If you **mean** to do something, you intend to do it. *I meant to phone you, but I didn't have time.*

ADJECTIVE **5** Someone who is **mean** does not like spending money or sharing.

meaning meanings

NOUN The **meaning** of a word or sentence is the thing or idea that it is explaining. *Do you know the meaning of the proverb "Look before you leap"?*

meanwhile

ADVERB **Meanwhile** means while something else is happening.

a b c d e f g h i j k l Mm n o p q r s t u v w x y z

measles

NOUN **Measles** is an illness caught especially by children. It gives you a fever and red spots on your skin.

measure measures, measuring, measured

VERB **1** If you **measure** something, you find out how large or heavy it is.

NOUN **2** A **measure** is a unit in which something such as size or speed is expressed. *Kilometres are a measure of distance.*
See *Measures* on page 270.

measurement measurements

NOUN A **measurement** is a result that you get by measuring something.

meat meats

NOUN **Meat** is the flesh of animals that is cooked and eaten.

mechanical

ADJECTIVE A **mechanical** object has moving parts and is used to do a physical task.

medal medals

NOUN A **medal** is a small metal disc or cross given as an award for bravery or as a prize for sport.

medical

ADJECTIVE **Medical** means to do with medicine or the care of people's health.

medicine medicines

NOUN **Medicine** is a tablet or liquid given to people who are ill to make them better.

medium

ADJECTIVE **Medium** means somewhere in the middle of two extremes. *He's of medium height – neither tall nor short.*

meet meets, meeting, met

VERB If you **meet** someone, you go to the same place at the same time as they do.

meeting meetings

NOUN A **meeting** is when a group of people meet to talk about particular things.

melon melons

NOUN A **melon** is a large fruit that is sweet and juicy inside. It has a thick, hard green or yellow skin.
See *Fruit* on page 257.

melt melts, melting, melted

VERB When something like ice **melts**, it changes from a solid into a liquid because it has become warmer.

member members

NOUN A **member** of a group is one of the people, animals or things belonging to that group.
membership NOUN

memorize memorizes, memorizing, memorized; also spelt memorise

VERB If you **memorize** something, you learn it so that you can repeat it exactly using only your memory.

memory memories

NOUN **1** Your **memory** is what allows you to remember things.

NOUN **2** A **memory** is something you remember from the past.

men

NOUN **Men** is the plural of **man**.

mend mends, mending, mended

VERB If you **mend** something that is broken or does not work, you put it right so that it can be used again.

mental

ADJECTIVE **Mental** means to do with your mind or brain. For example, mental maths is working out the answers to calculations in your head.

mention mentions, mentioning, mentioned

VERB If you **mention** something, you talk about it briefly.

menu menus

NOUN **1** A **menu** is a list of food that you can order in a restaurant.

NOUN **2** A **menu** on a computer is a list of choices.

mercury

NOUN **Mercury** is a silver-coloured metal. Liquid mercury is used in thermometers.

mercy

NOUN If you show **mercy** to someone, you do not hurt or punish them.

mermaid mermaids

NOUN In stories, a **mermaid** is a woman with a fish's tail.

merry merrier, merriest

ADJECTIVE **Merry** means happy and cheerful.

mess messes

NOUN If you say something is a **mess**, you mean it is very untidy.

messy ADJECTIVE

message messages

NOUN A **message** is words that you send or leave when you cannot speak directly to someone.

messenger messengers

NOUN A **messenger** is a person who takes a message to someone.

met

VERB **Met** is the past tense of **meet**.

metal metals

NOUN A **metal** is a hard, strong material that melts when it is heated, such as iron, gold or steel. Metals are used to make things like jewellery, tools, cars and machines.

meter meters

NOUN A **meter** is an instrument for measuring something, such as the amount of gas that you have used.

method methods

NOUN A **method** is a particular way of doing something.

metre metres

NOUN **1** A **metre** (m) is a measure of length. It is equal to 100 centimetres.

NOUN **2** In poetry, **metre** is the rhythmic arrangement of words and syllables.

metric

ADJECTIVE **Metric** relates to the system of measurement that uses metres, kilograms and litres.

miaow

NOUN A **miaow** is the short high-pitched sound that a cat makes.

mice

NOUN **Mice** is the plural of **mouse**.

micro-

PREFIX **Micro-** means small.

See **Prefixes** on page 264.

microchip microchips

NOUN A **microchip** is a small piece of silicon on which electronic circuits for a computer are printed.

microphone microphones

NOUN A **microphone** is a piece of equipment that is used to make sounds louder, or to record them.

microscope microscopes

NOUN A **microscope** is a piece of equipment which makes small objects appear much larger.

microscopic ADJECTIVE

a
b
c
d
e
f
g
h
i
j
k
l
Mm
n
o
p
q
r
s
t
u
v
w
x
y
z

a b c d e f g h i j k l **Mm** **n o p q r s t u v w x y z**

microwave microwaves

NOUN A **microwave** is a type of oven which cooks food very quickly.

mid-

PREFIX **Mid-** is used to form words that refer to the middle part of a place or period of time, for example "midday". See *Prefixes* on page 264.

midday

NOUN **Midday** is 12 o'clock (noon) in the middle of the day.

middle middles

NOUN **1** The **middle** of something is the part furthest from the edges.
ADJECTIVE **2** The **middle** one in a series or a row is the one that has an equal number of people or things on each side of it.

midnight

NOUN **Midnight** is 12 o'clock at night.

might

VERB **1** If you say something **might** happen, you are not sure if it will.
VERB **2** If you say something **might** be true, you are not sure about it.

migrate migrates, migrating, migrated

VERB When birds, fish or animals **migrate**, they move to another place at a particular time of year so that they can find food.

mild milder, mildest

ADJECTIVE **1** Something that is **mild** is gentle and does no harm. *You need to use a mild shampoo.*
ADJECTIVE **2** **Mild** weather in the winter is warmer than usual.

mile miles

NOUN A **mile** is a unit of distance equal to about one and a half kilometres.

military

ADJECTIVE **Military** means to do with the armed forces of a country.

milk

NOUN **Milk** is the white liquid that female mammals make in their bodies to feed their young. People drink milk from cows and use it to make butter, cheese and yogurt.

mill mills

NOUN **1** A **mill** is a building in which grain is crushed to make flour. The photo shows a water mill. The water makes the mill wheel turn.

NOUN **2** A **mill** is also a factory used for making things such as cotton or paper.

millennium millennia or millenniums

NOUN A **millennium** is a period of 1000 years.

millilitre millilitres

NOUN A **millilitre** is a measure of volume and capacity. There are 1000 millilitres in a litre.

millimetre millimetres

NOUN A **millimetre** (mm) is a measure of length. There are 1000 millimetres in a metre. There are 10 millimetres in a centimetre.

million millions

NOUN A million is the number 1 000 000.

millionaire millionaires

NOUN A **millionaire** is a person who has more than a million pounds or dollars.

mince

NOUN **Mince** is meat which has been cut into very small pieces.

mincemeat

NOUN **Mincemeat** is a sticky mixture of dried fruit and other sweet things.

mind minds, minding, minded

NOUN **1** Your **mind** is your ability to think, together with your memory and all the thoughts you have.

NOUN **2** If you **change your mind**, you change a decision you have made.

VERB **3** If you **mind** about something, it worries you or makes you angry.

mine mines

PRONOUN **1** **Mine** refers to something belonging to the person who is speaking or writing. *That book is **mine**.*

NOUN **2** A **mine** is a place under the ground where people dig out things like diamonds, coal or other minerals.

NOUN **3** A **mine** can be a bomb hidden in the ground or underwater, which explodes when people or things touch it.

mineral minerals

NOUN **Minerals** are substances such as tin, salt or coal that are formed naturally in rocks and in the earth.

mini-

PREFIX **Mini-** is used to form nouns that refer to something smaller or less important than similar things, for example a minibus.

See *Prefixes* on page 264.

minibus minibuses

NOUN A **minibus** is a van with seats in the back that is used as a small bus.

minister ministers

NOUN **1** A **minister** is an important member of the government of a country.

NOUN **2** A **minister** is also a person in charge of a church.

minor

ADJECTIVE Something that is **minor** is not very important or serious. *She had a **minor** accident.*

mint mints

NOUN **1** **Mint** is a small plant. Its leaves have a strong taste and smell, and are used in cooking.

NOUN **2** A **mint** is a kind of sweet.

NOUN **3** A **mint** is also a place where coins are made.

minus

PREPOSITION **1** You use **minus** to show that one number is being subtracted from another. For example, ten minus six equals four (written $10 - 6 = 4$).

ADJECTIVE **2** Minus is used when talking about temperatures below 0° Celsius. *The temperature is **minus** two degrees.*

minute minutes

(*said* **min**-nit) NOUN **1** A **minute** is a unit of time equal to 60 seconds.

(*said* my-**nyoot**) ADJECTIVE **2** Something **minute** is extremely small.

miracle miracles

NOUN **1** A **miracle** is a wonderful event, believed to have been caused by God.

NOUN **2** A **miracle** can also be any very surprising event. *By some **miracle** he got to school early.*

mirror mirrors

NOUN A **mirror** is a piece of glass that reflects light. When you look in a mirror you can see yourself.

mis-

PREFIX **Mis-** is added to some words to form other words, often ones that refer to things being done wrongly, for example "misprint" or "misunderstand".

See *Prefixes* on page 264.

misbehave misbehaves, misbehaving, misbehaved

VERB If a child **misbehaves**, they are naughty or behave badly.

a b c d e f g h i j k l **Mm** n o p q r s t u v w x y z

mischief

mischief
NOUN **Mischief** is silly things that some children do to annoy other people.

mischievous
ADJECTIVE **1** A **mischievous** person likes to have fun by embarrassing people or playing tricks.
ADJECTIVE **2** A **mischievous** child is often naughty but does not do any real harm.

miserable
ADJECTIVE Someone who is **miserable** is unhappy.
miserably ADVERB

misery
NOUN **Misery** is great unhappiness.

misfortune **misfortunes**
NOUN **Misfortune** is bad luck.

mislay **mislays, mislaying, mislaid**
VERB If you **mislay** something, you forget where you have put it.

mislead **misleads, misleading, misled**
VERB To **mislead** someone is to give them an idea that is not true.

misprint **misprints**
NOUN A **misprint** is a mistake in something that has been printed, for example "cow" instead of "cot".

miss **misses, missing, missed**
VERB **1** If you are aiming at something and **miss**, you fail to hit it.
VERB **2** If you **miss** a bus or train, you are too late to get on it.
VERB **3** If you **miss** somebody, you are lonely without them.

Miss
NOUN **Miss** is used before the name of a girl or an unmarried woman.

missile **missiles**
NOUN A **missile** is a weapon that goes through the air and explodes when it reaches its target.

missing
ADJECTIVE If something is **missing**, it is not in its usual place and you cannot find it.

misspell **misspells, misspelling, misspelt or misspelled**
VERB If you **misspell** a word, you spell it wrongly.

mist **mists**
NOUN A **mist** is a large number of tiny drops of water in the air. When there is a mist, you cannot see very far.
misty ADJECTIVE

mistake **mistakes**
NOUN A **mistake** is something that is done wrong.

misunderstand **misunderstands, misunderstanding, misunderstood**
VERB If you **misunderstand** someone, you do not understand them properly.

mix **mixes, mixing, mixed**
VERB If you **mix** things, you stir them or put them together. *The children made paste by mixing flour and water.*

mixture **mixtures**
NOUN A **mixture** is several different things mixed up.

moan **moans, moaning, moaned**
VERB If you **moan**, you make a low sad sound because you are in pain or trouble.

moat **moats**
NOUN A **moat** is a wide water-filled ditch around a building such as a castle.

mobile **mobiles**
ADJECTIVE **1** If you are **mobile**, you are able to travel or move to another place.
NOUN **2** A **mobile** is a decoration that you hang up so that it moves around when a breeze blows.

mobile phone **mobile phones**
NOUN A **mobile phone** is a telephone you can carry about.

model **models**
NOUN **1** A **model** is a small copy of something. It shows what it looks like or how it works.
NOUN **2** A **model** is also someone who shows clothes to people by wearing them.

modern
ADJECTIVE **Modern** is to do with new ideas and equipment. *We live in a* **modern** *house.*

modest
ADJECTIVE People who are **modest** do not boast about themselves.

moist **moister, moistest**
ADJECTIVE Something that is **moist** is slightly wet.
moisten VERB

moisture
NOUN **Moisture** is tiny drops of water in the air or on a surface.

mole **moles**
NOUN **1** A **mole** is a small burrowing animal with tiny eyes and dark silky fur.

NOUN **2** A **mole** is also a small dark lump on someone's skin.

moment **moments**
NOUN **1** A **moment** is a very short time.
NOUN **2** A **moment** is also a point in time when something happens. *At that* **moment***, the teacher came into the room.*

Monday **Mondays**
NOUN **Monday** is the day between Sunday and Tuesday.

money
NOUN **Money** is the coins or banknotes you use to buy something.

mongrel **mongrels**
NOUN A **mongrel** is a dog with parents of different breeds.

monitor **monitors**
NOUN A **monitor** is the part of a computer that contains the screen.

monkey **monkeys**
NOUN A **monkey** is an animal that lives in hot countries. It has a long tail and climbs trees.

monster **monsters**
NOUN A **monster** is an imaginary creature that is large and terrifying.

month **months**
NOUN A **month** is a measure of time. There are 12 months in a year.

mood **moods**
NOUN Your **mood** is the way you are feeling about things at a particular time, such as how cheerful or angry you are.

moon **moons**
NOUN The **moon** is a satellite that moves round the Earth. It shines in the sky at night. You can only see it because the moon's surface reflects sunlight.

moonlight
NOUN **Moonlight** is the light that comes from the moon at night.

moor **moors**
NOUN A **moor** is an open area of land covered mainly with grass and heather.

a b c d e f g h i j k l **Mm** n o p q r s t u v w x y z

moose

NOUN A **moose** is a large North American deer. Moose have very flat, branch-shaped horns called antlers.

mop mops

NOUN A **mop** is a tool for washing floors. It has a long handle with sponge or pieces of string fixed to the end.

more

ADJECTIVE OR ADVERB **More** means a greater number or amount of something. It is the comparative of "many" or "much". *Jill thinks football is more fun than maths. He's got more chips than me.*

morning mornings

NOUN **Morning** is the part of the day before noon.

mosque mosques

NOUN A **mosque** is a building where Muslims worship.

mosquito mosquitoes or mosquitos

NOUN A **mosquito** is a small flying insect that lives in damp places. The female bites people and other animals to suck their blood.
See *Insects* on page 259.

moss mosses

NOUN **Moss** is a small green plant without roots. It grows in flat clumps on trees, rocks and damp ground.

most

ADJECTIVE, ADVERB OR NOUN **Most** means the greatest number or amount of something. It is the superlative of "many" or "much". *I saw the most fantastic film. Most children like sweets. The most I can give you is three pieces.*

moth moths

NOUN A **moth** is an insect like a butterfly that usually flies at night.

mother mothers

NOUN A **mother** is a woman who has a child or children of her own.

motion motions

NOUN A **motion** is a movement.

motive motives

NOUN A **motive** is a reason for doing something. *There was no motive for the attack.*

motor motors

NOUN A **motor** is part of a vehicle or machine. The motor uses fuel to make the vehicle or machine work.

motorbike motorbikes

NOUN A **motorbike** is a two-wheeled vehicle that is driven by an engine.

motorway motorways

NOUN A **motorway** is a wide road built for fast travel over long distances.

mould moulds

NOUN **1 Mould** is a soft grey or green substance that can form on old food.
NOUN **2** A **mould** is a container used to make something into a particular shape, for example a jelly mould.

moult moults, moulting, moulted

VERB When an animal **moults**, it loses its hair or feathers so that new ones can grow.

mount mounts, mounting, mounted

VERB If you **mount** a horse, you climb on its back.

mountain mountains

NOUN A **mountain** is a very high piece of land with steep sides.

mouse mice

NOUN **1** A **mouse** is a small rodent with a long tail.

NOUN **2** A **mouse** is also a small object that you use to move the cursor on a computer screen.

moustache moustaches

NOUN A man's **moustache** is hair growing on his upper lip.

mouth mouths

NOUN **1** Your **mouth** is your lips, or the space behind them where your tongue and teeth are.

NOUN **2** The **mouth** of a cave or hole is the entrance to it.

NOUN **3** The **mouth** of a river is the place where it flows into the sea.

move moves, moving, moved

VERB **1** To **move** means to go to a different place or position.

VERB **2** To **move** something means to change its place or position.

movement NOUN

mow mows, mowing, mowed

VERB If a person **mows** an area of grass, they cut it with a lawnmower.

Mr (*said* **miss**-ter)

Mr is used before a man's name.

Mrs (*said* **miss**-iz)

Mrs is used before the name of a married woman.

Ms (*said* **miz**)

Ms can be used before a woman's name. Some women choose to be called Ms because it says nothing about whether they are married or not.

much

ADVERB **1** You use **much** to show that something is true to a great extent. *I feel much better now.*

ADVERB **2** If something does not happen **much**, it does not happen very often.

ADJECTIVE **3** You use **much** to ask questions or give information about the size or amount of something. *How much money do you need?*

mud

NOUN **Mud** is wet sticky earth.

muddy ADJECTIVE

muddle muddles

NOUN If things such as papers are in a **muddle**, they are all mixed up.

muffled

ADJECTIVE A **muffled** sound is quiet or difficult to hear.

mug mugs

NOUN A **mug** is a large deep cup, usually with straight sides and a handle.

multiple multiples

NOUN The **multiples** of a number are other numbers that it will divide into exactly. For example, 6, 9 and 12 are multiples of 3.

multiplication

NOUN **Multiplication** is when you multiply one number by another. The sign you use for multiplication is ×.

multiply multiplies, multiplying, multiplied

VERB **1** When something **multiplies**, it increases greatly in number. *Fleas multiply very fast.*

VERB **2** When you **multiply** a number, you make it bigger by a number of times. For example, two multiplied by three (two plus two plus two) equals six. 2 × 3 = 6 or 2 + 2 + 2 = 6

a
b
c
d
e
f
g
h
i
j
k
l
Mm
n
o
p
q
r
s
t
u
v
w
x
y
z

mum

Mm

mum mums
NOUN Your **mum** is your mother.

mumble mumbles, mumbling, mumbled
VERB If you **mumble**, you speak very quietly and not clearly.

mumps
NOUN **Mumps** is an illness caught especially by children. Your neck swells and your throat hurts.

munch munches, munching, munched
VERB If you **munch** something, you chew it steadily and thoroughly.

murder murders
NOUN **Murder** is the deliberate killing of a person.

murmur murmurs, murmuring, murmured
VERB If you **murmur**, you say something very softly.

muscle muscles
NOUN **Muscles** are the parts inside your body that you use when you move.

museum museums
NOUN A **museum** is a building where many interesting or valuable objects are kept and displayed.

mushroom mushrooms
NOUN A **mushroom** is a small fungus with a short thick stem and a round top. You can eat some kinds of mushroom, but others are poisonous.

music
NOUN **1** Music is a pattern of sounds made by people singing or playing instruments.

NOUN **2** Music is also the written symbols that stand for musical sounds.

musical
ADJECTIVE **Musical** means relating to playing or studying music. *He wants to learn to play a **musical** instrument.*

musician musicians
NOUN A **musician** is a person who plays a musical instrument well.

Muslim Muslims; also spelt Moslem
NOUN A **Muslim** is a person who follows the religion of Islam.

must
VERB If something **must** happen, it is important or necessary that it happens. *You **must** be home by 5 p.m.*

mustard
NOUN **Mustard** is a hot spicy yellow paste made from mustard seeds.

my
ADJECTIVE **My** refers to something belonging or relating to the person speaking or writing. *I held **my** breath.*

myself
PRONOUN **Myself** is used when the person speaking does something and no one else does it. *I hung the picture **myself**.*

mysterious
ADJECTIVE Something that is **mysterious** is strange and puzzling.

mystery mysteries
NOUN **1** A **mystery** is something strange that cannot be explained.
NOUN **2** A **mystery** is also a story in which strange things happen.

myth myths
NOUN A **myth** is a story which was made up long ago to explain natural events and religious beliefs.

Nn

nail **nails**

NOUN **1** A **nail** is a small piece of metal with a sharp point at one end, which you hammer into objects to hold them together.

NOUN **2** Your **nails** are the thin hard areas at the ends of your fingers and toes.

naked

ADJECTIVE Someone who is **naked** is not wearing any clothes.

name **names**

NOUN A **name** is what someone or something is called.

nappy **nappies**

NOUN A **nappy** is a thick piece of soft material wrapped round a baby's bottom to help keep it dry and clean.

narrative **narratives**

NOUN A **narrative** is a story or an account of events.

narrator **narrators**

NOUN A **narrator** is a person who tells a story or explains what is happening.

narrow **narrower, narrowest**

ADJECTIVE Something **narrow** is a short distance from one side to the other. *The stream was **narrow** enough to jump across.*

nasty **nastier, nastiest**

ADJECTIVE **1** Something that is **nasty** is very unpleasant.

ADJECTIVE **2** Someone who is **nasty** is very unkind.

nastily ADVERB

nation **nations**

NOUN A **nation** is a country with its own laws.

national

ADJECTIVE Something that is **national** is to do with the whole of a country. *The Observer is a **national** newspaper.*

native

ADJECTIVE **1** Your **native** country is the country where you were born.

ADJECTIVE **2** Your **native** language is the language that you first learned to speak.

ADJECTIVE **3** Animals or plants that are **native** to a place live there naturally. They have not been brought there by people.

natural

ADJECTIVE **1** **Natural** means existing or happening in nature. For example, an earthquake is a natural disaster.

ADJECTIVE **2** Something that is **natural** is normal and to be expected.

nature **natures**

NOUN **1** **Nature** is animals, plants and all the other things in the world not made by people.

NOUN **2** The **nature** of a person or thing is their basic character.

naughty **naughtier, naughtiest**

ADJECTIVE A child who is **naughty** behaves badly.

navigate **navigates, navigating, navigated**

VERB When someone **navigates**, they work out the direction in which a ship, plane or car should go, using maps and sometimes instruments.

navy navies

NOUN **1** A **navy** is the part of a country's armed forces that fights at sea.

ADJECTIVE **2** Something that is **navy** is a very dark blue.

See *Colours* on page 271.

near nearer, nearest

ADJECTIVE **1** Something that is **near** is not far away. *Where is the nearest garage?*

ADVERB **2** If you are **near** something or somewhere, you are not far away from it. *We must be getting nearer.*

nearly

ADVERB **Nearly** means almost but not quite. *I nearly caught him but he ran off.*

neat neater, neatest

ADJECTIVE Something that is **neat** is very tidy and clean.

necessary

ADJECTIVE Something that is **necessary** is needed or must be done.

necessarily ADVERB

neck necks

NOUN Your **neck** is the part of your body that joins your head to the rest of your body.

necklace necklaces

NOUN A **necklace** is a piece of jewellery that you wear around your neck.

need needs, needing, needed

VERB **1** If you **need** something, you must have it in order to live and be healthy.

VERB **2** Sometimes you **need** something to help you do a particular job. *Now I need a paintbrush.*

VERB **3** If you **need** to do something, you have to do it.

needle needles

NOUN **1** A **needle** is a small thin piece of metal used for sewing. It has a hole in one end and a sharp point at the other. You put thread through the hole.

NOUN **2** A **needle** is also a thin metal tube with a sharp point, that people like doctors use to give injections.

NOUN **3** **Needles** are long thin pieces of metal or plastic used for knitting.

NOUN **4** The thin leaves on pine trees are called **needles**.

negative negatives

ADJECTIVE **1** A **negative** sentence is one that has the word "no" or "not" in it.

ADJECTIVE **2** A **negative** number is less than zero.

NOUN **3** A **negative** is a film from a camera. You can get your photographs printed from negatives.

neglect neglects, neglecting, neglected

NOUN If you **neglect** something, you do not look after it.

neighbour neighbours

NOUN Your **neighbour** is someone who lives near you.

neighbourhood neighbourhoods

NOUN A **neighbourhood** is a district where people live. *This is a friendly neighbourhood.*

nephew nephews

NOUN Someone's **nephew** is a son of their sister or brother. See **niece**.

nerve nerves

NOUN **1** Your **nerves** are the long thin threads in your body that carry messages between your brain and the other parts of your body.

NOUN **2** **Nerve** is courage. *I wanted to go on the ride but I hadn't got the nerve.*

nervous

ADJECTIVE **1** If you are **nervous**, you are worried about doing something.

ADJECTIVE **2** A **nervous** person is easily frightened.

nest nests

NOUN A **nest** is a place that a bird or other animal makes for its babies.

net nets

NOUN **1** Net is material made from threads woven together with small spaces in between.

NOUN **2** The **net** is the same as the Internet.

NOUN **3** In maths, the **net** of a three-dimensional shape is the flat shape that you could fold to make the three-dimensional shape.

ADJECTIVE **4** The **net** weight of something is its weight without its wrapping.

netball

NOUN **Netball** is a game played by two teams of seven players. Each team tries to score goals by throwing a ball through a net at the top of a pole.

nettle nettles

NOUN A **nettle** is a wild plant covered with little hairs that sting.

never

ADVERB **Never** means at no time in the past or future. *You must **never** cross the road without looking carefully.*

new newer, newest

ADJECTIVE **1** Something that is **new** has just been made or bought. *They have built some **new** houses close to us.*

ADJECTIVE **2** New can mean different. *We've got a **new** car – it's only a year old.*

news

NOUN **News** is information about something that has just happened.

newspaper newspapers

NOUN A **newspaper** is sheets of paper that are printed and sold regularly. Newspapers contain news and articles.

newt newts

NOUN A **newt** is a small animal that looks like a lizard. It lives near water. *See Amphibians on page 259.*

next

ADJECTIVE **1** The **next** period or thing is the one that comes immediately after this one. *The **next** programme will follow after the break.*

ADJECTIVE **2** The **next** place is the one nearest to you. *She's in the **next** room.*

nib nibs

NOUN A **nib** is a small pointed piece of metal at the end of a pen. Ink comes out of the nib as you write.

nibble nibbles, nibbling, nibbled

VERB If you **nibble** something, you eat it slowly by taking small bites out of it.

nice nicer, nicest

ADJECTIVE **1** You say something is **nice** when you like it. *This cake is **nice**.*

ADJECTIVE **2** If you say the weather is **nice**, it is warm and pleasant.

ADJECTIVE **3** If you are **nice** to people, you are friendly and kind.

nickname nicknames

NOUN A **nickname** is a name that is given to a person by friends or family. *The baby's name is Sam but his **nickname** is Dribbler.*

niece nieces

NOUN Someone's **niece** is a daughter of their sister or brother. See **nephew**.

night nights

NOUN The **night** is the time between evening and morning when it is dark.

nightfall

NOUN **Nightfall** is the time of day when it starts to get dark.

a
b
c
d
e
f
g
h
i
j
k
l
m
Nn
o
p
q
r
s
t
u
v
w
x
y
z

nightingale **nightingales**
NOUN A **nightingale** is a small brown European bird. Nightingales sing after dark as well as during the day.

nightmare **nightmares**
NOUN A **nightmare** is a frightening dream.

no
1 You say **no** when you do not want something or do not agree. *"More tea?"* *"**No**, thank you."*
ADJECTIVE **2** You can use **no** to mean not any. *I had **no** help at all.*
ADVERB **3** You can use **no** to mean not. *Competition entries must be in **no** later than Friday.*

nobody
PRONOUN **Nobody** means not a single person.

nocturnal
ADJECTIVE An animal that is **nocturnal** is active mostly at night.

nod **nods, nodding, nodded**
VERB If you **nod**, you move your head quickly down and up to answer yes to a question, or to show that you agree.

noise **noises**
NOUN **1** A **noise** is a sound that someone or something makes.
NOUN **2** Noise is loud or unpleasant sounds.
noisy ADJECTIVE

non-
PREFIX Putting **non-** in front of a word makes it mean the opposite. *This is a **non**-smoking area.*
See *Prefixes* on page 264.

none
PRONOUN **None** means not any, or not one. ***None** of us wanted to go.*

non-fiction
NOUN **Non-fiction** is writing that is based on fact. For example, dictionaries are non-fiction. See **fiction**.

nonsense
NOUN **Nonsense** is words that do not make sense.

noon
NOUN **Noon** is 12 o'clock in the middle of the day.

no one also spelt **no-one**
PRONOUN **No one** means not a single person.

normal
ADJECTIVE Something that is **normal** is what you would expect.

north
NOUN **North** is one of the four main points of the compass. If you face the point where the sun rises, north is on your left. See **compass point**.
northern ADJECTIVE

north-east
NOUN **North-east** is halfway between north and east.

north-west
NOUN **North-west** is halfway between north and west.

nose **noses**
NOUN Your **nose** is the part of your face that sticks out above your mouth. It is used for smelling and breathing.

nostril **nostrils**
NOUN Your **nostrils** are the two openings at the end of your nose. You breathe through your nostrils.

a b c d e f g h i j k l m **Nn** o p q r s t u v w x y z

note notes

NOUN **1** A **note** is a short written message.
NOUN **2** You take **notes** to help you remember what has been said.
NOUN **3** A **note** is also a single sound in music.
NOUN **4** A bank **note** is a printed piece of paper that is used as money.

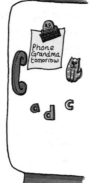

nothing

PRONOUN **Nothing** means not anything.

notice notices, noticing, noticed

VERB **1** If you **notice** something, you pay attention to it. *She noticed that it was raining.*
NOUN **2** A **notice** is a sign that tells people something. *The notice said, "Cameras are not allowed in the museum".*

nought

Nought is the number 0, or zero.

noun nouns

NOUN In grammar, a **noun** is a word which names a person, a thing or an idea. "James", "newt", and "success" are all nouns.
See Noun on page 262.

nourishment

NOUN **Nourishment** is the food that you need in order to grow and stay healthy.
nourishing ADJECTIVE

novel novels

NOUN A **novel** is a long written story that has been made up by the author. Novels are fiction.

November

NOUN **November** is the 11th month of the year. It has 30 days.

now

ADVERB **Now** means at the present time.

nowhere

ADVERB **Nowhere** means not anywhere.

nude

ADJECTIVE Someone who is **nude** is not wearing any clothes.

nudge nudges, nudging, nudged

VERB If you **nudge** somebody, you push them gently, usually with your elbow.

nuisance nuisances

NOUN If you say that someone or something is a **nuisance**, you mean they annoy you.

numb

ADJECTIVE If something is **numb**, it does not feel anything. *My foot is so cold it is numb.*

number numbers

NOUN A **number** is a word or sign that tells you how many of something there are.
See Number bank on page 272.

numeracy

NOUN **Numeracy** is the ability to understand and work with numbers.

numerous

ADJECTIVE If there are **numerous** things or people, there are a lot of them.

nurse nurses

NOUN A **nurse** is a person whose job is to care for people who are ill or injured.

nursery nurseries

NOUN **1** A **nursery** is a place where young children can be looked after during the day.
NOUN **2** A **nursery** can also be a place where plants are grown and sold.

nut nuts

NOUN **1** A **nut** is the hard fruit of certain trees such as walnuts and chestnuts.

NOUN **2** A **nut** is also a small piece of metal with a hole in it. It screws onto a bolt to fasten things together.

nylon

NOUN **Nylon** is a strong artificial material.

a
b
c
d
e
f
g
h
i
j
k
l
m
Nn
o
p
q
r
s
t
u
v
w
x
y
z

a
b
c
d
e
f
g
h
i
j
k
l
m
Oo
n
p
q
r
s
t
u
v
w
x
y
z

Oo

oak oaks
NOUN An **oak** is a large tree with nuts called acorns. The wood of oak trees is often used to make furniture.

oar oars
NOUN An **oar** is a wooden pole with a wide flat end, used for rowing a boat.

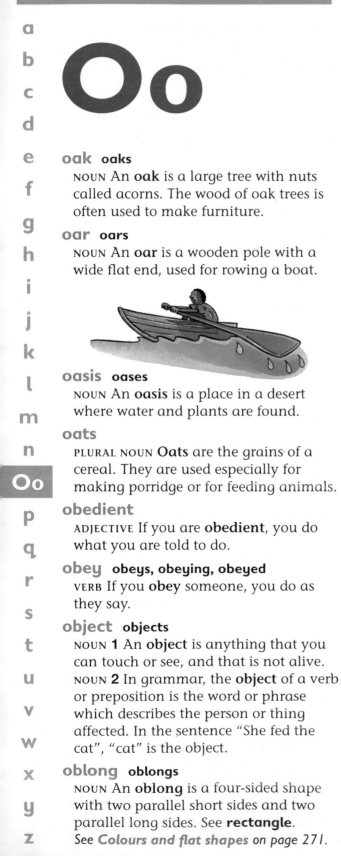

oasis oases
NOUN An **oasis** is a place in a desert where water and plants are found.

oats
PLURAL NOUN **Oats** are the grains of a cereal. They are used especially for making porridge or for feeding animals.

obedient
ADJECTIVE If you are **obedient**, you do what you are told to do.

obey obeys, obeying, obeyed
VERB If you **obey** someone, you do as they say.

object objects
NOUN **1** An **object** is anything that you can touch or see, and that is not alive.
NOUN **2** In grammar, the **object** of a verb or preposition is the word or phrase which describes the person or thing affected. In the sentence "She fed the cat", "cat" is the object.

oblong oblongs
NOUN An **oblong** is a four-sided shape with two parallel short sides and two parallel long sides. See **rectangle**.
See *Colours and flat shapes* on page 271.

observe observes, observing, observed
VERB If you **observe** something or somebody, you watch them carefully.

obstinate
ADJECTIVE Someone who is **obstinate** is determined to do what they want and will not change their mind.

obvious
ADJECTIVE Something that is **obvious** is easy to see or understand.

occasion occasions
NOUN An **occasion** is an important event or celebration.

occasional
ADJECTIVE **Occasional** means happening sometimes, but not regularly or often.
occasionally ADVERB

occupant occupants
NOUN The **occupant** of a place is the person who lives or works there.

occupy occupies, occupying, occupied
VERB **1** To **occupy** a place means to live, stay or work in it.
VERB **2** If something **occupies** you, you are busy doing it or thinking about it.
ADJECTIVE **3** If something like a chair is **occupied**, someone is using it.

occur occurs, occurring, occurred
VERB **1** When something **occurs**, it happens.
VERB **2** If something **occurs** to you, you suddenly think of it or realize it.

ocean oceans
NOUN An **ocean** is one of the five large seas on the earth's surface.

o'clock
ADVERB You say **o'clock** after numbers when you say a time that is exactly on the hour.

octagon octagons
NOUN An **octagon** is a flat shape with eight straight sides.
octagonal ADJECTIVE
See *Colours and flat shapes* on page 271.

October

NOUN **October** is the 10th month of the year. It has 31 days.

octopus octopuses

NOUN An **octopus** is a sea animal with eight long arms called tentacles.

odd odder, oddest

ADJECTIVE **1** If you say something is **odd**, you mean it is strange or unusual.

ADJECTIVE **2** **Odd** numbers are those which cannot be divided exactly by two. 13, 25 and 79 are odd numbers.

ADJECTIVE **3** **Odd** things are those which do not belong in a pair or a set. *You can't go out wearing **odd** socks.*

odds and ends PHRASE **Odds and ends** are small unimportant things. *His pockets were full of **odds and ends**.*

odour odours

NOUN An **odour** is a particular smell.

off

PREPOSITION **1** **Off** can show movement away from or out of a place. *They stepped **off** the plane.*

ADVERB **2** **Off** can mean not switched on. *He turned the radio **off**.*

ADVERB **3** **Off** can also mean time spent away from work. *He took the afternoon **off**.*

ADVERB **4** People use **off** to show a reduction. *All right, I'll take ten per cent **off**.*

ADJECTIVE **5** If food is **off**, it is going bad.

offend offends, offending, offended

VERB If you **offend** someone, you upset them by doing or saying something rude.

offensive ADJECTIVE

offer offers, offering, offered

VERB **1** If you **offer** something to someone, you ask them if they would like to have it.

VERB **2** If you **offer** to do something, you say you will do it without being asked.

office offices

NOUN An **office** is a room where people work at desks.

officer officers

NOUN **1** An **officer** is a member of the police, or of a government organization.

NOUN **2** An **officer** is also a person in the army, navy or air force who gives orders to other people.

official

ADJECTIVE Something that is **official** is written or done by the government or by someone else in charge.

often

ADVERB If something happens **often**, it happens many times.

ogre ogres

NOUN In fairy tales, an **ogre** is a man who is large, cruel and frightening.

oil oils

NOUN **1** **Oil** is a smooth thick liquid that is found under the ground. It is used to keep machines running smoothly, and also for fuel.

NOUN **2** **Oil** can also be made from plants or animals. This oil can sometimes be used for cooking.

ointment ointments

NOUN An **ointment** is an oily cream that you put on sore skin to help it get better.

old older, oldest

ADJECTIVE **1** Someone or something **old** has been in the world for many years.

ADJECTIVE **2** You say something is **old** if it has been used a lot, or you have had it for a long time. *These are my **old** shoes.*

ADJECTIVE **3** If you ask how **old** someone is, you want to know how long they have lived. *How **old** is your baby?*

a b c d e f g h i j k l m n **Oo** p q r s t u v w x y z

old-fashioned

ADJECTIVE Something **old-fashioned** belongs to the past and has been replaced by something more modern.

olive olives

NOUN An **olive** is a small green or black fruit. Olives are eaten as a snack, or used to make oil for cooking.

omelette omelettes

NOUN An **omelette** is a food made by beating eggs and cooking them.

once

ADVERB **1** If something happens **once**, it happens one time only.

ADVERB **2 Once** means at some time in the past. *Once, the Romans ruled in Britain.*

at once PHRASE If you do something **at once**, you do it straight away.

one

1 One is the number 1.

PRONOUN **2 One** refers to a particular thing or person. *I think Tim's idea is the best **one**.*

onion onions

NOUN An **onion** is a small round vegetable with a brown papery skin and a very strong taste.

only

ADJECTIVE **1 Only** means one and no more. *She was the **only** girl in the group.*

ADJECTIVE **2** An **only** child is someone who has no brothers or sisters.

ADVERB **3** You say **only** when you mean one person or thing and not others. *He's **only** interested in football.*

ADVERB **4** You can say **only** when something is not very important. *It was **only** a sparrow.*

ADVERB **5 Only** can be used when something was less than you expected. *It **only** took me ten minutes.*

onomatopoeia

NOUN **Onomatopoeia** is the use of words that sound like what they mean, for example "hiss" and "buzz".

opaque

ADJECTIVE If something is **opaque**, it does not let light through and you cannot see through it.

open opens, opening, opened

VERB **1** If you **open** a door, you move it so that people can go through it.

VERB **2** If you **open** a box or a bottle, you take the lid off or unfasten it.

VERB **3** When flowers **open**, you can see their petals.

ADJECTIVE **4** When a place such as a shop or library is **open**, you can use it.

opening openings

NOUN An **opening** is a hole or space that things or people can go through.

opera operas

NOUN An **opera** is a musical play in which most of the words are sung.

operate operates, operating, operated

VERB **1** When someone **operates** a machine, they make it work.

VERB **2** When doctors **operate**, they cut open a patient's body to remove or repair a damaged part.

operation operations

NOUN An **operation** is when doctors cut open a patient's body to remove or repair a damaged part.

opinion opinions

NOUN An **opinion** is what someone thinks about something.

opponent opponents

NOUN An **opponent** is someone who is against you in an argument or a contest.

opposite opposites

NOUN **1** The **opposite** of something is the thing that is most different from it. *Hot is the opposite of cold.*

PREPOSITION **2** If one person or thing is **opposite** another, they are on the other side of something. *In the train I sat opposite a small boy.*

optician opticians

NOUN An **optician** is someone who tests people's eyes, and sells glasses and contact lenses.

orange oranges

NOUN **1** An **orange** is a round fruit with a thick skin. Oranges are juicy and sometimes sweet.
See Fruit on page 257.

ADJECTIVE **2** Something that is **orange** has a colour between red and yellow.
See Colours on page 271.

orbit orbits, orbiting, orbited

VERB If something **orbits** a planet or the Sun, it goes round and round it.

orchard orchards

NOUN An **orchard** is an area of land where fruit trees are grown.

orchestra orchestras

NOUN An **orchestra** is a large group of musicians who play different instruments together.

order orders, ordering, ordered

NOUN **1** An **order** is something you are told to do.

VERB **2** If you **order** something, for example in a restaurant, you ask for it to be brought to you.

NOUN **3** Order is the way a set of things is organized. A dictionary is written in alphabetical order.

ordinary

ADJECTIVE Something that is **ordinary** is not special in any way.

organ organs

NOUN **1** An **organ** is a part of your body that does a special job, for example your heart, lungs or stomach.

NOUN **2** An **organ** is also a large musical instrument like a piano. It has pipes that air is forced through to make the sounds.

organic

ADJECTIVE Food that is **organic** has been produced without the use of chemicals.

organization organizations;
also spelt organisation

NOUN An **organization** is a large group of people who work together. For example, the police force is an organization.

a b c d e f g h i j k l m n **Oo** p q r s t u v w x y z

143

organize

organize organizes, organizing,
organized; also spelt organise
VERB **1** If you **organize** an event, you
plan and arrange it.
VERB **2** If you **organize** things, you
arrange them in a sensible order.

origin origins
NOUN **1** The **origin** of something is how
and why it started.
NOUN **2** You can refer to where someone
comes from as their **origin**. *She was of
Swedish origin.*

original
ADJECTIVE **1** Something that is **original** is
new and not a copy.
ADJECTIVE **2** If you say someone's ideas
are **original**, you mean they are clever
at thinking of new ways of doing things.

ornament ornaments
NOUN An **ornament** is an object that you
put somewhere because you think it is
nice to look at.

orphan orphans
NOUN An **orphan** is a child whose
parents are dead.

ostrich ostriches
NOUN An **ostrich** is the
largest living bird. It
cannot fly, but it can
run very fast. Ostriches
live in sandy places in
Africa. Their eggs are
large, weighing more
than a kilo each.

other
ADJECTIVE **1** When you say **other** things
or other people, you can mean more of
the same kind. *He found it hard to make
friends with other children.*
ADJECTIVE **2** You can also use **other** to
mean different. *We got lost last time.
I think we'll try some other way.*
every other PHRASE **Every other** means
one in every two. *We meet every other
week.*

otherwise
ADVERB You say **otherwise** to explain
what will happen if you do not do
something. *I'd better take an umbrella,
otherwise I'll get soaked.*

otter otters
NOUN An **otter** is an animal with brown
fur, short legs and a long tail. Otters
swim well and eat fish.

ought
VERB If you **ought** to do something, you
should do it. *I ought to leave early.*

our
ADJECTIVE **Our** refers to something
belonging or relating to the speaker or
writer and one or more other people.
We recently sold our house.

ourselves
PRONOUN **Ourselves** is used when the
people speaking do something and no
one else does it. *We made the beds
ourselves.*

out
ADVERB **1** **Out** means towards the
outside of a place. *Two dogs rushed out
of the house.*
ADVERB **2** **Out** can also mean not at
home. *She was out when I rang last night.*
ADVERB **3** **Out** can mean no longer
shining or burning. *The lights went out.*

outer
ADJECTIVE The **outer** parts of something
are the parts furthest from the centre.
*The outer layer of an onion is brown and
papery.*

outing outings
NOUN An **outing** is a short trip
somewhere to enjoy yourself.

outline outlines

NOUN An **outline** is the shape of something, especially when you cannot see any details.

outside

NOUN **1** The **outside** of something is the part which surrounds the rest of it. *The outside of the box had a picture on it.*

ADVERB **2** You can use **outside** with a verb to mean out of a building. *Let's go outside.*

PREPOSITION **3** You can use **outside** before a noun to say which building you are referring to. *The bicycle was chained up outside the church.*

oval ovals

NOUN **1** An **oval** is a shape like an egg.

ADJECTIVE **2** **Oval** describes something shaped like an egg, such as an oval mirror or oval frame.

See *Colours and flat shapes* on page 271.

oven ovens

NOUN The **oven** is the part of a cooker that you use for baking or roasting food.

over

PREPOSITION **1** **Over** something means directly above it or covering it. *He put his hands over his eyes.*

PREPOSITION **2** A view **over** an area is a view across that area. *The front windows look out over the sea.*

PREPOSITION **3** Something that is **over** a particular amount is more than that amount.

PREPOSITION **4** If something happens **over** a period of time, it happens during that period. *I went to London over Christmas.*

ADVERB **5** If you lean **over**, you bend your body in a particular direction.

ADVERB **6** You can use **over** to show movement from one place to another. *She went over to the door.*

over-

PREFIX **Over-** is placed in front of an adjective or a verb to mean too much or to too great an extent, for example "overestimate".

See *Prefixes* on page 264.

overalls

PLURAL NOUN **Overalls** are a piece of clothing with trousers and jacket in one. You wear overalls to protect your other clothes when you are working.

overboard

ADVERB If someone falls **overboard**, they fall over the side of a ship into the water.

overcoat overcoats

NOUN An **overcoat** is a thick warm coat that people wear in winter.

overdue

ADJECTIVE If someone or something is **overdue**, they are late. *My library book is overdue.*

overflow overflows, overflowing, overflowed

VERB **1** If a liquid **overflows**, it spills over the edges of its container.

VERB **2** If a river **overflows**, it flows over its banks.

a b c d e f g h i j k l m n **Oo** p q r s t u v w x y z

overgrown

overgrown

ADJECTIVE If a place is **overgrown**, it is thickly covered with plants and weeds, usually because it has not been looked after for a long time.

overhead

ADVERB Overhead means above you. *Seagulls were flying* **overhead**.

overhear overhears, overhearing, overheard

VERB If you **overhear** someone's conversation, you hear what they are saying to someone else.

overlap overlaps, overlapping, overlapped

VERB If one thing **overlaps** another, one part of it covers part of the other thing.

overseas

ADVERB If you go **overseas**, you go to a country which is on the other side of a sea or ocean.

oversleep oversleeps, oversleeping, overslept

VERB If you **oversleep**, you sleep longer than you meant to, and wake up late.

overtake overtakes, overtaking, overtook, overtaken

VERB If you **overtake** someone, you pass them because you are moving faster than they are.

owe owes, owing, owed

VERB **1** If you **owe** someone money, they have lent it to you and you have not yet paid it back.

VERB **2** If you **owe** someone something, such as thanks, you need to give it to them.

owl owls

NOUN An **owl** is a bird with a flat face and large eyes. Usually owls hunt at night for small animals.

own owns, owning, owned

VERB **1** If you **own** something, it belongs to you.

VERB **2** If you **own up** to something wrong, you say that you did it.

on your own PHRASE If you are **on your own**, you are alone.

If you do something **on your own**, you do it without any help.

owner owners

NOUN The **owner** of something is the person it belongs to.

ox oxen

NOUN **Oxen** are cattle which are used for carrying or pulling things.

oxygen

NOUN **Oxygen** is a gas that forms part of the air we breathe. Other animals and plants also need oxygen to live, and things will not burn without it.

oyster oysters

NOUN An **oyster** is a large flat shellfish. Some oysters produce pearls. See **pearl**.

ozone

NOUN **Ozone** is a form of oxygen.

ozone layer PHRASE The **ozone layer** is the part of the Earth's atmosphere that protects living things from the dangerous rays of the sun.

Pp

pace **paces**
NOUN **1** The **pace** of something is the speed at which it happens.
NOUN **2** A **pace** is a step that you take when you walk.

pack **packs, packing, packed**
VERB **1** When you **pack**, you put your clothes in a case or bag.
NOUN **2** A **pack** is a set of playing cards.
NOUN **3** A **pack** of wolves or other animals is a group that hunts together. See *Collective nouns* on page 262.

package **packages**
NOUN A **package** is a small parcel.

packaging
NOUN **Packaging** is the container that something is sold or sent in.

packet **packets**
NOUN A **packet** is a thin cardboard box or paper container.

pad **pads**
NOUN **1** A **pad** is a number of pieces of paper fixed together on one side.
NOUN **2** An animal's **pads** are the soft parts under its paws.

paddle **paddles, paddling, paddled**
VERB **1** If you **paddle** in the sea, you stand or walk in the shallow water.
VERB **2** If you **paddle** a small boat such as a canoe, you use a special type of oar called a paddle to move the boat along.

padlock **padlocks**
NOUN A **padlock** is a special kind of lock. You can use it to lock gates and bicycles.

page **pages**
NOUN A **page** is one side of a piece of paper in a book or newspaper.

pagoda **pagodas**
NOUN A **pagoda** is a tall building which is used as a temple. Pagodas can be seen in China, Japan and south-east Asia.

paid
VERB **Paid** is the past tense of **pay**.

pail **pails**
NOUN A **pail** is a bucket.

pain **pains**
NOUN A **pain** is an unpleasant feeling that you have in part of your body if you have been hurt or are ill.

painful
ADJECTIVE If you say that something is **painful**, you mean it is hurting you.
painfully ADVERB

paint **paints, painting, painted**
NOUN **1** **Paint** is a coloured liquid that you put onto a surface to make it look fresh.
VERB **2** When you **paint** a picture, you use paint to make a picture on paper or canvas.

painting **paintings**
NOUN A **painting** is a picture that has been painted.

pair **pairs**
NOUN **1** A **pair** is a set of two things that go together. *I need a new **pair** of shoes.*
NOUN **2** Some objects, such as trousers and scissors, have two main parts which are the same size and shape. This sort of object is also called a **pair**.

palace **palaces**
NOUN A **palace** is a large important house, especially one which is the home of a king, queen or president.

pale **paler, palest**
ADJECTIVE Something that is **pale** is light in colour, and not strong or bright.

palm

a
b
c
d
e
f
g
h
i
j
k
l
m
n
o
Pp
q
r
s
t
u
v
w
x
y
z

palm **palms**

NOUN **1** The **palm** of your hand is the inside surface of it. Your fingers and thumb are not part of your palm.

NOUN **2** A **palm** is a tree which grows in hot countries. It has long pointed leaves that grow out of the top of a tall trunk.

pan **pans**

NOUN A **pan** is a container with a long handle that is used for cooking.

pancake **pancakes**

NOUN A **pancake** is a thin flat cake made of flour, eggs and milk, which is fried.

panda **pandas**

NOUN A **panda** is an animal like a black and white bear that lives in the bamboo forests of China.

pane **panes**

NOUN A **pane** is a sheet of glass in a window or door.

panic **panics, panicking, panicked**

VERB If you **panic**, you suddenly get so worried you cannot act sensibly.

pant **pants, panting, panted**

VERB If you **pant**, you breathe quickly with your mouth open. You usually pant when you have been running fast.

panther **panthers**

NOUN **Panther** is another name for a black leopard.

pantomime **pantomimes**

NOUN A **pantomime** is a funny musical play for children.

pants

PLURAL NOUN **Pants** are a piece of clothing that you wear under your other clothes. They have two holes for your legs and elastic round the waist.

paper **papers**

NOUN **1** **Paper** is the material that you write on or wrap things in.

NOUN **2** A newspaper is also called a **paper**.

parable **parables**

NOUN A **parable** is a short story which aims to teach you something about the way you should behave.

parachute **parachutes**

NOUN A **parachute** is a large piece of thin cloth. It has strings fixed to it so that a person attached to it can float down to the ground from an aircraft.

parade **parades**

NOUN A **parade** is a lot of people marching in the road on a special day.

paraffin

NOUN **Paraffin** is a liquid used as a fuel in things like heaters and lamps.

paragraph **paragraphs**

NOUN A **paragraph** is a section of a piece of writing. Paragraphs begin on a new line.

parallel

ADJECTIVE Two lines or other things that are **parallel** are the same distance apart all the way along. *The road along the sea front is **parallel** with the sea.*

paralysed

ADJECTIVE Someone who is **paralysed** cannot move or feel some or all of their body.

parcel **parcels**

NOUN A **parcel** is one or more objects wrapped in paper. This is usually done so that it can be sent by post.

parent parents

NOUN Your **parents** are your mother and father.

park parks, parking, parked

NOUN **1** A **park** is an area of land with grass and trees, usually in a town. People go there to walk or play.

VERB **2** When someone **parks** a vehicle, they put it somewhere until they need it again.

parliament parliaments

NOUN The **parliament** of a country is the people who make the country's laws.

parrot parrots

NOUN A **parrot** is a brightly-coloured bird with a curved beak.

parsnip parsnips

NOUN A **parsnip** is a long, pointed, cream-coloured root vegetable. See *Vegetables* on page 256.

part parts

NOUN **1** A **part** of something is one of the pieces that it is made from. *We need a new **part** for the washing machine.*

NOUN **2** A **part** is also a particular bit of something such as an area or a body. *This **part** of the park is for young children only.*

NOUN **3** If you have a **part** in a play, you are one of the people in it.

participle participles

NOUN In grammar, a **participle** is a form of a verb. English has two participles – the past participle and the present participle. In the sentence "He has gone" the word "gone" is a past participle; in the sentence "She is winning" the word "winning" is a present participle.

particular

ADJECTIVE When you talk about a **particular** person or thing, you mean just that person or thing and not others of the same kind.

partly

ADVERB **Partly** means not completely. *The table was **partly** covered with a cloth.*

partner partners

NOUN Your **partner** is the person you are doing something with, for example when dancing or playing games.

party parties

NOUN A **party** is a group of people having fun together.

pass passes, passing, passed

VERB **1** If you **pass** someone, you go past them without stopping.

VERB **2** If you **pass** something to someone, you hand it to them.

VERB **3** If you **pass** a test or an exam, you are successful in it.

passage passages

NOUN **1** A **passage** is a long narrow space with walls on both sides.

NOUN **2** A **passage** is also a section in a piece of writing. *There's a wonderful **passage** in the book that describes their arrival at the castle.*

passenger passengers

NOUN A **passenger** is a person who travels in a vehicle but is not the driver.

passive

NOUN In grammar, the **passive** or **passive voice** is the form of the verb in which the person or thing to which an action is being done is the subject of the sentence. For example, the sentence "The ball was hit by the boy" is in the passive. See **voice**.

passport passports

NOUN A **passport** is a book with your name and photograph in it, that you need when you leave your own country.

a
b
c
d
e
f
g
h
i
j
k
l
m
n
o
Pp
q
r
s
t
u
v
w
x
y
z

password **passwords**

NOUN A **password** is a secret word or phrase that you must say to be allowed into a particular place.

past

NOUN **1** The **past** is the period of time before the present.

ADVERB **2** If you go **past** something, you move towards it and continue until you are on the other side.

PREPOSITION **3** You use **past** when you are telling the time. *It's ten **past** three.*

NOUN **4** In grammar, the **past tense** of a verb is the form used to show that something happened in the past.

pasta

NOUN **Pasta** is a type of food made from flour, eggs and water, which is formed into different shapes. Spaghetti, macaroni and noodles are types of pasta.

paste **pastes**

NOUN **Paste** is a thick wet mixture that is easy to spread.

pastime **pastimes**

NOUN A **pastime** is something you like to do in your free time.

pastry

NOUN **Pastry** is a food made of flour, fat and water, rolled flat and used for making pies.

pasture **pastures**

NOUN **Pasture** is land that is used for farm animals to graze on.

pat **pats, patting, patted**

VERB If you **pat** something, you hit it gently, usually with your open hand.

patch **patches**

NOUN A **patch** is a piece of material you put over a hole in something to mend it.

path **paths**

NOUN A **path** is a strip of ground that people walk on.

patience

NOUN **Patience** is being able to wait calmly for something, or to do something difficult without giving up.

patient **patients**

ADJECTIVE **1** If you are **patient**, you are able to wait calmly for something, or to do something difficult without giving up.

NOUN **2** A **patient** is someone who is being treated by a doctor.

patrol **patrols, patrolling, patrolled**

VERB When people like the police **patrol** a particular area, they go round it to make sure there is no trouble or danger.

pattern **patterns**

NOUN A **pattern** is a regular way something is organized. For example, lines and shapes can make patterns.

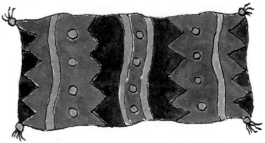

pause **pauses, pausing, paused**

VERB If you **pause** while you are doing something, you stop for a moment.

pavement **pavements**

NOUN A **pavement** is a path with a hard surface beside a road, so that people can walk in safety.

paw **paws**

NOUN A **paw** is the foot of some animals. Paws have claws at the front and soft pads underneath.

pay **pays, paying, paid**

VERB When a person **pays** someone, they give them money in exchange for work or for things that they have bought.

payment NOUN

PC PCs
NOUN **1** A **PC** is a personal computer.
NOUN **2** In Britain, a **PC** is also a police constable.

PE
NOUN **PE** is an abbreviation of **physical education**.

pea peas
NOUN **Peas** are round green seeds which are eaten as a vegetable. They grow inside a covering called a pod.
See *Vegetables* on page 256.

peace
NOUN **1 Peace** is a feeling of quiet and calm.
NOUN **2** When a country has **peace** or is **at peace**, it is not fighting a war.

peaceful
ADJECTIVE A **peaceful** place is quiet and calm.

peach peaches
NOUN A **peach** is a round juicy fruit with a large stone in the middle. It has sweet yellow flesh and a yellow and red skin.
See *Fruit* on page 257.

peacock peacocks
NOUN A **peacock** is a large male bird with bright blue and green feathers, and long tail feathers which it spreads in a fan. The female is called a peahen.

peak peaks
NOUN **1** The **peak** of a mountain is the pointed top of it.
NOUN **2** The **peak** of a cap is the part that sticks out at the front.

peanut peanuts
NOUN **Peanuts** are small hard seeds which grow under the ground. You can buy roasted and salted peanuts to eat.

pear pears
NOUN A **pear** is a sweet juicy fruit which grows on trees. It is narrow near its stalk, and wider and rounded at the bottom.
See *Fruit* on page 257.

pearl pearls
NOUN A **pearl** is a hard round object which grows inside the shell of an oyster. It is creamy-white in colour. Pearls are used to make valuable jewellery.

pebble pebbles
NOUN A **pebble** is a small smooth stone found on seashores and river beds.

peck pecks, pecking, pecked
VERB When a bird **pecks**, it bites at something with its beak.

peculiar
ADJECTIVE Something that is **peculiar** is strange or unusual.

pedal pedals
NOUN The **pedals** on a cycle are the two parts that you push with your feet to make it move.

pedestrian pedestrians
NOUN A **pedestrian** is a person who is walking.

peek peeks, peeking, peeked
VERB If you **peek** at something, you have a quick look at it.

peel peels, peeling, peeled
VERB If you **peel** fruit or vegetables, you remove the skin.

peep peeps, peeping, peeped
VERB If you **peep** at something, you look at it very quickly, and usually secretly.

peg pegs
NOUN **1** A **peg** is a thin piece of metal or plastic that is used to hang things on.
NOUN **2** A **peg** is also a small clip that is used to hold washing on a line.

a
b
c
d
e
f
g
h
i
j
k
l
m
n
o
Pp
q
r
s
t
u
v
w
x
y
z

pelican pelicans

NOUN A **pelican** is a water bird. Its large beak has a soft lower part like a pouch.

pen pens

NOUN A **pen** is a long thin tool that you use to write in ink.

pence

NOUN **Pence** is the plural of **penny**.

pencil pencils

NOUN A **pencil** is a long thin piece of wood with a dark material called graphite in the middle. It is used for writing or drawing.

pendulum pendulums

NOUN A **pendulum** is a large weight which hangs from a clock. It swings from side to side to keep the clock going at the right speed.

penguin penguins

NOUN A **penguin** is a large black and white bird found in the Antarctic. Penguins cannot fly. They use their wings for swimming in the water.

penis penises

NOUN Boys and men have a **penis**. It is used to get rid of waste liquid from the body. Men can also use their penis to help make babies.

penknife penknives

NOUN A **penknife** is a small knife with blades that fold back into the handle.

penny pennies or pence

NOUN A **penny** is a small British coin. A hundred pence are worth one pound. The abbreviation for pence is p.

pentagon pentagons

NOUN A **pentagon** is a flat shape that has five straight sides.
pentagonal ADJECTIVE
See *Colours and flat shapes* on page 271.

people

PLURAL NOUN **People** are men, women and children.

pepper peppers

NOUN **1 Pepper** is a hot-tasting powder which is used to flavour food.
NOUN **2** A **pepper** is a red, green or yellow vegetable. It can be cooked or eaten raw in salads.

per cent

PHRASE You use **per cent** to talk about amounts as a proportion of 100. For example, ten per cent (10%) means 10 out of every 100.

perch perches

NOUN A **perch** is a short piece of wood for a bird to stand on.

percussion

ADJECTIVE **Percussion** instruments are instruments that you play by hitting them. Drums and cymbals are percussion instruments.

perfect

ADJECTIVE **1** Something that is **perfect** is done so well it could not be done better.
ADJECTIVE **2** If you say something is **perfect**, you mean it is wonderful.
perfectly ADVERB

perform performs, performing, performed

VERB If someone **performs**, they do something to entertain an audience.

a b c d e f g h i j k l m n o **Pp** q r s t u v w x y z

performance performances

NOUN A **performance** is something done in front of people, like acting or dancing.

perfume perfumes

NOUN **1** A **perfume** is a pleasant smell.

NOUN **2** Perfume is a liquid that you put on your body so that you smell nice.

perhaps

ADVERB **1** If you say **perhaps** something will happen, you mean it might happen but you are not sure.

ADVERB **2** You can also say **perhaps** when you are suggesting something. *He's late – **perhaps** he missed the train.*

perimeter perimeters

NOUN The **perimeter** of a shape is the distance all round it.

period periods

NOUN A **period** is a particular length of time. *Mrs Smith will be away for a **period** of six months.*

periscope periscopes

NOUN A **periscope** is a tube with mirrors. When you look in one end, you can see what would otherwise be out of sight.

permanent

ADJECTIVE Something that is **permanent** lasts for ever, or for a very long time.

permission

NOUN If you have **permission** to do something, you are allowed to do it.

permit permits, permitting, permitted

VERB If someone **permits** you to do something, they allow you to do it.

persist persists, persisting, persisted

VERB If you **persist**, you go on doing something even when it is difficult or other people have told you to stop.

person people

NOUN A **person** is a man, woman or child.

personal

ADJECTIVE **Personal** matters relate to your feelings, relationships and health, which you may not want to talk about with other people.

persuade persuades, persuading, persuaded

VERB If someone **persuades** you to do something you did not want to do, you agree because they gave you a good reason.

persuasion NOUN

persuasive

ADJECTIVE **1** Someone who is **persuasive** is good at persuading others to believe or do a particular thing.

ADJECTIVE **2** Persuasive text aims to persuade the reader of something.

pest pests

NOUN A **pest** is an insect, rat or other small animal that causes damage.

pester pesters, pestering, pestered

VERB If you **pester** someone, you keep bothering them.

pet pets

NOUN A **pet** is a tame animal that you keep and look after in your home.

petal petals

NOUN A **petal** is part of a flower. Petals may have bright colours or scents to attract insects.

petrol

NOUN **Petrol** is a liquid used as fuel in motor vehicles.

phantom phantoms

NOUN A **phantom** is a ghost.

a
b
c
d
e
f
g
h
i
j
k
l
m
n
o
Pp
q
r
s
t
u
v
w
x
y
z

phone **phones**
NOUN **Phone** is an abbreviation of **telephone**.

photo **photos**
NOUN **Photo** is an abbreviation of **photograph**.

photocopier **photocopiers**
NOUN A **photocopier** is a machine that makes copies of documents.

photocopy **photocopies**
NOUN A **photocopy** is a copy of a document produced by a photocopier.

photograph **photographs**
NOUN A **photograph** is a picture that is made using a camera.

phrase **phrases**
NOUN A **phrase** is a short group of words used together.

physical
ADJECTIVE **1 Physical** means to do with things that can be touched or seen.
ADJECTIVE **2 Physical** also means to do with a person's body, rather than their mind.
physically ADVERB

piano **pianos**
NOUN A **piano** is a large musical instrument with black and white keys that you press with your fingers.

pick **picks, picking, picked**
VERB **1** To **pick** means to choose. *We need to **pick** three more people for our team.*
VERB **2** When you **pick** flowers or fruit, you take them off the plant.
VERB **3** If you **pick** something **up**, you lift it up from where it is.

pickle **pickles**
NOUN **Pickles** are vegetables or fruit that have been kept in vinegar or salt water.

picnic **picnics**
NOUN A **picnic** is a meal that you take with you and eat out of doors.

pictogram **pictograms**
NOUN **1** A **pictogram** is a picture or symbol used instead of a word or words.
NOUN **2** A **pictogram** is also a graph that uses pictures to show information.

picture **pictures**
NOUN A **picture** is a drawing, painting or photograph.

pie **pies**
NOUN A **pie** is fruit, vegetables, meat or fish baked in pastry.

piece **pieces**
NOUN A **piece** is a part of something.

pier **piers**
NOUN A **pier** is a long platform which sticks out over the sea. Piers often have some kind of entertainment on them.

pierce **pierces, piercing, pierced**
VERB If a sharp object **pierces** something, it goes through it and makes a hole in it.

pig **pigs**
NOUN A **pig** is a farm animal kept for its meat. It has pinkish skin and short legs.

pigeon **pigeons**
NOUN A **pigeon** is a large bird with grey feathers, often seen in towns.

piglet **piglets**
NOUN A **piglet** is a young pig.
*See **Young animals** on page 260.*

pile piles

NOUN A **pile** is a lot of things, such as books, which have been put one on top of the other.

pill pills

NOUN A **pill** is medicine made into a small round object that you swallow.

pillar pillars

NOUN A **pillar** is a tall post made of something such as stone or brick. It usually helps to hold up a building.

pillar box pillar boxes

NOUN A **pillar box** is an iron cylinder with a slot in it for letters.

pillow pillows

NOUN A **pillow** is a bag filled with soft material to rest your head on in bed.

pilot pilots

NOUN A **pilot** is a person who is trained to fly an aircraft.

pimple pimples

NOUN A **pimple** is a small red spot, especially on your face.

pin pins

NOUN A **pin** is a small thin piece of metal with a point at one end. Pins can be pushed through things such as pieces of paper or cloth, to hold them together.

pincers

PLURAL NOUN **1** The **pincers** of a crab or lobster are its front claws.
PLURAL NOUN **2** Pincers are also a tool used for gripping and pulling things.

pinch pinches, pinching, pinched

VERB If someone **pinches** you, they squeeze part of you quickly between their thumb and first finger.

pine pines

NOUN A **pine** is a tall evergreen tree with sharp thin leaves called needles.

pineapple pineapples

NOUN A **pineapple** is a large oval fruit with yellow flesh and a thick, lumpy skin. Pineapples grow in hot countries.

pink pinker, pinkest

ADJECTIVE Something that is **pink** has a colour between white and red.
See **Colours** on page 271.

pint pints

NOUN A **pint** is a measure for liquids. A pint is equal to just over half a litre.

pipe pipes

NOUN A **pipe** is a long hollow tube, usually made of metal or plastic. Pipes are used to carry liquid or gas.

pirate pirates

NOUN In the past, a **pirate** was a robber who stole from ships.

pistol pistols

NOUN A **pistol** is a small gun.

pit pits

NOUN **1** A **pit** is a large hole that has been dug in the ground.
NOUN **2** A **pit** is also a coal mine.

pitch pitches, pitching, pitched

NOUN **1** A **pitch** is an area of ground where a game such as hockey or football is played.
NOUN **2** The **pitch** of a sound is how high or low it is.
VERB **3** When you **pitch** a tent, you put it up so that you can use it.

pity

NOUN **1** If you feel **pity** for someone, you feel sorry for them.
NOUN **2** If you say something is a **pity**, you mean it is disappointing. *What a pity Mark isn't coming.*

a
b
c
d
e
f
g
h
i
j
k
l
m
n
o
Pp
q
r
s
t
u
v
w
x
y
z

a
b
c
d
e
f
g
h
i
j
k
l
m
n
o

Pp

q
r
s
t
u
v
w
x
y
z

pizza pizzas

NOUN A **pizza** is a flat round piece of dough covered with cheese, tomato and other savoury food.

place places

NOUN 1 A **place** is any building or area.
NOUN 2 A **place** is also the position where something belongs. *Please put the tools back in their right place.*

place value

NOUN In maths, the **place value** of a digit tells you what the digit is worth in hundreds, tens or units (HTU).

plague plagues

NOUN A **plague** is a disease that spreads quickly and kills many people.

plaice

NOUN A **plaice** is a flat sea fish.

plain plainer, plainest; plains

ADJECTIVE 1 A **plain** object has no pattern on it. *She wore a plain skirt.*
ADJECTIVE 2 If something is **plain**, it is clear and easy to see.
NOUN 3 A **plain** is a large, flat area of land with very few trees on it.

plait plaits, plaiting, plaited

VERB 1 If you **plait** three lengths of hair or rope together, you twist them over each other in turn.
NOUN 2 A **plait** is a length of hair that has been plaited.

plan plans, planning, planned

NOUN 1 If you have a **plan**, you have thought of a way of doing something.
NOUN 2 A **plan** is a drawing that shows what something looks like from above.
VERB 3 If you **plan** what you are going to do, you decide exactly how to do it.

plane planes

NOUN 1 A **plane** is a flying vehicle. It has wings and one or more engines. **Plane** is an abbreviation of **aeroplane**.
NOUN 2 A **plane** is also a tool used for smoothing wood.

planet planets

NOUN A **planet** is a large round object in space that moves around a star. Earth is one of the nine planets that go round the Sun.

plank planks

NOUN A **plank** is a long flat piece of wood.

plant plants, planting, planted

NOUN 1 A **plant** is any living thing that is not an animal. Plants can make their own food.
VERB 2 When you **plant** things, such as seeds, flowers or trees, you put them in the ground so that they will grow.

plaster plasters

NOUN 1 A **plaster** is a strip of sticky material used for covering small cuts.
NOUN 2 **Plaster** is a smooth paste that dries and forms a hard layer. It is used to cover walls and ceilings inside buildings.

plastic

NOUN 1 **Plastic** is a light artificial material that does not break easily. It is used to make all sorts of things, such as buckets, bowls and plates.
ADJECTIVE 2 Something that is **plastic** is made of plastic.

Plasticine

NOUN; TRADEMARK **Plasticine** is a soft material like clay, which can be used to make models.

plate plates

NOUN A **plate** is a flat dish for food.

platform **platforms**

NOUN **1** A **platform** is the area in a station where you wait for the train.

NOUN **2** A **platform** is also a raised area for people to stand on so that they can be seen more easily.

play **plays, playing, played**

VERB **1** When you **play**, you spend time doing things you enjoy.

VERB **2** When one person or team **plays** another, they take part in a game and each side tries to win.

VERB **3** If you **play** a musical instrument, you make musical sounds with it.

NOUN **4** A **play** is a story which is acted on the stage, or on radio or television.

player NOUN

playground **playgrounds**

NOUN A **playground** is a piece of land for children to play on.

playscript **playscripts**

NOUN A **playscript** is the written version of a play.

playtime

NOUN **Playtime** is a break in the school day when you can play.

pleasant

ADJECTIVE If something is **pleasant**, you enjoy it or like it.

please **pleases, pleasing, pleased**

VERB If you **please** someone, you make them feel happy.

pleasure

NOUN **Pleasure** is a feeling of happiness or enjoyment.

pleat **pleats**

NOUN A **pleat** is a permanent fold in fabric.

pleated ADJECTIVE

plenty

NOUN If there is **plenty** of something, there is more than enough of it.

pliers

PLURAL NOUN **Pliers** are a tool used for pulling out small things like nails, or for bending or cutting wire.

plot **plots, plotting, plotted**

NOUN **1** A **plot** is a secret plan.

NOUN **2** The **plot** of a film, novel or play is the story and the way it develops.

NOUN **3** A **plot** of land is a small piece that has been marked out for a special purpose such as building houses or growing vegetables.

VERB **4** If people **plot** something, they plan secretly to do it.

plough **ploughs**

NOUN A **plough** is a farming tool that is pulled across a field to turn the soil over.

pluck **plucks, plucking, plucked**

VERB **1** When someone **plucks** a musical instrument, such as a guitar, they pull the strings and let them go quickly.

VERB **2** When you **pluck** a feather, flower or fruit, you pull it from where it is growing.

plug **plugs, plugging, plugged**

NOUN **1** A **plug** is a thick piece of rubber or plastic that fits in the drain hole of a bath or washbasin.

NOUN **2** A **plug** is also a small object that joins pieces of equipment to the electricity supply.

VERB **3** If someone **plugs** a hole, they block it with something.

plum **plums**

NOUN A **plum** is a small fruit with a thin, dark red or yellow skin and juicy flesh. It has a large stone in the middle.
See Fruit on page 257.

a
b
c
d
e
f
g
h
i
j
k
l
m
n
o
Pp
q
r
s
t
u
v
w
x
y
z

plumber

plumber **plumbers**
NOUN A **plumber** is a person who fits and mends water pipes.

plump **plumper, plumpest**
ADJECTIVE Someone or something that is **plump** is rather fat.

plunge **plunges, plunging, plunged**
VERB If someone **plunges** into the water, they dive or throw themselves into it.

plural **plurals**
NOUN **Plural** means more than one. *The **plural** of "boy" is "boys". The **plural** of "box" is "boxes".* See **singular**.

plus
PREPOSITION **1** You use **plus** (+) to show that one number is being added to another. *Two **plus** two equals four.*
PREPOSITION **2** You can use **plus** when you mention an additional item. *You get a television **plus** a free radio.*

p.m.
ADVERB **p.m.** is the time between 12 noon and 12 midnight. See **a.m.**

poach **poaches, poaching, poached**
VERB If you **poach** an egg, you remove its shell and cook the egg gently in boiling water.

pocket **pockets**
NOUN A **pocket** is a small bag that is sewn into clothing.

pod **pods**
NOUN A **pod** is a seed cover. Peas and beans grow inside pods. See **pea**.

poem **poems**
NOUN A **poem** is a piece of writing in short lines, which sometimes rhyme. The lines usually have a particular rhythm.

poet **poets**
NOUN A **poet** is a person who writes poems.

poetry
NOUN **Poetry** is writing in which the lines have a rhythm and sometimes rhyme.

point **points, pointing, pointed**
NOUN **1** The **point** of something such as a pin is the sharp end of it.
NOUN **2** A **point** is a position or time. *I'll call you at some **point** during the day.*
NOUN **3** The **point** of doing something is the reason for doing it. *The **point** of playing is to have fun.*
NOUN **4** In a game or sport, a **point** is part of the score.
NOUN **5** The decimal **point** in a number is the dot separating the whole number from the fraction.
VERB **6** If you **point** at something, you show where it is by using your finger.
VERB **7** If something **points** in a particular direction, it faces that way.

pointed
ADJECTIVE Something that is **pointed** has a point at one end.

poison **poisons**
NOUN **Poison** is something that harms or kills people or animals if it gets into their body.
poisonous ADJECTIVE

poke **pokes, poking, poked**
VERB If you **poke** something, you push it hard with your finger.

polar bear **polar bears**
NOUN A **polar bear** is a large white bear that lives near the North Pole.

pole **poles**
NOUN **1** A **pole** is a long round post, used especially for holding things up.
NOUN **2** A **pole** is also one of the two points on the Earth that are the furthest from the equator. They are known as the North Pole and the South Pole.

police

PLURAL NOUN The **police** are an organization whose job is to protect people and their belongings, and to make sure that people obey the law.
policeman NOUN   **policewoman** NOUN

police officer   **police officers**

NOUN A **police officer** is a policeman or policewoman.

polish   **polishes, polishing, polished**

NOUN **1 Polish** is a substance that you put on an object to clean and shine it.
VERB **2** If you **polish** something, you put polish on it or rub it with a cloth to make it shine.

polite

ADJECTIVE Someone who is **polite** is well-behaved and thinks about other people's feelings.

politician   **politicians**

NOUN A **politician** is a person involved in the government of a country.

politics

NOUN **Politics** is the study of the way in which a country is governed.

pollen

NOUN **Pollen** is a fine, yellow powder in flowers that the wind or insects carry to other flowers to make seeds.

pollution

NOUN **Pollution** is making things like the air and water dirty and dangerous to live in or use.

poly-

PREFIX **Poly-** means many or much. For example, a polygon is a shape with many sides.
See *Prefixes* on page 264.

polyester

NOUN **Polyester** is an artificial fibre used especially to make clothes.

polygon   **polygons**

NOUN A **polygon** is a flat shape with three or more straight sides.

polyhedron   **polyhedrons** or **polyhedra**

NOUN A **polyhedron** is a solid shape with four or more faces.

polythene

NOUN **Polythene** is a thin plastic material that is often made into bags.

pond   **ponds**

NOUN A **pond** is a small lake.

pony   **ponies**

NOUN A **pony** is a kind of horse which is smaller than an ordinary horse.

ponytail   **ponytails**

NOUN A **ponytail** is long hair which is tied behind the head and hangs down like a tail.

pool   **pools**

NOUN A **pool** is a small area of still or slow-moving water.

poor   **poorer, poorest**

ADJECTIVE **1** Someone who is **poor** has very little money and few belongings.
ADJECTIVE **2** Something that is **poor** is not good. *If my work is poor, I have to do it again.*

pop   **pops**

NOUN **1 Pop** is modern music played and enjoyed especially by young people.
NOUN **2** A **pop** is a short sharp sound.

popcorn

NOUN **Popcorn** is a snack made from a type of corn that pops open when heated.

poppy   **poppies**

NOUN A **poppy** is a plant with a large red flower on a hairy stem.

popular

ADJECTIVE If someone or something is **popular**, they are liked by a lot of people.

a
b
c
d
e
f
g
h
i
j
k
l
m
n
o
Pp
q
r
s
t
u
v
w
x
y
z

population

NOUN **1** The **population** of a country or area is all the people who live in it.

NOUN **2** The **population** of a place is also the number of people who live there.

porch **porches**

NOUN A **porch** is a sheltered place at the entrance to a building.

porcupine **porcupines**

NOUN A **porcupine** is an animal with lots of stiff hairs called quills on its back.

pork

NOUN **Pork** is meat from a pig.

porpoise **porpoises**

NOUN A **porpoise** is a sea mammal that looks like a dolphin or a small whale.

porridge

NOUN **Porridge** is a thick sticky food made from oats cooked in water or milk.

port **ports**

NOUN A **port** is a place where boats come to load and unload.

portable

ADJECTIVE Something that is **portable** is made to be easily carried, for example a portable television.

porter **porters**

NOUN A **porter** is a person whose job is to look after the entrance of a building, greeting and directing visitors.

portion **portions**

NOUN A **portion** of food is the amount that is given to one person at a meal.

portrait **portraits**

NOUN A **portrait** is a picture of a person.

position **positions**

NOUN **1** The **position** of someone or something is the place where they are.

NOUN **2** Someone's **position** can also be the way they are sitting or standing. *Try to stay in that **position** while I draw you.*

positive

ADJECTIVE **1** If you are **positive** about something, you are very sure about it.

ADJECTIVE **2** **Positive** numbers are those which are greater than zero.

possess **possesses, possessing, possessed**

VERB If you **possess** something, you have it or own it.

possession NOUN

possible

ADJECTIVE **1** Something that is **possible** can be done.

ADJECTIVE **2** You can also use **possible** to talk about something that may happen but is not certain. *It's **possible** we might go abroad next year.*

possibly ADVERB

possum **possums**

NOUN A **possum** is a marsupial with thick fur and a long tail.

post **posts, posting, posted**

NOUN **1** **Post** is letters or parcels that are collected and delivered.

NOUN **2** A **post** is a strong piece of wood or metal fixed upright in the ground.

VERB **3** If you **post** a letter, you send it to someone by putting it in a postbox.

postbox **postboxes**

NOUN A **postbox** is a metal box with a slot in it where you can post letters.

postcard **postcards**

NOUN A **postcard** is a piece of thin card, often with a picture on one side, that you can use to send a message to someone.

postcode postcodes

NOUN A **postcode** is the letters and numbers at the end of an address to help the sorting of mail.

poster posters

NOUN A **poster** is a large notice or picture that is put on a wall or notice board.

postman postmen

NOUN A **postman** is a man whose job is to deliver letters and parcels sent by post.

post office post offices

NOUN A **post office** is a building where you can take things to be posted.

postpone postpones, postponing, postponed

VERB If you **postpone** something, you put it off until later. *We had to **postpone** the picnic because the weather was so bad.*

pot pots

NOUN A **pot** is a round container for things like paint or jam, or for growing plants in.

potato potatoes

NOUN A **potato** is a round vegetable that grows under the ground. Potatoes can be boiled, baked or fried.
See Vegetables on page 256.

pottery

NOUN **Pottery** is objects such as dishes and ornaments that are made from clay.

pouch pouches

NOUN **1** A **pouch** is a small bag for keeping things in.
NOUN **2** A **pouch** can also be a pocket of skin on an animal. Female kangaroos and other marsupials have a pouch on their stomach. Their babies grow in this pouch. Hamsters have pouches in their cheeks for storing food.

pounce pounces, pouncing, pounced

VERB When an animal **pounces** on something, it leaps on it and grabs it.

pound pounds

NOUN **1** The **pound** (£) is a unit of money in Britain and in some other countries.
NOUN **2** A **pound** is also a unit of weight equal to just under half a kilogram.

pour pours, pouring, poured

VERB **1** If you **pour** a liquid out of a container, you make it flow out by tipping the container.
VERB **2** When it is raining heavily, you can say that it is **pouring**.

powder

NOUN **Powder** is something that has been ground into tiny pieces.

power powers

NOUN **1** If someone or something has **power**, they have control over other people.
NOUN **2** The **power** of something, such as the wind or the sea, is its strength.

powerful

ADJECTIVE If someone or something is **powerful**, they are very strong.

practical

ADJECTIVE **1** **Practical** people are good at working with their hands.
ADJECTIVE **2** **Practical** ideas are ones that are likely to work.

practice

NOUN **Practice** is doing something many times so that you get better at it.

practise practises, practising, practised

VERB If you **practise**, you do something again and again, in order to get better at it. *She has been **practising** this piece of music for months.*

praise praises, praising, praised

VERB If someone **praises** you for something you have done, they say how well you have done it.

a b c d e f g h i j k l m n o **Pp** q r s t u v w x y z

pram

pram **prams**

NOUN A **pram** is a small carriage that a baby can be pushed around in.

prawn **prawns**

NOUN A **prawn** is a small edible shellfish with a long tail.

pray **prays, praying, prayed**

VERB When someone **prays**, they speak to the god they believe in, to give thanks or to ask for help.

prayer **prayers**

NOUN A **prayer** is the words someone says when they are praying.

pre-

PREFIX **Pre-** is used to form words that describe something as taking place before a particular time or event. *We shop early to miss the **pre-**Christmas rush.* See *Prefixes* on page 264.

precious

ADJECTIVE Something that is **precious** is worth a lot of money.

precipice **precipices**

NOUN A **precipice** is a steep side on a mountain or rock.

precise

ADJECTIVE Something that is **precise** is exact and accurate in every detail. *Take **precise** measurements of the room.* **precisely** ADVERB

predator **predators**

NOUN A **predator** is an animal that kills and eats other animals.

predict **predicts, predicting, predicted**

VERB If someone **predicts** an event, they say that it will happen in the future.

prefer **prefers, preferring, preferred**

VERB If you **prefer** someone or something, you like that person or thing better than another.

prefix **prefixes**

NOUN A **prefix** is a letter or group of letters added to the beginning of a word to make a new word, for example "dis-", "pre-" and "un-". See *Prefixes* on page 264.

pregnant

ADJECTIVE A woman who is **pregnant** is expecting a baby.

prehistoric

ADJECTIVE Something that is **prehistoric** belongs to the time before history was written down.

preparations

PLURAL NOUN **Preparations** are all the things that have to be done before an event. *The children were busy with **preparations** for the school play.*

prepare **prepares, preparing, prepared**

VERB **1** If you **prepare** for something that is going to happen, you get ready for it. VERB **2** If you **prepare** someone or something, you get them ready.

preposition **prepositions**

NOUN In grammar, a **preposition** is a word such as "by", "for" or "with", that goes in front of a noun group. In the sentence "She fell into the pond", "into" is a preposition and "the pond" is a noun group.

present **presents, presenting, presented**

NOUN **1** A **present** is something that you give to someone for them to keep. ADJECTIVE **2** If someone is **present** somewhere, they are there. NOUN **3** The **present** is the time now. VERB **4** If someone **presents** you with something, they give it to you. *The mayor **presented** her with a certificate.* VERB **5** The person who **presents** a show introduces each part or each guest. NOUN **6** The **present tense** of a verb is the form used to show something is happening now.

preserve preserves, preserving, preserved
VERB **1** If you **preserve** something, you do something to keep it the way it is.
VERB **2** To **preserve** food means to stop it from going bad.

president presidents
NOUN The **president** of a country or an organization is the head of it.

press presses, pressing, pressed
VERB **1** If you **press** something against something else, you hold it there firmly.
He **pressed** *the phone against his ear.*
NOUN **2** Newspapers and the journalists who work for them are called the **press**.

pressure
NOUN **Pressure** is the force of one thing pressing or pushing on another.

pretend pretends, pretending, pretended
VERB If you **pretend**, you act as though something is true although it is not.
Let's **pretend** *to be working.*

pretty prettier, prettiest
ADJECTIVE Someone who is **pretty** is nice to look at.

prevent prevents, preventing, prevented
VERB If you **prevent** someone from doing something, you stop them doing it.

prey
NOUN The **prey** of an animal is the creatures that it hunts for food.
bird of prey PHRASE A **bird of prey** is a bird such as an eagle or a hawk, that kills and eats smaller birds and animals.

price prices
NOUN The **price** of something is the amount of money that you must pay to buy it.

prick pricks, pricking, pricked
VERB To **prick** something means to make a tiny hole with something sharp.

prickle prickles
NOUN **Prickles** are small sharp points or thorns on plants.

pride
NOUN **1** **Pride** is the good feeling you have when you have done something well.
NOUN **2** A **pride** of lions is a group of lions that live together.
See **Collective nouns** *on page 262.*

prime minister prime ministers
NOUN The **prime minister** of a country is the leader of that country's government.

prince princes
NOUN A **prince** is the son of a king or queen.

princess princesses
NOUN A **princess** is the daughter of a king or queen, or the wife of a prince.

print prints, printing, printed
VERB **1** When someone **prints** something such as a poster or a newspaper, they use a machine to make lots of copies of it.
VERB **2** If you **print** words, you write in letters that are not joined together.

printer printers
NOUN **1** A **printer** is a machine that is linked to a computer to print information on paper.
NOUN **2** A **printer** is also a person who prints things like books and magazines.

print-out print-outs
NOUN A **print-out** is a printed copy of information from a computer.

prism prisms
NOUN **1** A **prism** is an object made of clear glass with many flat sides. It separates light passing through it into the colours of the rainbow.
NOUN **2** A **prism** is also any three-dimensional shape that has the same size and shape of face at each end.

a
b
c
d
e
f
g
h
i
j
k
l
m
n
o
Pp
q
r
s
t
u
v
w
x
y
z

prison

prison prisons

NOUN A **prison** is a building where people are kept when they have broken the law.

prisoner prisoners

NOUN 1 A **prisoner** is someone who is kept in prison as a punishment.

NOUN 2 A **prisoner** is also someone who has been captured by an enemy.

private

ADJECTIVE If something is **private**, it is for one person or group only. *All the rooms have a private bath.*

in private PHRASE If you do something **in private**, you do it without other people being there.

prize prizes

NOUN A **prize** is something that is given to someone as a reward.

probable

ADJECTIVE Something that is **probable** is likely to be true, or likely to happen.

probably ADVERB

problem problems

NOUN 1 A **problem** is something that is difficult.

NOUN 2 A **problem** is also something, like a puzzle, that you have to work out.

process processes

NOUN A **process** is a series of actions for doing or making something.

procession processions

NOUN A **procession** is a line of people walking or riding through the streets on a special occasion.

prod prods, prodding, prodded

VERB If you **prod** something, you push it with your finger.

produce produces, producing, produced

VERB 1 To **produce** something means to make it.

VERB 2 If you **produce** an object from somewhere such as a pocket, you bring it out so that it can be seen.

VERB 3 Someone who **produces** a play, film or television programme gets it ready to show to the public.

product products

NOUN 1 A **product** is something that is made to be sold.

NOUN 2 In maths, the **product** of two numbers is the answer you get when you multiply them together. For example, the product of four and two is eight.

profit profits

NOUN A **profit** is the money you gain when you sell something for more than it cost you to make or buy.

program programs

NOUN A **program** is a set of instructions that a computer uses in order to do particular things.

programme programmes

NOUN 1 A radio or television **programme** is the thing that is being broadcast.

NOUN 2 A **programme** is a plan of things that will take place.

progress progresses, progressing, progressed

NOUN 1 **Progress** is moving forward or getting better at something. *I'm making progress with my spelling.*

VERB 2 If you **progress**, you get better at something.

project projects

NOUN A **project** is work that you do to learn about something and then write about it.

promise promises, promising, promised

VERB If you **promise** to do something, you mean you really will do it.

prong prongs

NOUN The **prongs** of a fork are the long pointed parts.

pronoun pronouns

NOUN **1** In grammar, a **pronoun** is a word that is used to replace a noun.

NOUN **2 Personal pronouns** replace the subject or object of a sentence. In the sentence "She caught a fish", "she" is a personal pronoun.

NOUN **3 Possessive pronouns** replace the subject or object when you want to show who owns it. In the sentence "This book is mine", "mine" is a possessive pronoun.

See *Pronoun* on page 263.

pronounce pronounces, pronouncing, pronounced

VERB To **pronounce** a word means to say it in a particular way.

pronunciation

NOUN **Pronunciation** is the way a word is usually said.

proof

NOUN **Proof** of something is the facts that show that it is true or that it exists.

prop props, propping, propped

VERB If you **prop** an object somewhere, you support it against something.

propeller propellers

NOUN A **propeller** is the blades that turn to drive an aircraft or ship.

proper

ADJECTIVE **1 Proper** means right. *Put those things back in the **proper** place.*

ADJECTIVE **2** You can also use **proper** to mean real. *You need a **proper** screwdriver for that job.*

properly

ADVERB If something is done **properly**, it is done correctly.

proper noun proper nouns

NOUN A **proper noun** is the name of a particular person or place. It starts with a capital letter. "Ben" and "London" are both proper nouns.

See *Noun* on page 262.

property properties

NOUN **1** Someone's **property** is the things that belong to them.

NOUN **2** A **property** is a building and the land belonging to it.

prophet prophets

NOUN A **prophet** is a person who predicts what will happen in the future.

proportion proportions

NOUN The **proportion** of one amount to another is its size in comparison with the other amount. *There was a large **proportion** of boys in the class.*

prose

NOUN **Prose** is written language that is not poetry or a play.

protect protects, protecting, protected

VERB To **protect** someone or something is to prevent them from being harmed. **protection** NOUN

protein proteins

NOUN **Protein** is a substance found in meat, eggs and milk that is needed by bodies for growth.

protest protests

NOUN A **protest** is something you say or do to show that you disagree with something.

proud prouder, proudest

ADJECTIVE If you feel **proud**, you feel glad about something you have done, or about something that belongs to you. *She was **proud** of her new bike.*

a
b
c
d
e
f
g
h
i
j
k
l
m
n
o
Pp
q
r
s
t
u
v
w
x
y
z

prove proves, proving, proved

VERB When you **prove** something, you show that it is definitely true.

proverb proverbs

NOUN A **proverb** is a short sentence that people say which gives advice about life. For example, the proverb "Look before you leap" means that you should think carefully before you do something.

provide provides, providing, provided

VERB If you **provide** something for someone, you give it to them so that they have it when they need it.

prune prunes, pruning, pruned

VERB 1 When someone **prunes** a tree, they cut off some of the branches so that it will grow better.

NOUN 2 A **prune** is a dried plum.

psalm psalms

NOUN A **psalm** is a poem or prayer from the Bible.

pub pubs

NOUN A **pub** is a building where people go to drink and talk with their friends.

public

ADJECTIVE Something that is **public** can be used by anyone. For example, anyone can pay to travel on public transport, such as trains and buses.

publish publishes, publishing, published

VERB When a company **publishes** a book, newspaper or magazine, they print copies of it and sell them.
publisher NOUN

pudding puddings

NOUN A **pudding** is a sweet food which is usually eaten after the main part of a meal.

puddle puddles

NOUN A **puddle** is a small shallow pool of liquid.

pull pulls, pulling, pulled

VERB 1 When you **pull** something, you hold it firmly and move it towards you.

VERB 2 When you **pull** a curtain, you move it across a window.

VERB 3 When a vehicle **pulls away**, **pulls out** or **pulls in**, it moves in that direction.

pulley pulleys

NOUN A **pulley** is for lifting heavy weights. The weight is attached to a rope or a chain which passes over a wheel.

pullover pullovers

NOUN A **pullover** is a jumper.

pulse

NOUN Your **pulse** is the regular beating of blood through your body. You can feel your pulse in your neck or wrist.

pump pumps, pumping, pumped

NOUN 1 A **pump** is a machine that is used to force gas or liquid to move the way it is wanted.

VERB 2 To **pump** is to force gas or liquid somewhere using a pump. *I must **pump** up these balloons.*

pumpkin pumpkins

NOUN A **pumpkin** is a very large, orange-coloured vegetable with a thick skin. It is soft inside, with a lot of seeds.

pun puns

NOUN A **pun** is a joke using a word which has two different meanings. For example, the sentence "My dog's a champion boxer" has a pun on the word "boxer".

punch punches, punching, punched

VERB If you **punch** someone, you hit them hard with your fist.

punctual

ADJECTIVE Someone who is **punctual** arrives somewhere or does something at exactly the right time.

punctuation

NOUN **Punctuation** is the marks such as full stops and commas that you use in writing.
punctuate VERB
See *Punctuation* on page 264.

puncture punctures

NOUN A **puncture** is a small hole in a tyre. When a tyre has a puncture, the air inside escapes and the tyre goes flat.

punish punishes, punishing, punished

VERB To **punish** someone means to make them suffer because they have done something wrong.
punishment NOUN

pupil pupils

NOUN **1** The **pupils** at a school are the children who go there.
NOUN **2** Your **pupils** are the small round black holes in the centre of your eyes.

puppet puppets

NOUN A **puppet** is a kind of doll that you can move. Some puppets have strings which you can pull. Others are made so that you can put your hand inside.

puppy puppies

NOUN A **puppy** is a young dog.
See *Young animals* on page 260.

purchase purchases, purchasing, purchased

VERB When you **purchase** something, you buy it.

pure purer, purest

ADJECTIVE Something that is **pure** is not mixed with anything else.

purple

ADJECTIVE Something that is **purple** is of a reddish-blue colour.
See *Colours* on page 271.

purpose purposes

NOUN A **purpose** is the reason for doing something.
on purpose PHRASE If you do something **on purpose**, you mean to do it. It does not happen by accident.

purr purrs, purring, purred

VERB When a cat **purrs**, it keeps making a low sound that shows it is happy.

purse purses

NOUN A **purse** is a small bag that people keep their money in.

push pushes, pushing, pushed

VERB When you **push** something, you press it hard.

pushchair pushchairs

NOUN A **pushchair** is a small folding chair on wheels in which a baby or toddler can be wheeled around.

put puts, putting, put

VERB **1** When you **put** something somewhere, you move it there.
VERB **2** If you **put** something **off**, you delay doing it.
VERB **3** If you **put** a light **out**, you make it stop shining.

puzzle puzzles, puzzling, puzzled

VERB **1** If something **puzzles** you, you do not understand it.
NOUN **2** A **puzzle** is a game or question that needs a lot of thought to solve it.

pyjamas

PLURAL NOUN **Pyjamas** are loose trousers and a top that people wear in bed.

pyramid pyramids

NOUN **1** A **pyramid** is a solid shape with a flat base and flat triangular faces that meet at the top in a point.
See *Solid shapes* on page 271.
PLURAL NOUN **2** The **Pyramids** are ancient stone structures built over the bodies of Egyptian kings and queens.

a
b
c
d
e
f
g
h
i
j
k
l
m
n
o
Pp
q
r
s
t
u
v
w
x
y
z

a
b
c
d
e
f
g
h
i
j
k
l
m
n
o
p
Qq
r
s
t
u
v
w
x
y
z

Qq

quack quacks, quacking, quacked
VERB When a duck **quacks**, it makes a loud harsh sound.

quadrilateral quadrilaterals
NOUN A **quadrilateral** is a flat shape with four straight sides.
See *Colours and flat shapes* on page 271.

quaint quainter, quaintest
ADJECTIVE Something that is **quaint** is unusual and rather pretty.

qualify qualifies, qualifying, qualified
VERB **1** When someone **qualifies**, they pass the examination they need to do a particular job.
VERB **2** You **qualify** if you get enough points in a competition to go on to the next stage.

quality qualities
NOUN The **quality** of something is how good or bad it is, compared with other things of the same kind.

quantity quantities
NOUN A **quantity** is an amount you can measure or count. *We shall need a huge quantity of food for the weekend.*

quarrel quarrels
NOUN A **quarrel** is an angry argument.

quarry quarries
NOUN A **quarry** is a deep hole that has been dug in a piece of land. Quarries are dug to provide materials such as stone for building and other work.

quarter quarters
NOUN A **quarter** is one of four equal parts of something.
See *Fractions* on page 272.

quay quays
(*said* **kee**)
NOUN A **quay** is a place where boats are tied up to be loaded or unloaded.

queen queens
NOUN **1** A **queen** is a woman who rules a country. Queens are not chosen by the people. They are born into a royal family.
NOUN **2** The wife of a king is also called a **queen**.
NOUN **3** In the insect world, a **queen** is a large female bee, ant or wasp which can lay eggs.

query queries, querying, queried
NOUN **1** A **query** is a question.
VERB **2** If you **query** something, you ask about it because you think it might not be right.

question questions
NOUN A **question** is words you say or write when you want to ask something.

question mark question marks
NOUN A **question mark** is the punctuation mark (**?**) which you use in writing at the end of a question.
See *Punctuation* on page 264.

questionnaire questionnaires
NOUN A **questionnaire** is a list of questions which asks for information for a survey.

queue queues
NOUN A **queue** is a line of people or vehicles waiting for something.

quiche quiches
NOUN A **quiche** is a sort of tart with a filling of eggs, and cheese or other food.

quick quicker, quickest

ADJECTIVE **1** Someone or something that is **quick** moves very fast.

ADJECTIVE **2** Something that is **quick** lasts only a short time. *I'll have a **quick** look at it.*

quickly

ADVERB Things that happen **quickly** happen very fast.

quiet quieter, quietest

ADJECTIVE **1** Someone or something that is **quiet** makes only a little noise or no noise at all.

ADJECTIVE **2** Quiet also means peaceful. *Let's have a **quiet** evening at home.*

quilt quilts

NOUN A **quilt** is a soft cover for a bed.

quit quits, quitting, quit

VERB **1** If you **quit** something, you stop doing it. ***Quit** teasing me!*

VERB **2** If you **quit**, you leave. *My dad has just **quit** his job.*

VERB **3** If you **quit** a file on a computer, you close it.

quite

ADVERB **1** Quite means rather. *I think he's **quite** nice.*

ADVERB **2** Quite can also mean completely. *The work is now **quite** finished.*

quiver quivers, quivering, quivered

VERB **1** If something **quivers**, it trembles.

NOUN **2** A **quiver** is a container for carrying arrows.

quiz quizzes

NOUN A **quiz** is a game or test. Someone tries to find out how much you know by asking you questions.

quotation quotations

NOUN A **quotation** is an extract from a book or speech that you use in your own work.

quotation marks

PLURAL NOUN Quotation marks are punctuation marks (" ") or (' ') used in writing to show where speech begins and ends.

quote quotes, quoting, quoted

VERB **1** If you **quote** something that someone has written or said, you repeat their exact words.

NOUN **2** A **quote** is a piece out of a book or speech.

quotient quotients

NOUN In maths, a **quotient** is a whole number you get when you divide one number into another. For example, if you divide eight by two, the quotient is four.

a
b
c
d
e
f
g
h
i
j
k
l
m
n
o
p
Qq
r
s
t
u
v
w
x
y
z

a
b
c
d
e
f
g
h
i
j
k
l
m
n
o
p
q

Rr

s
t
u
v
w
x
y
z

Rr

rabbit rabbits
NOUN A **rabbit** is a small furry animal with long ears.

race races, racing, raced
NOUN **1** A **race** is a competition to see who is the fastest.

NOUN **2** A **race** is also a large group of people who look alike in some way. For example, different races have different skin colour, or differently shaped eyes.

VERB **3** If you **race** someone, you try to beat them in a race.

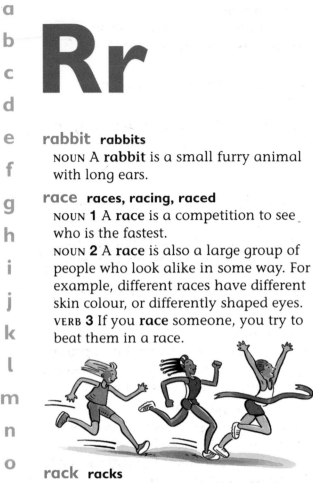

rack racks
NOUN A **rack** is a frame that is used for holding things or for hanging things on.

racket rackets
NOUN **1** A **racket** is a bat with an oval frame and strings across and down it. It is used in tennis and similar games.

NOUN **2** If someone makes a **racket**, they make a loud unpleasant noise.

radar
NOUN **Radar** is a way of showing the position and speed of ships and aircraft when they cannot be seen. Radio signals give the information on a screen.

radiator radiators
NOUN **1** A **radiator** is a hollow metal object that can be filled with liquid in order to heat a room.

NOUN **2** In a car, the **radiator** holds the water that is used to cool the engine.

radio radios
NOUN A **radio** is a piece of equipment which receives sounds through the air. You can use a radio to listen to programmes that are broadcast.

radish radishes
NOUN A **radish** is a small salad vegetable with a red skin and white flesh. *See Vegetables on page 256.*

radius radii
NOUN The **radius** of a circle is the length of a straight line drawn from its centre to any point on its edge.

raffle raffles
NOUN A **raffle** is a competition. You buy a numbered ticket and win a prize if your number is chosen.

raft rafts
NOUN A **raft** is a floating platform. Rafts are often made of large pieces of wood fixed together.

rag rags
NOUN **1** A **rag** is a piece of old cloth that you can use to clean or wipe things.

NOUN **2** Rags are old torn clothes.

rage
NOUN **Rage** is great anger. *Dad's face showed his rage.*

ragged
ADJECTIVE Clothes that are **ragged** are old and torn.

raid raids
NOUN A **raid** is a sudden attack against an enemy.

rail rails
NOUN **1** A **rail** is a horizontal bar that is firmly fixed to posts. Rails are used as fences, or for people to lean on.

NOUN **2** Rails are the heavy metal bars that trains run on.

railing railings
NOUN A **railing** is a kind of fence made from metal bars.

railway railways

NOUN A **railway** is a route along which trains travel on metal rails.

rain rains, raining, rained

NOUN **1** Rain is water that falls from the clouds in small drops.

VERB **2** When it is **raining**, rain is falling.

rainbow rainbows

NOUN A **rainbow** is an arch of different colours that sometimes appears in the sky when the sun shines through rain.

rainforest rainforests

NOUN A **rainforest** is a dense forest in a tropical area where there is a lot of rain.

raise raises, raising, raised

VERB **1** If you **raise** something, you move it so that it is higher.

VERB **2** If you **raise** your voice, you speak more loudly.

VERB **3** To **raise** money for a cause means to get people to give money towards it.

raisin raisins

NOUN A **raisin** is a dried grape.

rake rakes

NOUN A **rake** is a garden tool with a row of metal teeth fixed to a long handle.

ram rams, ramming, rammed

VERB **1** If one vehicle **rams** another, it crashes into it.

NOUN **2** A **ram** is an adult male sheep.

Ramadan

NOUN **Ramadan** is the ninth month of the Muslim year, when Muslims eat and drink nothing from sunrise to sunset.

ramp ramps

NOUN A **ramp** is a sloping surface between two places at different levels.

ran

VERB **Ran** is the past tense of **run**.

ranch ranches

NOUN In the United States, a **ranch** is a large farm for raising cattle, sheep or horses.

rang

VERB **Rang** is the past tense of **ring**.

range ranges

NOUN **1** The **range** of something is the area or distance over which it can be used.

NOUN **2** A **range** is a row of hills or mountains.

rank ranks

NOUN A **rank** is a position that a person holds in an organization. The higher the rank, the more important they are.

rap raps, rapping, rapped

VERB **1** If you **rap** something, you hit it with a series of quick blows.

NOUN **2** Rap is a style of poetry spoken to music with a strong beat.

rapid

ADJECTIVE Something that is **rapid** is very quick.

rare rarer, rarest

ADJECTIVE Something that is **rare** is not often seen, or does not happen very often.

rash rashes

NOUN A **rash** is a lot of spots that appear on your skin in certain illnesses.

raspberry raspberries

NOUN A **raspberry** is a small red fruit which is soft and juicy, with a lot of small seeds called pips. *See Fruit on page 257.*

rat rats

NOUN A **rat** is a rodent with a long tail.

rather

ADVERB 1 **Rather** means quite. *I'm rather angry about that.*

ADVERB 2 You can say **rather** if there is something else you want to do. *I don't want to go out. I'd rather watch television.*

rattle rattles, rattling, rattled

VERB 1 When something **rattles**, it makes short rapid knocking sounds. *Can you stop that window rattling?*

NOUN 2 A baby's **rattle** is a toy that makes a noise when it is shaken.

raw

ADJECTIVE Food that is **raw** is not cooked.

ray rays

NOUN A **ray** is a line of light.

razor razors

NOUN A **razor** is a tool that people use for shaving.

re-

PREFIX **Re-** is added to words to show that something is done again. For example, to "reread" means to read again. *See Prefixes on page 264.*

reach reaches, reaching, reached

VERB 1 When you **reach** a place, you arrive there.

VERB 2 If you **reach** somewhere, you stretch out your hand. *He reached across the table for the salt.*

react reacts, reacting, reacted

VERB When you **react** to something, you behave in a particular way because of it. *He reacted badly to the news.*

reaction NOUN

read reads, reading, read

VERB 1 When you **read**, you look at words and understand what they mean.

VERB 2 When you **read aloud**, you say the words that are written.

reading readings

NOUN **Reading** is the activity of reading books or other written material.

ready

ADJECTIVE If someone or something is **ready**, they are properly prepared for doing something.

real

ADJECTIVE 1 Something that is **real** is true. It is not imaginary. *I've seen a real princess.*

ADJECTIVE 2 You also say **real** when you mean the thing itself and not a copy. *I've got a lovely toy pony. But Jenny's got a real one.*

realize realizes, realizing, realized; also spelt realise

VERB If you **realize** something, you work it out or notice it. *I've just realized you must be Tara's sister.*

really

ADVERB You can use **really** to make something you are saying stronger. *I really don't like that boy.*

rear

NOUN The **rear** of something is the part that is at the back of it.

rearrange rearranges, rearranging, rearranged

VERB To **rearrange** something means to organize or arrange it in a different way.

reason reasons

NOUN The **reason** for something is why it happens. *I'm sorry I'm late, but there is a good reason.*

reasonable

ADJECTIVE 1 People who are **reasonable** behave in a fair and sensible way.

ADJECTIVE 2 A price that is **reasonable** seems fair and not too high.

reasonably ADVERB

rebel rebels, rebelling, rebelled
VERB To **rebel** means to fight against authority.
rebellious ADJECTIVE

receive receives, receiving, received
VERB When you **receive** something, you get it after it has been given or sent to you.

recent
ADJECTIVE Something that is **recent** happened only a short time ago.
recently ADVERB

recipe recipes
NOUN A **recipe** is a list of ingredients and instructions for cooking something.

recite recites, reciting, recited
VERB When you **recite** something like a poem, you say it aloud from memory.

reckon reckons, reckoning, reckoned
VERB If you **reckon** that something is true, you think it is true.

recognize recognizes, recognizing, recognized; also spelt **recognise**
VERB If you **recognize** someone, you realize that you know who they are.

recommend recommends, recommending, recommended
VERB If you **recommend** something to someone, you tell them it is good.

record records, recording, recorded
NOUN **1** If you keep a **record** of something, you keep a written account or store information in a computer.
NOUN **2** A **record** is also the best that has been done so far.
VERB **3** If someone **records** information, they write it down, put it onto tape or film, or into a computer.
VERB **4** To **record** sound means to put it on tape or compact disc.

recorder recorders
NOUN A **recorder** is a small musical instrument which you play by blowing into one end and putting your fingers over the holes.

recover recovers, recovering, recovered
VERB When you **recover** from something such as an illness, you become well again.

recreation
NOUN **Recreation** is all the things that you like doing in your spare time.
recreational ADJECTIVE

rectangle rectangles
NOUN A **rectangle** is a flat shape with four straight sides and four right angles.
rectangular ADJECTIVE
See *Colours and flat shapes* on page 271.

recycle recycles, recycling, recycled
VERB To **recycle** used products means to process them so they can be used again.

red redder, reddest
ADJECTIVE Something that is **red** is the colour of a ripe tomato.
See *Colours* on page 271.

redraft redrafts, redrafting, redrafted
VERB If you **redraft** a piece of text, you make another draft.

reduce reduces, reducing, reduced
VERB To **reduce** something means to make it smaller in size or amount.

a b c d e f g h i j k l m n o p q **Rr** s t u v w x y z

reed

reed reeds

NOUN A **reed** is a plant with a tall hollow stem. Reeds grow in or near water.

reef reefs

NOUN A **reef** is a long line of rocks that is just below the surface of the sea.

reel reels

NOUN A **reel** is a round object that you wrap thread, wire or film around.

refer refers, referring, referred

VERB If you **refer** to someone or something, you mention them.

referee referees

NOUN A **referee** is a person whose job is to make sure that the players in a game follow the rules properly.

reference book reference books

NOUN A **reference book** is a book that gives you information in a way that is easy to find. Dictionaries and encyclopedias are reference books.

refill refills, refilling, refilled

NOUN 1 A **refill** is a full container that replaces an empty one. *Have you got a refill for this pen?*

VERB 2 If you **refill** something, you fill it again after it has been emptied.

reflect reflects, reflecting, reflected

VERB 1 When a surface **reflects** rays of something like light or heat, the rays bounce back from the surface.

VERB 2 When a mirror **reflects** a person or thing, it shows what they look like.

reflection reflections

NOUN A **reflection** is what you see when you look in a mirror or shiny surface.

refreshing

ADJECTIVE Something that is **refreshing** makes you feel energetic or cool again after you have been tired or hot.

refreshments

PLURAL NOUN **Refreshments** are drinks and snacks.

refrigerator refrigerators

NOUN A **refrigerator** is a large cooled container in which you store food to keep it fresh. A refrigerator is often called a **fridge** for short.

refuse refuses, refusing, refused

(*said* rif-**yooz**) VERB 1 If you **refuse** to do something, you say you will not do it. (*said* **ref**-yoos) NOUN 2 **Refuse** is rubbish or waste.

region regions

NOUN A **region** is a large area of land.

register registers, registering, registered

NOUN 1 A **register** is an official list or record of things.

VERB 2 When something is **registered**, it is recorded on an official list. *The car was registered in my mother's name.*

regret regrets, regretting, regretted

VERB If you **regret** something, you wish it had not happened.

regular

ADJECTIVE 1 Something that is **regular** does not change its pattern, for example a regular heartbeat.

ADJECTIVE 2 A **regular** polygon has all its angles and sides equal.

rehearsal rehearsals

NOUN A **rehearsal** is a practice of a play, dance or piece of music, to prepare for a public performance.

reign reigns, reigning, reigned

VERB 1 When a king or queen **reigns**, they rule a country.

NOUN 2 The **reign** of a king or queen is the period during which they reign.

rein reins

NOUN A **rein** is one of the leather straps that are used to control a horse.

reindeer

NOUN A **reindeer** is a large deer that lives in cold northern countries.

relate relates, relating, related

VERB If something **relates** to something else, it is connected or concerned with it.

related

ADJECTIVE **1** People who are **related** belong to the same family.

ADJECTIVE **2** If one thing is **related** to another, there is a connection between them. *A graph shows how two sets of numbers are **related**.*

relation relations

NOUN If someone is your **relation**, they belong to the same family as you.

relative relatives

NOUN If someone is your **relative**, they belong to the same family as you.

relax relaxes, relaxing, relaxed

VERB When you **relax**, you stop worrying and feel more calm.

release releases, releasing, released

VERB If someone **releases** a person or animal that has been trapped or held in some way, they set them free.

reliable

ADJECTIVE If something or someone is **reliable**, you can depend on them.

relief

NOUN **Relief** is the feeling you have if you do not need to worry about something any more.

relieved

ADJECTIVE If you are **relieved**, you are glad because you can stop worrying about something.

religion religions

NOUN A **religion** is a set of beliefs about a god, or about several gods.
religious ADJECTIVE

reluctant

ADJECTIVE If you are **reluctant** to do something, you do not want to do it.
reluctantly ADVERB

rely relies, relying, relied

VERB **1** If you **rely** on someone, you need them and depend on them.
VERB **2** If you can **rely** on someone to do something, you can trust them to do it.

remain remains, remaining, remained

VERB **1** If you **remain** in a place, you stay there and do not go away.
PLURAL NOUN **2** The **remains** of something are the parts that are left after most of it has been destroyed. *They found the **remains** of an ancient pyramid.*

remainder

NOUN **1** The **remainder** of something is the part that is left. *He gulped down the **remainder** of his coffee.*
NOUN **2** In maths, the **remainder** is the amount left over when one number cannot be exactly divided by another. For example, if nine is divided by four, the answer is two remainder one.

remark remarks, remarking, remarked

VERB If you **remark** on something, you mention it. *The teacher **remarked** on his strange haircut.*

remarkable

ADJECTIVE Someone or something that is **remarkable** is unusual in some way so that people notice them and feel surprised.

remember remembers, remembering, remembered

VERB If you can **remember** something, you can bring it back into your mind. *Can you **remember** that actor's name?*

a
b
c
d
e
f
g
h
i
j
k
l
m
n
o
p
q
Rr
s
t
u
v
w
x
y
z

a
b
c
d
e
f
g
h
i
j
k
l
m
n
o
p
q

Rr

s
t
u
v
w
x
y
z

remind **reminds, reminding, reminded**
VERB **1** If someone or something **reminds** you to do something, they make you remember it. *That reminds me – I must get a card for Auntie Mary.*
VERB **2** If someone **reminds** you of someone else, something about them makes you think of the other person.

remote **remoter, remotest**
ADJECTIVE **Remote** areas are far away from places where most people live.

remote control
NOUN **Remote control** is a system of controlling a machine from a distance, using radio or electronic signals.

removal **removals**
NOUN **1** The **removal** of something is the act of taking it away or getting rid of it.
NOUN **2** A **removal company** takes furniture from one building to another when people move house.

remove **removes, removing, removed**
VERB If you **remove** something from somewhere, you take it off or away.

rent **rents**
NOUN **Rent** is the amount of money you pay regularly for a house or flat.

repair **repairs, repairing, repaired**
VERB If you **repair** something that is broken or not working, you mend it.

repeat **repeats, repeating, repeated**
VERB If you **repeat** something, you say it or do it again.
repetition NOUN

replace **replaces, replacing, replaced**
VERB **1** If you **replace** something, you put it back where it was before.
VERB **2** If you **replace** something that is old, lost or broken, you get a new one.

reply **replies, replying, replied**
VERB When you **reply**, you answer someone.

report **reports, reporting, reported**
VERB **1** If you **report** that something has happened, you tell someone about it. *He reported the theft to the police.*
NOUN **2** A **report** is an account of an event or situation.

reporter **reporters**
NOUN A **reporter** is someone who works for a newspaper, radio or television. Their job is to find out what is happening in the world so that their report can be printed or broadcast.

represent **represents, representing, represented**
VERB **1** If you **represent** someone, you act for them. *The class chose Meena to represent them.*
VERB **2** If a sign or symbol **represents** something, it stands for it.

reptile **reptiles**
NOUN A **reptile** is a cold-blooded animal with a scaly skin. Female reptiles lay eggs. Snakes and crocodiles are reptiles. See **Reptiles** on page 259.

request **requests, requesting, requested**
VERB **1** If you **request** something, you ask for it politely.
NOUN **2** A **request** is a polite demand for something.

require **requires, requiring, required**
VERB If you **require** something, you need it.

rescue **rescues, rescuing, rescued**
VERB If you **rescue** someone, you save them from danger.

research researches, researching, researched
NOUN **1** **Research** is studying something and trying to find out facts about it.
VERB **2** If you **research** something, you try to discover facts about it.

resent resents, resenting, resented
VERB If you **resent** something, you feel angry about it.

reserve reserves, reserving, reserved
VERB If you **reserve** something, like a book at the library, you arrange for it to be kept for you.

reservoir reservoirs
NOUN A **reservoir** is a lake that is used for storing drinking water for an area.

resign resigns, resigning, resigned
VERB If someone **resigns** from a job, they say they want to leave it.

resist resists, resisting, resisted
VERB If you **resist** something, you fight against it and do not give up.

resource resources
NOUN The **resources** of a country, organization or person are the materials, money or skills they have.

respect respects, respecting, respected
VERB If you **respect** someone, you look up to them and think their opinions are important.

respectable
ADJECTIVE Someone who is **respectable** behaves in a way that other people think is right.

respond responds, responding, responded
VERB When you **respond** to someone, you react to them by doing or saying something.
response NOUN

responsible
ADJECTIVE **1** If you are **responsible** for something, it is your job to deal with it, and you are to blame if it goes wrong.

ADJECTIVE **2** A **responsible** person behaves properly and sensibly.

rest rests, resting, rested
VERB **1** When you **rest**, you sit or lie down and keep still for a while.
NOUN **2** A **rest** is a period of time when you do not work.
NOUN **3** The **rest** is all the things in a group that are left. *I've done some of the washing-up. I'll do the rest tomorrow.*

restaurant restaurants
NOUN A **restaurant** is a place where meals are served.

restless
ADJECTIVE If you feel **restless**, you find it hard to relax.

result results
NOUN **1** A **result** is something that happens because of something else. *The milk boiled over and the result was a real mess.*
NOUN **2** A **result** is also the score at the end of a game.

retire retires, retiring, retired
VERB When someone **retires**, they stop doing their job, usually because they are getting old.

retreat retreats, retreating, retreated
VERB If you **retreat** from something difficult or dangerous, you move backwards away from it. *The army retreated from the enemy.*

return returns, returning, returned
VERB **1** When you **return** to a place, you go back there after you have been away.
VERB **2** If you **return** something to someone, you give it back to them.
NOUN **3** A **return** is a ticket for the journey to a place and back again.

a
b
c
d
e
f
g
h
i
j
k
l
m
n
o
p
q
Rr
s
t
u
v
w
x
y
z

reveal

reveal reveals, revealing, revealed
VERB If you **reveal** something that has been secret or hidden, you tell people about it or show it to them.

revenge
NOUN **Revenge** is something a person does to hurt someone who has hurt them.

reverse reverses, reversing, reversed
VERB **1** If a car **reverses**, it goes backwards.
VERB **2** If you **reverse** the order of things, you put them in the opposite order.

revise revises, revising, revised
VERB **1** If you **revise** something, you alter it or correct it.
VERB **2** When you **revise**, you read something again so that you can learn it for a test.
revision NOUN

revolver revolvers
NOUN A **revolver** is a small gun.

reward rewards
NOUN A **reward** is something you are given for doing well.

rhinoceros rhinoceroses
NOUN A **rhinoceros** is a large African or Asian animal with a thick skin and one or two horns on its nose. Rhinoceroses are often called **rhinos** for short.

rhyme rhymes, rhyming, rhymed
VERB If two words **rhyme**, they have a similar sound. For example, "dog" rhymes with "log".

rhythm rhythms
NOUN **Rhythm** is a regular pattern of sound or movement. Music and dancing have rhythm.

rib ribs
NOUN Your **ribs** are the curved bones that go from your backbone to your chest.

ribbon ribbons
NOUN A **ribbon** is a long narrow piece of fine cloth. It is used for tying things together, or as a decoration.

rice
NOUN **Rice** is white or pale brown grains which are boiled and eaten.

rich richer, richest
ADJECTIVE Someone who is **rich** has a lot of money or valuable things.

rid
get rid of PHRASE When you **get rid of** something that you do not want, you remove it or throw it away.

riddle riddles
NOUN A **riddle** is a kind of puzzle. You ask a question which has a funny answer.

ride rides, riding, rode, ridden
NOUN **1** A **ride** is a journey using a bus, car, train, horse or bicycle.
VERB **2** When a person **rides** a horse or a bicycle, they sit on it and control it.
VERB **3** When you **ride** in a vehicle such as a car, you travel in it.

ridiculous
ADJECTIVE If you say something is **ridiculous**, you mean it is foolish.

right
ADJECTIVE **1** If something is **right**, it is correct.
ADJECTIVE OR ADVERB **2** Right means on or towards the right side of something. Most people write with their right hand.

right angle right angles
NOUN A **right angle** is an angle or turn of 90 degrees.

rigid
ADJECTIVE Something that is **rigid** is very stiff and does not bend or stretch.

rim rims

NOUN **1** The **rim** of a container, such as a cup, is the edge round the top.

NOUN **2** The **rim** of a round object, such as a wheel, is the outside edge of it.

rind rinds

NOUN The **rind** of a fruit such as an orange or a lemon is its thick outer skin.

ring rings, ringing, rang, rung

NOUN **1** A **ring** is an ornament that people wear on a finger.

NOUN **2** Anything in the shape of a circle can be called a **ring**.

VERB **3** If you **ring** someone, you phone them.

VERB **4** When a bell **rings**, it makes a loud clear sound.

rinse rinses, rinsing, rinsed

VERB When you **rinse** something, you wash it in clean water with no soap.

rip rips, ripping, ripped

VERB If someone **rips** something, they tear it violently.

ripe riper, ripest

ADJECTIVE When fruit or grain is **ripe**, it is ready to be eaten or harvested.

ripple ripples

NOUN A **ripple** is a little wave on the surface of water.

rise rises, rising, rose, risen

VERB **1** If something **rises**, it moves upwards.

VERB **2** When the sun or the moon **rises**, it appears above the horizon.

risk risks

NOUN A **risk** is a danger that something bad might happen.

take a risk PHRASE If someone **takes a risk**, they do something knowing that it could be dangerous.

risky ADJECTIVE

rival rivals

NOUN Your **rival** is someone who is trying to win the same things as you are.

river rivers

NOUN A **river** is a large amount of fresh water flowing towards the sea.

road roads

NOUN A **road** is a long piece of hard ground, specially treated so that people and vehicles can travel along it easily.

roam roams, roaming, roamed

VERB If you **roam**, you wander around without any particular purpose.

roar roars, roaring, roared

VERB If something **roars**, it makes a very loud noise like a lion. *The car **roared** off down the road.*

roast roasts, roasting, roasted

VERB When someone **roasts** meat or other food, they cook it in an oven or over a fire.

rob robs, robbing, robbed

VERB If someone **robs** you, they steal something from you.

robber NOUN   **robbery** NOUN

robin robins

NOUN A **robin** is a small brown bird with a red neck and chest.

robot robots

NOUN A **robot** is a machine which is programmed to move and perform tasks automatically.

rock rocks, rocking, rocked

NOUN **1** Rock is the very hard material that is in the earth. Cliffs and mountains are made of rock.

NOUN **2** A **rock** is a large piece of rock.

VERB **3** When something **rocks**, it moves slowly backwards and forwards, or from side to side.

NOUN **4** Rock or **rock music** is music with a very strong beat.

NOUN **5** Rock is also a sweet shaped into long hard sticks.

rocky ADJECTIVE

rocket rockets

NOUN **1** A **rocket** is a space vehicle, usually shaped like a long pointed tube.

NOUN **2** Rockets are fireworks that explode when they are high in the air.

rod rods

NOUN A **rod** is a long thin pole or bar, usually made of wood or metal. *His uncle gave him a new fishing rod.*

rode

VERB **Rode** is the past tense of **ride**.

rodent rodents

NOUN A **rodent** is a small mammal with sharp front teeth for gnawing. Rats, mice, squirrels and hamsters are rodents.

roll rolls, rolling, rolled

VERB **1** When something **rolls**, or when you roll it, it moves along a surface, turning over and over.

NOUN **2** A **roll** of something like paper is a long piece of it that has been rolled into a tube.

NOUN **3** A **roll** is a small loaf of bread for one person.

Rollerblade Rollerblades

NOUN; TRADEMARK **Rollerblades** are roller skates which have the wheels set in one straight line on the bottom of the boot.

roller skate roller skates

NOUN **Roller skates** are shoes with four small wheels underneath.

roof roofs

NOUN **1** The **roof** of a building or car is the covering on top of it.

NOUN **2** The **roof** of your mouth or of a cave is the highest part.

room rooms

NOUN **1** A **room** is a section in a building, divided from other rooms by walls.

NOUN **2** If there is plenty of **room**, there is a lot of space.

root roots

NOUN **1** A **root** is the part of a plant that grows underground.

NOUN **2** The **root** of a hair, tooth or nail is the part that you cannot see because it is covered with skin.

root word root words

NOUN A **root word** is a word to which prefixes and suffixes can be added to make other words. In the word "clearly", the root word is "clear".

rope ropes

NOUN **Rope** is thick strong string.

rose roses

NOUN **1** A **rose** is a flower. Most roses grow on thorny stems.

VERB **2** Rose is also the past tense of **rise**.

rot rots, rotting, rotted

VERB **1** When vegetables and other foods **rot**, they go bad.

VERB **2** When wood **rots**, it goes soft and can easily be pulled to pieces.

rotate rotates, rotating, rotated

VERB When something **rotates**, it turns with a circular movement.

rotten

ADJECTIVE Something that is **rotten** has gone bad or soft so that it cannot be used.

rough rougher, roughest

ADJECTIVE **1** If something is **rough**, the surface is uneven and not smooth.

ADJECTIVE **2** If someone is being **rough**, they are not being gentle.

ADJECTIVE **3** A **rough** estimate is not meant to be exact.

ADJECTIVE **4** A **rough** draft is an early version of something you are writing.

roughly

ADVERB **1** If you say **roughly**, you mean approximately. *There are **roughly** twice as many boys as girls in this club.*

ADVERB **2** If someone speaks **roughly** to you, they sound angry and aggressive.

round rounder, roundest

ADJECTIVE **1** Something **round** is shaped like a ball or a circle.

PREPOSITION **2** If something is **round** something else, it surrounds it. *There was a wall **round** the garden.*

PREPOSITION **3** If something moves **round** you, it keeps moving in a circle with you in the centre.

ADVERB **4** If you turn or look **round**, you turn so you are facing a different way.

round up or **round down** PHRASE If you **round a number**, you raise it up or lower it down to the nearest 10, 100 or 1000. *If you **round** 34 to the nearest ten, it would be 30. 675 **rounded up** to the nearest hundred is 700.*

roundabout roundabouts

NOUN **1** A **roundabout** is a place where several roads meet, with a circle in the centre which vehicles have to go round.

NOUN **2** A **roundabout** is also a large machine at a fair that children can sit on and go round and round.

rounders

NOUN **Rounders** is a game in which players run between posts after hitting the ball.

route routes

NOUN A **route** is a way from one place to another. *David took his usual **route** to school.*

routine routines

ADJECTIVE **1** **Routine** things happen regularly.

NOUN **2** Your **routine** is the usual way that you do things.

row rows, rowing, rowed
(*rhymes with* **snow**)

NOUN **1** A **row** of people or things is several of them arranged in a line.

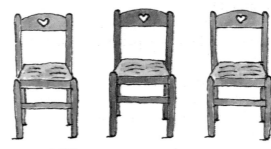

VERB **2** When you **row** a boat, you use oars to make it move through the water.

(*rhymes with* **now**) NOUN **3** A **row** is a noisy argument.

royal

ADJECTIVE **1** Someone who is **royal** belongs to the family of a king or queen.

ADJECTIVE **2** Something that is **royal** is connected with a royal family.

rub rubs, rubbing, rubbed

VERB When you **rub** something, you wipe it hard.

rubber rubbers

NOUN **1** **Rubber** is a strong stretchy material that is made from the sap of a tree. It is used to make things like tyres.

NOUN **2** A **rubber** is a small piece of rubber used to get rid of pencil marks.

rubbish

NOUN **1** **Rubbish** is waste material, such as used paper or empty tins.

NOUN **2** If you say something is **rubbish**, you think it is of very poor quality. *This new television programme is **rubbish**.*

ruby rubies

NOUN A **ruby** is a dark red jewel.

rudder rudders

NOUN A **rudder** is a piece of wood or metal on the back of a boat or plane which is moved to make the boat or plane turn.

rude **ruder, rudest**
ADJECTIVE If someone is **rude**, they behave badly and are not polite. *It's **rude** to stare at people.*

rug **rugs**
NOUN A **rug** is a piece of thick material like a small carpet.

rugby
NOUN **Rugby** is a game played with an oval ball. Two teams try to score points by carrying the ball across a line, or by kicking the ball over a bar.

ruin **ruins, ruining, ruined**
VERB 1 To **ruin** something means to spoil it completely. *Mark and Joe **ruined** my party by fighting.*
NOUN 2 The **ruins** of a building are the parts of it that are left after it has fallen down or been badly damaged.

rule **rules, ruling, ruled**
VERB 1 To **rule** a country means to be in charge of the way the country works.
NOUN 2 **Rules** tell you what you are allowed to do and what you are not allowed to do. They are used in games, and in places such as schools.

ruler **rulers**
NOUN 1 A **ruler** is a person who rules a country.
NOUN 2 A **ruler** is also a long flat piece of wood or plastic with straight edges, used for measuring or drawing straight lines.

rumour **rumours**
NOUN A **rumour** is a story or piece of information which a lot of people are talking about, but which may not be true.

run **runs, running, ran, run**
VERB 1 When you **run**, you move quickly, leaving the ground during each stride.

VERB 2 When liquid **runs**, it flows. *Don't leave the hot water **running**.*
VERB 3 Someone who **runs** something, like a school or country, is in charge of it.
VERB 4 When a vehicle such as a train or bus **runs** somewhere, it travels at set times. *The bus **runs** every 20 minutes.*
VERB 5 If you **run** out of something, you have no more of it left.

rung **rungs**
NOUN 1 A **rung** is a wooden or metal step on a ladder.
VERB 2 **Rung** is the past participle of **ring**.

running
NOUN 1 **Running** is the activity of running, especially as a sport.
ADJECTIVE 2 **Running** water is flowing rather than standing still.

runway **runways**
NOUN A **runway** is a long narrow strip of ground at an airport which planes use when they take off or land.

rush **rushes, rushing, rushed**
VERB If you **rush** somewhere, you go there quickly.

rust **rusts, rusting, rusted**
NOUN 1 **Rust** is a reddish-brown substance that forms on iron or steel which has been in contact with water.
VERB 2 When something **rusts**, rust forms on it.
rusty ADJECTIVE

rustle **rustles, rustling, rustled**
VERB When something **rustles**, it makes soft sounds as it moves. *Dry leaves **rustled** underfoot.*

rut **ruts**
NOUN A **rut** is a deep groove in the ground made by the wheels of a vehicle.

Ss

sack **sacks**
NOUN A **sack** is a large strong bag made of cloth or plastic.

sad **sadder, saddest**
ADJECTIVE If you are **sad**, you are unhappy because something has happened that you do not like.

saddle **saddles**
NOUN A **saddle** is a seat for a rider on a horse or bicycle.

safari **safaris**
NOUN A **safari** is a journey to see wild animals.

safari park **safari parks**
NOUN A **safari park** is a large protected area of land where wild animals live and move around freely.

safe **safer, safest; safes**
ADJECTIVE **1** If you are **safe**, you are not in any danger.
ADJECTIVE **2** If something is in a **safe** place, it cannot be lost or stolen.
NOUN **3** A **safe** is a strong metal cupboard with special locks. People keep money or valuable things in a safe.
safety NOUN

said
VERB **Said** is the past tense of **say**.

sail **sails, sailing, sailed**
NOUN **1** A **sail** is a large piece of material fixed to a boat. The wind blows against the sail and pushes the boat along.

NOUN **2** A **sail** is also one of the flat pieces of wood on the top of a windmill.
VERB **3** To **sail** a boat means to make it move across water using its sails.

sailor **sailors**
NOUN A **sailor** is a person who works on a ship as a member of the crew.

salad **salads**
NOUN A **salad** is a mixture of raw vegetables, for example lettuce, cucumber and tomatoes.

sale **sales**
NOUN **1** The **sale** of anything is the selling of it for money.
NOUN **2** A **sale** is a time when a shop sells things at less than their usual price.

saliva
NOUN **Saliva** is the liquid in your mouth that helps you eat food.

salmon
NOUN A **salmon** is a large silvery fish. Salmon live in the sea, but they swim up rivers to lay their eggs.

salt
NOUN **Salt** is a white powder or crystal with a bitter taste. Salt is found in the earth and in sea water. It is used to flavour or preserve food.

salute **salutes, saluting, saluted**
NOUN **1** A **salute** is a sign of respect used especially in the armed forces.
VERB **2** If you **salute** someone, you give them a salute.

same
ADJECTIVE **1** If two things are the **same**, they are exactly like each other in some way. *Look! Your dress is the same as mine.*
ADJECTIVE **2** **Same** means one shared thing and not two different ones. *Amy and I are in the same class.*

sample **samples**
NOUN A **sample** of something is a small quantity of it that you can try.

a
b
c
d
e
f
g
h
i
j
k
l
m
n
o
p
q
r
Ss
t
u
v
w
x
y
z

sand

sand

NOUN **Sand** is tiny grains of rock, shells and other material. Most deserts and beaches are made of sand.

sandal sandals

NOUN **Sandals** are light shoes for warm weather. The soles are held on by straps which go over your foot.

sandpit sandpits

NOUN A **sandpit** is a shallow box in the ground with sand in it, where small children can play.

sandwich sandwiches

NOUN A **sandwich** is two slices of bread with a layer of food in between.

sang

VERB **Sang** is the past tense of **sing**.

sank

VERB **Sank** is the past tense of **sink**.

sap

NOUN **Sap** is the liquid that carries food through plants and trees.

sardine sardines

NOUN A **sardine** is a small sea fish.

sari saris

NOUN A **sari** is a piece of clothing worn especially by Asian women.

sat

VERB **Sat** is the past tense of **sit**.

satchel satchels

NOUN A **satchel** is a leather or cloth bag with a long strap.

satellite satellites

NOUN **1** A **satellite** is a natural object in space that moves around a larger object. The moon is a satellite of the Earth.

NOUN **2** A **satellite** is also an object sent into space to send signals back to Earth.

satellite dish satellite dishes

NOUN A **satellite dish** is an aerial which receives signals from an artificial satellite.

satellite television

NOUN **Satellite television** is where the programmes are sent from an artificial satellite. They can be received using a satellite dish.

satisfactory

ADJECTIVE Something that is **satisfactory** is good enough for its purpose.

satisfy satisfies, satisfying, satisfied

VERB To **satisfy** someone means to give them enough of something to make them pleased or contented.

Saturday Saturdays

NOUN **Saturday** is the day between Friday and Sunday.

sauce sauces

NOUN A **sauce** is a thick liquid served with other food to add to the taste.

saucepan saucepans

NOUN A **saucepan** is a deep metal cooking pot, usually with a long handle. Most saucepans have lids.

saucer saucers

NOUN A **saucer** is a small plate on which you stand a cup.

sausage sausages

NOUN A **sausage** is a finely minced meat mixture put into a skin.

savage

ADJECTIVE A **savage** animal is wild and fierce.

save saves, saving, saved

VERB **1** If you **save** someone or something, you help them to escape from harm or danger. *He fell in the river and his father dived in to save him.*

VERB **2** If you **save** money, you gradually collect it by not spending it all.

184

savings

PLURAL NOUN Your **savings** are the money you have saved.

saw **saws, sawing, sawed, sawn**

VERB **1** Saw is the past tense of **see**.

NOUN **2** A **saw** is a tool for cutting wood and other materials. It has a blade with sharp teeth along one edge.

VERB **3** If you **saw** something, you cut it with a saw.

sawdust

NOUN **Sawdust** is the dust and small bits of wood made when wood is sawn.

say **says, saying, said**

VERB When you **say** something, you speak words.

scald **scalds, scalding, scalded**

VERB If you **scald** yourself, you burn yourself with very hot liquid or steam.

scale **scales**

NOUN **1** The **scale** of a map is how its size relates to the place in the real world.

NOUN **2** The **scales** of a fish or reptile are the small pieces of hard skin covering its body.

scales

PLURAL NOUN **Scales** are a piece of equipment you use for weighing things.

scamper **scampers, scampering, scampered**

VERB When people or small animals **scamper**, they move quickly and lightly.

scan **scans, scanning, scanned**

VERB **1** If you **scan** a piece of writing, you look through it quickly.

VERB **2** If a machine **scans** something, it examines it using a beam of light, X-rays or sound waves.

scar **scars**

NOUN A **scar** is a mark that is left on the skin after a wound has healed.

scarce **scarcer, scarcest**

ADJECTIVE Something that is **scarce** is not often found.

scare **scares, scaring, scared**

VERB Someone or something that **scares** you makes you feel frightened.

scarecrow **scarecrows**

NOUN A **scarecrow** is an object in the shape of a person, put in a field of crops to frighten birds away.

scared

ADJECTIVE If you are **scared**, you are frightened.

scarf **scarves**

NOUN A **scarf** is a piece of cloth that you wear round your neck to keep you warm.

scarlet

ADJECTIVE Something **scarlet** is a bright red colour.

scatter **scatters, scattering, scattered**

VERB **1** If you **scatter** things, you throw or drop a lot of them all over an area.

VERB **2** If people **scatter**, they suddenly move away in different directions.

scene **scenes**

NOUN **1** The **scene** of an event is the place where it happened. *The police went to the scene of the crime.*

NOUN **2** A **scene** is part of a play or film in which things happen in one place.

scenery

NOUN **1** Scenery is what you can see when you are out in the country.

NOUN **2** Scenery is also all the cloths and boards that are used as a background for the stage in a theatre.

a
b
c
d
e
f
g
h
i
j
k
l
m
n
o
p
q
r
Ss
t
u
v
w
x
y
z

scent

scent **scents**
NOUN A **scent** is a pleasant smell.

scheme **schemes, scheming, schemed**
NOUN **1** A **scheme** is a plan for doing something.
VERB **2** When people **scheme**, they make secret plans.

school **schools**
NOUN **1** A **school** is a place for teaching and learning.
NOUN **2** You can refer to a large group of dolphins or fish as a **school**.
See **Collective nouns** on page 262.

science
NOUN **Science** is the study of plants and animals, materials, and things like electricity, forces, light and sound.

science fiction
NOUN **Science fiction** is stories about events happening in the future or in other parts of the universe.

scientist **scientists**
NOUN A **scientist** is a person who finds out why things happen by doing tests and by careful study.

scissors
PLURAL NOUN **Scissors** are a cutting tool with two sharp blades.

scoop **scoops, scooping, scooped**
VERB **1** If you **scoop** something up, you pick it up using a spoon or the palm of your hand.
NOUN **2** A **scoop** is an object like a large spoon which is used for picking up food such as ice cream.

score **scores, scoring, scored**
VERB **1** If someone **scores**, they get a goal or other point in a game.
NOUN **2** The **score** in a game is the total number of points made by the two teams or players.

scowl **scowls, scowling, scowled**
VERB If you **scowl**, you look very cross.

scramble **scrambles, scrambling, scrambled**
VERB If you **scramble** over rough or difficult ground, you move over it quickly, using your hands to help you.

scrap **scraps**
NOUN A **scrap** of something is a small piece of it. *I need a **scrap** of paper.*

scrapbook **scrapbooks**
NOUN A **scrapbook** is a book in which you stick things such as pictures or newspaper articles.

scrape **scrapes, scraping, scraped**
VERB If you **scrape** something, you take off its surface by pulling a rough or sharp object over it.

scratch **scratches, scratching, scratched**
VERB **1** If you **scratch** your skin, you rub your fingernails against it.
VERB **2** If you **scratch** something, you damage it by making small cuts on it. *I fell into the hedge and **scratched** my bike.*
NOUN **3** A **scratch** is a small cut.

scream **screams, screaming, screamed**
VERB If you **scream**, you shout or cry in a loud high-pitched voice.

screech **screeches, screeching, screeched**
VERB To **screech** means to make an unpleasant high-pitched noise. *The car wheels **screeched**.*

screen **screens**
NOUN A **screen** is a flat surface on which pictures or words are shown, for example a television or computer screen.

screw screws, screwing, screwed

NOUN **1** A **screw** is a small sharp piece of metal used for fixing things together.

VERB **2** If you **screw** things together, you fix them together using screws.

VERB **3** If you **screw** something onto something else, you fix it there by twisting it round and round. *He screwed the top back onto the bottle of water.*

screwdriver screwdrivers

NOUN A **screwdriver** is a tool used for turning screws.

scribble scribbles, scribbling, scribbled

VERB If you **scribble**, you write quickly and roughly.

script scripts

NOUN The **script** of a play or film is the written version of it.

scrub scrubs, scrubbing, scrubbed

VERB If you **scrub** something, you rub it hard with a stiff brush and water.

sculptor sculptors

NOUN A **sculptor** is someone who makes sculptures.

sculpture sculptures

NOUN **1** A **sculpture** is a statue or model made by shaping stone, clay or other materials.

NOUN **2** Sculpture is the art of making sculptures.

sea seas

NOUN The **sea** is the salty water that covers about three-quarters of the earth.

seagull seagulls

NOUN **Seagulls** are common white, grey and black birds that live near the sea.

seahorse seahorses

NOUN A **seahorse** is a small fish which swims upright, with a head that looks like a horse's head.

seal seals, sealing, sealed

NOUN **1** A **seal** is a large mammal with flippers that lives partly on land and partly in the sea.

VERB **2** If you **seal** an envelope, you stick down the flap.

seam seams

NOUN A **seam** is the line where two pieces of material are sewn together.

search searches, searching, searched

VERB If you **search** for something, you try to find it by looking carefully.

seaside

NOUN The **seaside** is a place by the sea, especially one where people go for their holidays.

season seasons

NOUN A **season** is one of the four parts of a year: spring, summer, autumn and winter.

seat seats

NOUN A **seat** is a place where you can sit, for example a chair or a stool.

seat belt seat belts

NOUN A **seat belt** is a strap that you fasten across your body for safety when travelling in a car, coach or aircraft.

seaweed

NOUN **Seaweed** is a plant that grows in the sea.

a
b
c
d
e
f
g
h
i
j
k
l
m
n
o
p
q
r
Ss
t
u
v
w
x
y
z

second **seconds**

ADJECTIVE **1** The **second** item in a series is the one counted as number two.

NOUN **2** A **second** is a short period of time. There are 60 seconds in a minute.

second person

NOUN In grammar, the **second person** is the person who is addressed in speech or writing. It is expressed as "you".

secret **secrets**

NOUN A **secret** is something that only a few people know and that they are not to tell other people.

section **sections**

NOUN A **section** of something is one of the separate parts it is divided into.

secure

ADJECTIVE **1** If you feel **secure**, you feel safe and confident.

ADJECTIVE **2** If something is **secure**, it is fixed firmly in position.

security NOUN

see **sees, seeing, saw, seen**

VERB **1** If you **see** something, you are looking at it or you notice it.

VERB **2** To **see** something also means to understand it. *I see what you mean.*

VERB **3** If you **see** someone, you visit them or meet them. *I went to see the doctor.*

seed **seeds**

NOUN The **seeds** of a plant are the small hard parts from which new plants grow.

seek **seeks, seeking, sought**

VERB If you **seek** someone or something, you try to find them.

seem **seems, seeming, seemed**

VERB **1** If you say that someone **seems**, for example, to be happy or sad, you mean that is the way they look. *Tim seems to be a bit upset today.*

VERB **2** If something **seems** a certain way, that is the way it feels to you. *I only waited for ten minutes but it seemed like hours.*

seen

VERB **Seen** is the past participle of **see**.

seesaw **seesaws**

NOUN A **seesaw** is a long plank. A child sits on each end and they move up and down in turn.

segment **segments**

NOUN A **segment** of something is a small part of it.

seize **seizes, seizing, seized**

VERB If you **seize** something, you grab it firmly.

select **selects, selecting, selected**

VERB When you **select** someone or something, you choose them.

selfish

ADJECTIVE People who are **selfish** only think about themselves. They do not care about other people.

sell **sells, selling, sold**

VERB When someone **sells** something, they give it in exchange for money.

Sellotape

NOUN; TRADEMARK **Sellotape** is a transparent sticky tape.

semi-

PREFIX Putting **semi-** in front of a word makes it mean half or partly. For example, a "semicircle" is half of a circle.

See *Prefixes* on page 264.

semicircle **semicircles**

NOUN A **semicircle** is half of a circle.

See *Colours and flat shapes* on page 271.

semicolon semicolons
NOUN A **semicolon** is the punctuation mark (;) which is used in writing to separate different parts of a sentence or list, or to show a pause.
See *Punctuation* on page 264.

semifinal semifinals
NOUN The **semifinals** are the two matches in a competition played to decide who plays in the final.

send sends, sending, sent
VERB **1** When you **send** something to someone, you arrange for it to be delivered to them.
VERB **2** If someone **sends** someone somewhere, they tell them to go there. *She was sent home because she was ill.*
VERB **3** If someone **sends** for you, you get a message to go and see them.

senior
ADJECTIVE People who are **senior** are older or more important.

sensation sensations
NOUN A **sensation** is a physical feeling.

sense senses
NOUN **1** Your **senses** are your power to see, hear, smell, touch and taste.
NOUN **2 Sense** is knowing the right thing to do. *You should have had more sense.*
NOUN **3** If something makes **sense**, you can understand it.

sensible
ADJECTIVE People who are **sensible** know what is the right thing to do.
sensibly ADVERB

sensitive
ADJECTIVE **1** If someone or something is **sensitive**, they are easily hurt. *He is very sensitive about his big ears.*
ADJECTIVE **2** If you are **sensitive** to other people's feelings, you understand them.

sent
VERB **Sent** is the past tense of **send**.

sentence sentences
NOUN A **sentence** is a group of words that mean something.

separate separates, separating, separated
ADJECTIVE **1** If two things are **separate**, they are not connected.
VERB **2** To **separate** people or things means to part them. *Separate the yolk from the white.*

September
NOUN **September** is the ninth month of the year. It has 30 days.

sequel sequels
NOUN A **sequel** to a book or film is another book or film which continues the story.

sequence sequences
NOUN A **sequence** of events is a number of them coming one after the other.

series
NOUN **1** A **series** is a number of things of the same kind that follow each other.
NOUN **2** A radio or television **series** is a set of programmes about the same thing.

serious
ADJECTIVE **1** People who are **serious** are often quiet and do not laugh very much.
ADJECTIVE **2** Things that are **serious** are important and need careful thought.
ADJECTIVE **3** A **serious** problem or situation is very bad and worrying.

servant servants
NOUN A **servant** is someone paid to work in another person's house.

a
b
c
d
e
f
g
h
i
j
k
l
m
n
o
p
q
r
Ss
t
u
v
w
x
y
z

serve **serves, serving, served**
VERB **1** If you **serve** food or drink to people, you give it to them.
VERB **2** To **serve** customers in a shop means to help them to buy what they want.

service **services**
NOUN A **service** is something useful that a person or company does for people.

serviette **serviettes**
NOUN A **serviette** is a small piece of cloth or paper that you use to wipe your hands and mouth when you are eating.

set **sets, setting, set**
NOUN **1** A **set** is a number of things of the same kind that belong together, for example a set of golf clubs or a set of tools.
VERB **2** When something such as jelly or concrete **sets**, it becomes firm or hard.
VERB **3** When the sun **sets**, it goes down behind the horizon.
VERB **4** When you **set** a clock or control, you adjust it to a particular position.

settee **settees**
NOUN A **settee** is a long, comfortable seat for two or more people.

setting **settings**
NOUN The **setting** of a story or play is where it takes place. *That old castle would make a great setting for a creepy story.*

settle **settles, settling, settled**
VERB **1** If you **settle**, you sit or make yourself comfortable.
VERB **2** If something such as dust or snow **settles**, it sinks slowly and becomes still.
VERB **3** If you **settle** something, you decide it.

several
ADJECTIVE **Several** people or things means a number of them. *He was gone for several hours.*

severe
ADJECTIVE **Severe** is used to describe something extremely bad or unpleasant. *She woke with severe toothache.*

sew **sews, sewing, sewed, sewn**
VERB When someone **sews**, they join pieces of cloth together by using a needle and thread.

sewer **sewers**
NOUN A **sewer** is a large underground pipe that carries rainwater and waste away from houses and other buildings.

sex **sexes**
NOUN The two **sexes** are the two groups that people and other living things are divided into. One sex is male and the other is female. Only female animals can have babies.

shabby **shabbier, shabbiest**
ADJECTIVE Something that is **shabby** looks old and nearly worn out.

shade **shades, shading, shaded**
NOUN **1** Shade is the darkness in a place where the sun cannot reach. *She sat in the shade of an apple tree.*
NOUN **2** A **shade** is something that covers a light to stop it shining in your eyes.
VERB **3** If you **shade** something, you stop the sun from shining on it.
NOUN **4** Shade is how dark or light a colour is. *I love this shade of blue.*

shadow **shadows**
NOUN A **shadow** is a dark shape. It is formed when something opaque blocks the light coming from a lamp, a torch or the sun.

shake shakes, shaking, shook, shaken
VERB **1** If you **shake** something, or it shakes, it moves quickly from side to side or up and down.
VERB **2** If your voice **shakes**, it trembles because you are nervous or angry.

shaky shakier, shakiest
ADJECTIVE If someone or something is **shaky**, they are weak and unsteady.
shakily ADVERB

shallow shallower, shallowest
ADJECTIVE Something that is **shallow**, such as a hole, a container or water, measures only a short distance from top to bottom.

shame
NOUN **1** **Shame** is an unhappy feeling that people have when they have done something wrong or foolish.
NOUN **2** If you say something is a **shame**, you mean you are sorry about it. *It's a shame you can't come round.*

shampoo shampoos
NOUN **Shampoo** is a soapy liquid that you use for washing your hair.

shape shapes
NOUN **1** The **shape** of something is the form of its outline, for example whether it is round or square.
NOUN **2** A **shape** is something that has its outside edges joining in a particular way. Shapes can be flat (two-dimensional), like a circle or a triangle, or solid (three-dimensional), like a cube or sphere. *See Colours and flat shapes and Solid shapes on page 271.*

share shares, sharing, shared
VERB **1** If you **share** something with another person, you both use it. *She shared a bedroom with her sister.*
VERB **2** If you **share** something among a group of people, you divide it so that everyone gets some.
NOUN **3** A **share** of something is a portion of it.

shark sharks
NOUN **Sharks** are large powerful fish with sharp teeth.

sharp sharper, sharpest
ADJECTIVE **1** A **sharp** object has a fine edge or point that is good for cutting or piercing things.
ADJECTIVE **2** A **sharp** person is quick to notice or understand things.
ADJECTIVE **3** A **sharp** pain is sudden and hurts a lot.

sharpen sharpens, sharpening, sharpened
VERB If you **sharpen** something, you make its edge or point sharper.

shatter shatters, shattering, shattered
VERB If something **shatters**, it breaks into a lot of small pieces.

shave shaves, shaving, shaved
VERB When a man **shaves**, he removes hair from his face with a razor.

shawl shawls
NOUN A **shawl** is a large piece of woollen cloth. Shawls are worn by women over their shoulders or head. They are also used to wrap babies in.

shear shears, shearing, sheared, shorn
VERB To **shear** a sheep means to cut the wool off it.

shears
PLURAL NOUN **Shears** are a tool like a large pair of scissors, used especially for cutting hedges.

shed sheds, shedding, shed
NOUN **1** A **shed** is a small building used for storing things.
VERB **2** When a tree **sheds** its leaves, they fall off.

a b c d e f g h i j k l m n o p q r **Ss** t u v w x y z

191

sheep

sheep
NOUN A **sheep** is a farm animal with a thick woolly coat. Sheep are kept for meat or wool.

sheet sheets
NOUN **1** A **sheet** is a large piece of thin cloth which is put on a bed.
NOUN **2** A **sheet** of something, such as paper or glass, is a thin flat piece.

shelf shelves
NOUN A **shelf** is something flat which is fixed to a wall or inside a cupboard. It is for putting things on.

shell shells
NOUN **1** The **shell** of an egg or nut is the hard covering round it.

NOUN **2** The **shell** of an animal such as a tortoise is the hard covering on its back.

shelter shelters, sheltering, sheltered
NOUN **1** A **shelter** is a small building or covered place where people or animals can be safe from bad weather or danger.
VERB **2** If you **shelter** in a place, you stay there and are safe.

shepherd shepherds
NOUN A **shepherd** is a person who looks after sheep.

sheriff sheriffs
NOUN **1** In America, a **sheriff** is a person who keeps the law in a county.
NOUN **2** In Scotland, a **sheriff** is the senior judge of a county or district.
NOUN **3** In Australia, a **sheriff** is an officer of the Supreme Court.

shield shields, shielding, shielded
NOUN **1** A **shield** is a large piece of strong material like metal or plastic which soldiers or policemen carry to protect themselves.
VERB **2** To **shield** someone means to protect them from something.

shift shifts, shifting, shifted
VERB **1** If you **shift** something, you move it.
VERB **2** If something **shifts**, it moves.
NOUN **3** A **shift** is a set period during which people work in a factory or hospital. *My dad works the night shift.*

shimmer shimmers, shimmering, shimmered
VERB If something **shimmers**, it shines with a faint flickering light, for example as the moon does on water.

shin shins
NOUN Your **shin** is the front part of your leg, between your knee and your ankle.

shine shines, shining, shone
VERB **1** When something **shines**, it gives out a bright light.
VERB **2** If you make an object **shine**, you make it bright by polishing it.
shiny ADJECTIVE

ship ships
NOUN A **ship** is a large boat which carries passengers or cargo.

shirt shirts
NOUN A **shirt** is a light piece of clothing for the top part of your body, with a collar, sleeves, and buttons down the front.

shiver shivers, shivering, shivered
VERB When you **shiver**, your body shakes slightly, usually because you are cold or frightened.

shoal shoals
NOUN A **shoal** of fish is a large group of them swimming together.
See *Collective nouns* on page 262.

a b c d e f g h i j k l m n o p q r **Ss** t u v w x y z

shock **shocks, shocking, shocked**

NOUN **1** If you have a **shock**, something happens suddenly which upsets you.

VERB **2** If you **shock** someone, you give them an unpleasant surprise.

shocking ADJECTIVE

shoe **shoes, shoeing, shod**

NOUN **1** **Shoes** are strong coverings for your feet.

VERB **2** To **shoe** a horse means to fix horseshoes onto its hooves.

shoelace **shoelaces**

NOUN A **shoelace** is a long piece of material like string that is used to fasten a shoe.

shone

VERB **Shone** is the past tense of **shine**.

shook

VERB **Shook** is the past tense of **shake**.

shoot **shoots, shooting, shot**

NOUN **1** A **shoot** is a new part growing from a plant or tree.

VERB **2** To **shoot** means to fire a bullet from a gun, or an arrow from a bow.

VERB **3** If someone **shoots** in a game such as football, they try to score a goal.

VERB **4** When a film is **shot**, it is filmed.

shop **shops, shopping, shopped**

NOUN **1** A **shop** is a place where things are sold.

VERB **2** When you **shop**, you go to the shops to buy things.

shopping NOUN

shopkeeper **shopkeepers**

NOUN A **shopkeeper** is a person who owns or looks after a small shop.

shore **shores**

NOUN The **shore** of a sea or lake is the land along the edge of it.

short **shorter, shortest**

ADJECTIVE **1** Someone who is **short** is not as tall as most other people.

ADJECTIVE **2** Something that is **short** is not very long.

PHRASE **3** If one word is **short for** another, it is a quick way of saying it. *Phone is **short for** telephone.*

shorts

PLURAL NOUN **Shorts** are trousers with short legs.

shot **shots**

VERB **1** **Shot** is the past tense of **shoot**.

NOUN **2** A **shot** is when a gun is fired.

NOUN **3** In football and tennis, a **shot** is the act of kicking or hitting the ball.

should

VERB **1** You use **should** to say that something ought to happen. *You **should** write a thank-you letter.*

VERB **2** You also use **should** to say that you expect something to happen. *We **should** have heard by now.*

shoulder **shoulders**

NOUN Your **shoulders** are the parts of your body between your neck and the tops of your arms.

shout **shouts, shouting, shouted**

VERB If you **shout** something, you say it very loudly.

shove **shoves, shoving, shoved**

VERB If you **shove** someone or something, you push them roughly.

shovel **shovels, shovelling, shovelled**

NOUN **1** A **shovel** is a tool like a spade with a rounded blade.

VERB **2** If you **shovel** earth or snow, you move it with a shovel.

a
b
c
d
e
f
g
h
i
j
k
l
m
n
o
p
q
r
Ss
t
u
v
w
x
y
z

show

show shows, showing, showed, shown
VERB 1 If you **show** someone something, you let them see it. *Show me your passport.*
VERB 2 If you **show** someone how to do something, you do it yourself so that they can watch you.
VERB 3 If something **shows**, people can see it. *Do you think that mark will show?*
VERB 4 If you **show** your feelings, you let people see them.
NOUN 5 A **show** is something that you watch at the theatre or on television.

shower showers
NOUN 1 A **shower** is a piece of equipment which sprays you with water so that you can wash yourself.
NOUN 2 A **shower** is also a short period of rain or snow.

shrank
VERB **Shrank** is the past tense of **shrink**.

shred shreds, shredding, shredded
NOUN 1 A **shred** of paper or material is a small narrow piece of it. *He tore the paper into shreds.*
VERB 2 If you **shred** something, you cut or tear it into small pieces.

shriek shrieks, shrieking, shrieked
VERB If you **shriek**, you give a sudden sharp scream.

shrill shriller, shrillest
ADJECTIVE A **shrill** sound is loud and high-pitched, like a whistle.

shrimp shrimps
NOUN A **shrimp** is a small edible shellfish with a long tail and many legs.

shrink shrinks, shrinking, shrank, shrunk
VERB If something **shrinks**, it becomes smaller.

shrivel shrivels, shrivelling, shrivelled
VERB When something **shrivels**, it becomes dry and curled up.

shrug shrugs, shrugging, shrugged
VERB If you **shrug** your shoulders, you raise them slightly to show that you are not interested in something.

shrunk
VERB **Shrunk** is the past participle of **shrink**.

shudder shudders, shuddering, shuddered
VERB If you **shudder**, you tremble with fear or horror.

shuffle shuffles, shuffling, shuffled
VERB 1 If you **shuffle**, you walk without lifting your feet properly off the ground.
VERB 2 If you **shuffle** a pack of cards, you mix them up before you begin a game.

shut shuts, shutting, shut
VERB 1 If you **shut** something, such as a door, you move it so that it fills a gap.
VERB 2 When a shop **shuts** you can no longer go into it.
ADJECTIVE 3 If something is **shut**, it is closed.

shy shier, shiest
ADJECTIVE A **shy** person is nervous with people they do not know well.

sick sicker, sickest
ADJECTIVE If you are **sick**, you are ill.

side sides
NOUN 1 The **side** of something is to the left or right of it. *He parted his hair on the left side.*
NOUN 2 The **side** of something can be the edge of it. *A triangle has three sides.*
NOUN 3 The **sides** of a river are its banks.
NOUN 4 The **sides** of a piece of paper are its front and back.
NOUN 5 The two **sides** in a game are the teams playing against each other.
ADJECTIVE 6 A **side** road is a small road leading off a larger one.

sideways
ADVERB **Sideways** means moving or facing towards one side. *She had to squeeze sideways through the gap.*

sigh sighs, sighing, sighed
VERB When you **sigh**, you breathe out heavily. People usually sigh when they are tired, sad or bored.

sight
NOUN **Sight** is being able to see.

sign signs, signing, signed
VERB **1** If you **sign** something, you write your name on it.
NOUN **2** A **sign** is a mark that means something, for example a plus sign (+).
NOUN **3** **Signs** can be words, pictures or symbols that tell you something.

NOUN **4** You can make a **sign** with your body that means something to other people. For example, if you shake your head it is a sign that you mean "No".

signal signals, signalling, signalled
NOUN **1** A **signal** is a message that is given by signs. For example, a flashing light is a signal that a driver is turning left or right.
VERB **2** If you **signal** to someone, you do something to give them a message.

signature signatures
NOUN Your **signature** is the way you write your own name.

sign language
NOUN **Sign language** is a way of communicating using your hands. It is often used by deaf people.

Sikh Sikhs
NOUN A **Sikh** is a person who believes in Sikhism, an Indian religion which teaches that there is only one God.

silence
NOUN **Silence** is when there is no noise.

silent
ADJECTIVE **1** If someone or something is **silent**, they are not saying anything or making any noise.
ADJECTIVE **2** A **silent** letter is one that is written but not pronounced, for example, the "g" in the word "gnat". See *Silent letters* on page 261.

silhouette silhouettes
NOUN A **silhouette** is the outline of a dark shape against a light background.

silk silks
NOUN **Silk** is a fine soft cloth. It is made from threads produced by a kind of caterpillar called a silkworm.
silky ADJECTIVE

silly sillier, silliest
ADJECTIVE If someone says you are **silly**, they mean you are behaving in a foolish or childish way.

silver
NOUN **Silver** is a greyish-white metal used for making jewellery.

similar
ADJECTIVE If things are **similar**, they are rather alike.

simile similes
NOUN A **simile** is an expression in which a person or thing is described as being similar to someone or something else. "She went as red as a beetroot" is a simile.

simple simpler, simplest
ADJECTIVE Something that is **simple** is easy to do or understand.
simply ADVERB

simplify simplifies, simplifying, simplified
VERB To **simplify** something means to make it easier to do or understand.

a
b
c
d
e
f
g
h
i
j
k
l
m
n
o
p
q
r
Ss
t
u
v
w
x
y
z

since

PREPOSITION **1 Since** means from a particular time until now. *I've been waiting **since** half past three.*

CONJUNCTION **2 Since** also means because. *I had a drink, **since** I was feeling thirsty.*

sincere

ADJECTIVE If you are **sincere**, you say things that you really mean.

sincerely ADVERB

sing sings, singing, sang, sung

VERB **1** If you **sing** a song, you make music with your voice.

VERB **2** When birds **sing**, they make pleasant sounds.

single

ADJECTIVE **1 Single** means one of something. *We can't park here. It's a **single** yellow line.*

ADJECTIVE **2** People who are **single** are not married.

ADJECTIVE **3** A **single** bed or bedroom is for one person.

ADJECTIVE **4** A **single** ticket only allows you to travel one way.

singular

NOUN **Singular** means one. *The **singular** of "girls" is "girl". The **singular** of "children" is "child".* See **plural**.

sink sinks, sinking, sank, sunk

NOUN **1** A **sink** is a large basin with water taps and a drain.

VERB **2** If something **sinks**, it moves slowly down until it disappears, especially below the surface of water.

VERB **3** To **sink** something sharp into an object means to make it go deeply into it. *The tiger **sank** its teeth into his leg.*

sip sips, sipping, sipped

VERB If you **sip** a drink, you drink it a little at a time.

sir

NOUN **Sir** is a polite way of addressing a man. *Please **sir**, can I leave early?*

siren sirens

NOUN A **siren** is something that makes a loud wailing noise as a warning. Fire engines, police cars and ambulances have sirens.

sister sisters

NOUN Your **sister** is a girl or woman who has the same parents as you.

sit sits, sitting, sat

VERB **1** When you **sit**, you put your bottom on something such as a chair or the floor.

VERB **2** When a bird **sits** on its eggs, it covers them with its body to hatch them.

site sites

NOUN A **site** is a piece of ground that is used for a particular purpose. *Let's stop at the next camp **site**.*

situation situations

NOUN **1** A **situation** is the place where something is. *Our hotel was in a lovely **situation**.*

NOUN **2** A **situation** is the things that are happening to you. *You have put me in a difficult **situation**.*

size sizes

NOUN The **size** of something is how big or small it is.

sizzle sizzles, sizzling, sizzled

VERB If something **sizzles**, it makes a hissing sound. *The meat **sizzled** in the frying pan.*

skate skates

NOUN **1 Skates** are ice skates or roller skates.

NOUN **2** A **skate** is an edible flat sea fish.

skateboard skateboards

NOUN A **skateboard** is a narrow board on wheels which you stand on and ride for fun.

skeleton skeletons

NOUN Your **skeleton** is all the bones in your body joined together. It supports your body and protects your organs.

sketch sketches

NOUN A **sketch** is a quick drawing.

ski skis

NOUN **Skis** are long pieces of wood, metal or plastic that you fasten to special boots so that you can move easily on snow.

skid skids, skidding, skidded

VERB If a vehicle **skids**, it slides out of control, for example because the road is wet or icy.

skill skills

NOUN **Skill** is the ability to do something well.

skilful ADJECTIVE

skim skims, skimming, skimmed

VERB **1** If you **skim** something from the surface of a liquid, you remove it.
VERB **2** If you **skim** a piece of writing, you read it to get a general idea of what it is about.

skin skins

NOUN **1** Your **skin** is the natural covering of your body.
NOUN **2** The **skin** of a fruit or vegetable is its outer covering.

skinny skinnier, skinniest

ADJECTIVE Someone **skinny** is very thin.

skip skips, skipping, skipped

VERB **1** When you **skip**, you move along almost as though you were dancing, with little jumps.

VERB **2** If you **skip** with a rope, you swing the rope over your head and under your feet while jumping.
VERB **3** If you **skip** something, you miss it out. *I'm going to skip lunch.*
NOUN **4** A **skip** is a large metal container for holding rubbish and rubble.

skirt skirts

NOUN A **skirt** is a piece of clothing worn by women and girls. It hangs from the waist.

skull skulls

NOUN Your **skull** is the bony part of your head. It protects your brain, which is inside it.

sky skies

NOUN The **sky** is the space around the earth which you can see when you stand outside and look upwards.

skyscraper skyscrapers

NOUN A **skyscraper** is a very tall building.

slab slabs

NOUN A **slab** is a thick flat piece of something such as stone or concrete.

slack slacker, slackest

ADJECTIVE Something that is **slack** is loose, and not firmly stretched.

slam slams, slamming, slammed

VERB If you **slam** a door, you shut it hard so that it makes a loud noise.

slang

NOUN **Slang** is words that you use in everyday talk but not when you are writing or being polite.

slant slants, slanting, slanted

VERB If something **slants**, it is not straight but lies at an angle.

a
b
c
d
e
f
g
h
i
j
k
l
m
n
o
p
q
r
Ss
t
u
v
w
x
y
z

slap slaps, slapping, slapped
VERB If you **slap** someone, you hit them with the palm of your hand.

slate slates
NOUN **Slate** is a dark grey rock that can be split into thin layers. It is often used for roofs.

sledge sledges
NOUN A **sledge** is a vehicle on runners used for travelling over snow.

sleek sleeker, sleekest
ADJECTIVE Hair or fur that is **sleek** is smooth and shiny.

sleep sleeps, sleeping, slept
VERB When you **sleep**, you close your eyes and your whole body rests.
sleepy ADJECTIVE

sleet
NOUN **Sleet** is a mixture of snow and rain.

sleeve sleeves
NOUN The **sleeves** of a coat or jumper are the parts that cover your arms.

sleigh sleighs
NOUN A **sleigh** is a sledge pulled by animals.

slept
VERB **Slept** is the past tense of **sleep**.

slice slices, slicing, sliced
NOUN **1** A **slice** is a thin piece of food that has been cut from a larger piece.
VERB **2** If you **slice** food, you cut it into thin pieces.

slide slides, sliding, slid
VERB **1** When something **slides**, it moves smoothly over a surface.
NOUN **2** A **slide** is a piece of playground equipment for sliding down.

slight slighter, slightest
ADJECTIVE Something that is **slight** is small. *She has a slight cut.*
slightly ADVERB

slim slimmer, slimmest
ADJECTIVE Someone who is **slim** has a body that is thin but not too thin.

slime
NOUN **Slime** is a thick slippery substance which covers a surface and which looks unpleasant. *The pond was covered in green slime.*
slimy ADJECTIVE

sling slings, slinging, slung
NOUN **1** A **sling** is a piece of cloth which you hang from your neck to support a broken or injured arm.
VERB **2** If you **sling** something somewhere, you throw it carelessly.

slip slips, slipping, slipped
VERB **1** If you **slip**, you accidentally slide and lose your balance.
VERB **2** If you **slip** somewhere, you go there quickly and quietly. *She slipped out of the house.*
NOUN **3** A **slip** of paper is a small piece of paper.

slipper slippers
NOUN **Slippers** are soft loose shoes that people wear in the house.

slippery
ADJECTIVE Something that is **slippery** is smooth, wet or greasy. It is difficult to keep hold of or to walk on.

slit slits, slitting, slit
VERB **1** If you **slit** something, you make a long narrow cut in it. *He slit open the envelope.*
NOUN **2** A **slit** is a long narrow opening in something.

slope slopes

NOUN A **slope** is a flat surface which has one end higher than the other.

slot slots

NOUN A **slot** is a narrow opening in something, usually for putting coins in.

slow slower, slowest

ADJECTIVE **1** Something that is **slow** moves along without much speed.

ADJECTIVE **2** If a watch or clock is **slow**, it shows a time that is earlier than the correct time.

slowly ADVERB

slug slugs

NOUN A **slug** is a small slow-moving animal with a long slimy body, like a snail but without a shell.

sly slyer, slyest

ADJECTIVE Someone who is **sly** is good at tricking people in a not very nice way.

smack smacks, smacking, smacked

VERB If a person **smacks** someone, they hit them with an open hand.

small smaller, smallest

ADJECTIVE Something that is **small** is not as large as other things of the same kind.

smart smarter, smartest

ADJECTIVE Someone who is **smart** looks neat and clean.

smash smashes, smashing, smashed

VERB **1** If something **smashes**, it falls and hits the ground. It makes a loud noise and breaks into lots of pieces. *The cup **smashed** when she dropped it.*

VERB **2** If someone or something **smashes** an object, they drop it or hit it so that it breaks into lots of pieces.

smell smells, smelling, smelled or smelt

VERB **1** When you **smell** something, you notice it with your nose.

VERB **2** If something **smells** nice or nasty, people's noses tell them about it.

NOUN **3** Your sense of **smell** is your ability to smell things.

smile smiles, smiling, smiled

VERB When you **smile**, the corners of your mouth move upwards and you look happy.

smoke smokes, smoking, smoked

NOUN **1** **Smoke** is a mixture of gas and small particles sent into the air when something burns.

VERB **2** If something is **smoking**, smoke is coming from it.

smooth smoother, smoothest

ADJECTIVE **1** Something which is **smooth** has no roughness, lumps or holes in it.

ADJECTIVE **2** A **smooth** ride is one that is comfortable because there are no bumps.

smother smothers, smothering, smothered

VERB **1** If someone **smothers** a fire, they cover it with something in order to put it out.

VERB **2** If a lot of things **smother** something, they cover it all over. *The grass was **smothered** in daisies.*

smudge smudges, smudging, smudged

NOUN **1** A **smudge** is a dirty mark left on something.

VERB **2** If you **smudge** something, you make it dirty by touching it.

smug smugger, smuggest

ADJECTIVE Someone who is **smug** is too pleased with how good or clever they are.

smuggle smuggles, smuggling, smuggled

VERB To **smuggle** things or people into or out of a place means to take them there secretly, or against the law.

snack snacks

NOUN A **snack** is a small amount of food that you eat quickly. *I had an apple and some crisps for a **snack**.*

a b c d e f g h i j k l m n o p q r **Ss** t u v w x y z

snag snags

NOUN A **snag** is a small problem.

snail snails

NOUN A **snail** is a small slow-moving animal with a shell on its back.

snake snakes

NOUN A **snake** is a long thin reptile with scales on its skin and no legs.
See *Reptiles* on page 259.

snap snaps, snapping, snapped

VERB **1** If something **snaps**, it breaks suddenly with a sharp cracking noise.
VERB **2** If a dog **snaps** at you, it tries to bite you.
VERB **3** If someone **snaps** at you, they speak crossly.
NOUN **4** **Snap** is a children's card game.

snarl snarls, snarling, snarled

VERB When an animal **snarls**, it makes a fierce sound in its throat while showing its teeth.

snatch snatches, snatching, snatched

VERB If you **snatch** something, you take it quickly and suddenly.

sneak sneaks, sneaking, sneaked

VERB If you **sneak** somewhere, you go there very quietly, being careful that other people do not see or hear you.

sneer sneers, sneering, sneered

VERB If a person **sneers** at something, they show that they don't like it much.

sneeze sneezes, sneezing, sneezed

VERB When you **sneeze**, you blow out suddenly through your nose, making a loud noise.

sniff sniffs, sniffing, sniffed

VERB If you **sniff**, you breathe in through your nose hard enough to make a sound.

snooze snoozes, snoozing, snoozed

VERB If you **snooze**, you sleep lightly for a short time, especially during the day.

snore snores, snoring, snored

VERB When people **snore**, they breathe very noisily while they are sleeping.

snorkel snorkels

NOUN A **snorkel** is a tube that you breathe through when your face is just under the surface of the sea.

snow snows, snowing, snowed

NOUN **1** **Snow** is flakes of ice crystals which fall from the sky in cold weather.
VERB **2** When it **snows**, snow falls from the sky.

snowball snowballs

NOUN A **snowball** is a ball of snow for throwing.

snowflake snowflakes

NOUN A **snowflake** is a soft piece of falling snow.

snowman snowmen

NOUN A **snowman** is a pile of snow that is made to look like a person.

snug snugger, snuggest

ADJECTIVE If you feel **snug**, you are warm and comfortable.

snuggle snuggles, snuggling, snuggled

VERB If you **snuggle** somewhere, you cuddle up to something or someone.

soak soaks, soaking, soaked

VERB **1** When liquid **soaks** something, it makes it very wet.
VERB **2** When something **soaks** up a liquid, the liquid is drawn up into it.

soap soaps

NOUN **Soap** is a substance made of natural oils and fats, used for washing yourself.

soar soars, soaring, soared

VERB If something soars into the air, it goes quickly up into it.

sob sobs, sobbing, sobbed

VERB When someone **sobs**, they cry in a noisy way, breathing in short breaths.

soccer

NOUN **Soccer** is another word for the game of football.

society societies

NOUN **1** Society is people in general.
NOUN **2** A **society** is an organization for people who have the same interests.

sock socks

NOUN A **sock** is a soft piece of clothing which covers your foot and ankle.

socket sockets

NOUN A **socket** is a place on a wall or on a piece of electrical equipment into which you can put a plug or bulb.

sofa sofas

NOUN A **sofa** is a long comfortable seat for more than one person. Sofas have a back, and usually arms.

soft softer, softest

ADJECTIVE **1** Something that is **soft** changes shape easily when you touch it.
ADJECTIVE **2** A **soft** sound or voice is quiet and gentle.
ADJECTIVE **3** A **soft** light or colour is not too bright.

software

NOUN **Software** is computer programs.

soggy soggier, soggiest

ADJECTIVE Something that is **soggy** is wet and often heavy.

soil

NOUN **Soil** is the top layer of earth, which plants can grow in.

solar

ADJECTIVE **1** Solar is used to describe something that is to do with the sun.
ADJECTIVE **2** Solar power uses the sun's energy to provide light and heat.

sold

VERB **Sold** is the past tense of **sell**.

soldier soldiers

NOUN A **soldier** is a person in an army.

sole soles

NOUN **1** The **sole** of your foot, shoe or sock is the underneath surface of it.

NOUN **2** A **sole** is also a flat sea fish.

solemn

ADJECTIVE Someone or something that is **solemn** is serious, rather than cheerful.

solid

ADJECTIVE **1** Something that is **solid** is firm and always keeps its shape. Metal, wood and rock are all solid.
ADJECTIVE **2** Something **solid** is not hollow.
ADJECTIVE **3** A **solid** shape is a three-dimensional shape such as a cylinder or a cone.
See *Solid shapes* on page 271.

solution solutions

NOUN **1** A **solution** is the answer to a problem.
NOUN **2** A **solution** can also be a liquid in which something, like a powder, has been dissolved.

a
b
c
d
e
f
g
h
i
j
k
l
m
n
o
p
q
r
Ss
t
u
v
w
x
y
z

solve

solve solves, solving, solved
VERB If you **solve** a problem, you find an answer to it.

some
ADJECTIVE You use **some** to talk about an amount when you are not saying how much there is. *There's **some** money on the table.*

somebody
PRONOUN You use **somebody** to talk about a person without saying exactly who you mean.

somehow
ADVERB You use **somehow** to talk about a way of doing something when you do not know exactly how.

someone
PRONOUN You use **someone** to talk about a person without saying exactly who you mean.

somersault somersaults
NOUN A **somersault** is a forwards or backwards roll in which you place your head on the ground and bring your body over it.

something
PRONOUN You use **something** to talk about a thing without saying exactly what you mean. *We need **something** to hold the door open.*

sometimes
ADVERB **Sometimes** means occasionally, rather than always or never.

somewhere
ADVERB 1 **Somewhere** is used to talk about a place without saying exactly where it is. *It must be around **somewhere**.*
ADVERB 2 **Somewhere** can be used to give an approximate amount, number or time. *It was **somewhere** between 11 o'clock and midnight.*

son sons
NOUN A boy is the **son** of his parents.

song songs
NOUN A **song** is a piece of music with words.

soon sooner, soonest
ADVERB **Soon** means in the near future.

soot
NOUN **Soot** is a black powder that comes from burning coal or wood.

sore sorer, sorest
ADJECTIVE If part of your body is **sore**, it hurts. *Her throat was so **sore** she couldn't talk.*

sorrow sorrows
NOUN **Sorrow** is feeling very sad.

sorry sorrier, sorriest
ADJECTIVE 1 If you feel **sorry** about something, you feel disappointed or sad. *I was **sorry** to leave all my friends.*
ADJECTIVE 2 If you feel **sorry** for someone, you feel sad for them.

sort sorts, sorting, sorted
NOUN 1 The different **sorts** of something are the different types of it.
VERB 2 If you **sort** things, you put them into groups. *Sort your socks into pairs.*
all sorts PHRASE **All sorts** of things means lots of different things.

sought
VERB **Sought** is the past tense of **seek**.

sound sounds
NOUN A **sound** is something that you hear.

soup soups
NOUN **Soup** is liquid food made by boiling meat, fish or vegetables in water.

sour sourer, sourest
ADJECTIVE 1 Something that is **sour** tastes sharp.
ADJECTIVE 2 **Sour** milk is no longer fresh.

a b c d e f g h i j k l m n o p q r **Ss** t u v w x y z

source sources

NOUN **1** The **source** of something is the place that it has come from.

NOUN **2** The **source** of a river or stream is the place where it begins.

south

NOUN **South** is one of the four main points of the compass. If you face the point where the sun rises, south is on your right. See **compass point**.
southern ADJECTIVE

south-east

NOUN **South-east** is halfway between south and east.

south-west

NOUN **South-west** is halfway between south and west.

souvenir souvenirs

NOUN A **souvenir** is something you keep to remind you of a person or place.

sow sows, sowing, sowed

(*rhymes with* **no**) VERB **1** To **sow** seeds means to plant them in the ground. (*rhymes with* **now**) NOUN **2** A **sow** is an adult female pig.

space spaces

NOUN **1** Space is the area that is empty in a place, building or container. *There's enough* **space** *for a bigger chair in my room.*

NOUN **2** Space is also the place far above the Earth where there is no air.

spaceship spaceships

NOUN A **spaceship** is a vehicle that carries people through space.

spacesuit spacesuits

NOUN A **spacesuit** is a special suit that is worn by an astronaut, which covers the whole body.

spade spades

NOUN A **spade** is a tool for digging, with a flat metal blade and a long handle.

spaghetti

NOUN Spaghetti is long thin pieces of pasta.

span spans

NOUN The **span** of something is the total length of it from end to end. For example, when a bird stretches its wings, the distance from wing tip to wing tip is called its "wing span".

spanner spanners

NOUN A **spanner** is a tool with a specially shaped end that fits round a nut to turn it.

spare spares, sparing, spared

ADJECTIVE **1** Something that is **spare** is extra to what is needed. *Do you have a* **spare** *pencil you can lend me?*

VERB **2** If you **spare** something, you make it available. *Can you* **spare** *me some time?*

spark sparks

NOUN A **spark** is a tiny piece of fire. It can fly up from something burning, or it can be caused by electricity.

sparkle sparkles, sparkling, sparkled

VERB If something **sparkles**, it shines with a lot of small bright points of light.

sparrow sparrows

NOUN A **sparrow** is a small bird with brown and grey feathers.

spawn

NOUN Spawn is a jelly-like substance containing the eggs of fish or amphibians.

speak speaks, speaking, spoke, spoken

VERB **1** When you **speak**, you use your voice to say words.

VERB **2** If you **speak** a foreign language, you know it and can use it.

spear spears, spearing, speared
NOUN **1** A **spear** is a weapon consisting of a long pole with a sharp point.
VERB **2** To **spear** something means to push or throw a pointed object into it. *He speared a potato with his fork.*

special
ADJECTIVE **1** Something that is **special** is more important or better than other things of its kind.
ADJECTIVE **2** **Special** can also mean that something is for a particular use. *You need a special tool for this job.*

speck specks
NOUN A **speck** is a tiny piece of something. *There wasn't a speck of dust anywhere.*

spectator spectators
NOUN A **spectator** is a person who is watching something.

speech speeches
NOUN **1** **Speech** is the ability to speak or the act of speaking.
NOUN **2** A **speech** is a formal talk given to an audience.
NOUN **3** In a play, a **speech** is a group of lines spoken by one of the characters.

speech bubble speech bubbles
NOUN A **speech bubble** is drawn to show what someone is saying in a picture. There is a line round the words, with a little tail near the mouth of the speaker.

This is a speech bubble!

speechless
ADJECTIVE If you are **speechless**, you cannot speak for a short time, usually because something has amazed you.

speech marks
PLURAL NOUN **Speech marks** are punctuation marks (" ") or (' ') used in writing to show where speech begins and ends.
See **Punctuation** on page 264.

speed speeds, speeding, sped or speeded
NOUN **1** The **speed** of something is how fast it moves.
VERB **2** Someone who is **speeding** is moving very fast, or too fast.

spell spells, spelling, spelt or spelled
VERB **1** When you **spell** a word, you name or write its letters in order.
NOUN **2** A **spell** is a short time. *We're in for a spell of bad weather.*
NOUN **3** A **spell** is also the words used to perform magic.

spelling
NOUN The **spelling** of a word is the correct order of letters in it.

spend spends, spending, spent
VERB **1** When you **spend** money, you buy things with it.
VERB **2** To **spend** time or energy means to use it.

sphere
NOUN A **sphere** is an object or shape that is like a ball.
spherical ADJECTIVE
See **Solid shapes** on page 271.

spice spices
NOUN A **spice** is the powder or seeds from a particular plant which people put in food to give it flavour.
spicy ADJECTIVE

spider spiders
NOUN A **spider** is a small animal with eight legs. Some spiders make webs that they use to catch insects for food.

spike spikes
NOUN A **spike** is a long piece of metal with a sharp point at one end.

spill **spills, spilling, spilled** or **spilt**
VERB If you **spill** a liquid, you let it flow out of a container by mistake.

spin **spins, spinning, spun**
VERB **1** If something **spins**, it turns round and round quickly.
VERB **2** When someone **spins**, they make thread by twisting together pieces of fibre using a machine.
VERB **3** When spiders **spin**, they give out a sticky thread and make it into a web.

spinach
NOUN **Spinach** is a vegetable with large green leaves.
See *Vegetables* on page 256.

spine **spines**
NOUN **1** Your **spine** is your backbone.
NOUN **2 Spines** are long sharp points on an animal's body or on a plant.

spiral **spirals**
NOUN A **spiral** is a continuous curve which winds round and round, with each curve above or outside the previous one.

spire **spires**
NOUN The **spire** of a church is the tall cone-shaped structure on top.

spite **spites, spiting, spited**
VERB If you do something to **spite** someone, you do it deliberately to hurt or annoy them.
in spite of PHRASE When you say that you are doing something **in spite of** something else, you mean that you are not going to let it stop you. *In spite of the rain, I'm still going out.*

spiteful
ADJECTIVE A **spiteful** person does or says nasty things to people to hurt them.
spitefully ADVERB

splash **splashes, splashing, splashed**
VERB **1** If you **splash** around in water, you disturb the water in a noisy way.

VERB **2** If liquid **splashes** something, it scatters over it in a lot of small drops.
NOUN **3** A **splash** is the sound made when something hits or falls into water.

splendid
ADJECTIVE **Splendid** means extremely good.

splinter **splinters, splintering, splintered**
NOUN **1** A **splinter** is a thin sharp piece of wood or glass which has broken off a larger piece.
VERB **2** If something **splinters**, it breaks into thin sharp pieces.

split **splits, splitting, split**
VERB **1** If something is **split**, it divides into two or more. *The village was **split** in two by the new road.*
VERB **2** If people **split** something between them, they share it.

spoil **spoils, spoiling, spoiled** or **spoilt**
VERB **1** If you **spoil** something, you damage it, or make it less good than it was.
VERB **2** To **spoil** children means to give them everything they want, so that they become selfish.

spoke **spokes**
VERB **1 Spoke** is the past tense of **speak**.
NOUN **2** The **spokes** of a wheel are the bars which connect the hub to the rim.

spoken
VERB **Spoken** is the past participle of **speak**.

sponge **sponges**
NOUN **1** A **sponge** is a soft thing with holes in it. It soaks up water and you use it for washing things.

NOUN **2** A **sponge** or **sponge cake** is a very light cake.

a
b
c
d
e
f
g
h
i
j
k
l
m
n
o
p
q
r
Ss
t
u
v
w
x
y
z

spoon

spoon spoons

NOUN A **spoon** is a tool like a small shallow bowl with a long handle. It is used for eating, mixing or serving food.

sport sports

NOUN **Sports** are games that you play which exercise your body.

spot spots, spotting, spotted

NOUN **1 Spots** are small round marks on a surface. Some fabrics have a pattern of spots.

NOUN **2** A **spot** can be a particular place. *This would be a nice spot for a picnic.*

NOUN **3** A **spot** can also be a small raised mark on a person's skin.

VERB **4** If you **spot** something, you notice it.

spotless

ADJECTIVE Something that is **spotless** is perfectly clean.

spout spouts

NOUN A **spout** is a tube with an end like a lip, for pouring liquid. *Teapots have a spout.*

sprang

VERB **Sprang** is the past tense of **spring**.

sprawl sprawls, sprawling, sprawled

VERB If you **sprawl**, you sit or lie with your legs and arms spread out.

spray sprays, spraying, sprayed

NOUN **1 Spray** is lots of small drops of liquid splashed or forced into the air.

VERB **2** To **spray** a liquid over something means to cover it with small drops of the liquid.

spread spreads, spreading, spread

VERB **1** If you **spread** something, you arrange it over a surface. *They spread their wet clothes out to dry.*

VERB **2** If you **spread** something, such as butter, you put a thin layer of it onto something.

VERB **3** If you **spread** parts of your body, such as your arms, you stretch them out until they are far apart.

spring springs, springing, sprang, sprung

NOUN **1 Spring** is the season between winter and summer.

NOUN **2** A **spring** is a coil of wire which returns to its shape after being pressed or pulled.

NOUN **3** A **spring** is also a place where water comes up through the ground.

VERB **4** To **spring** means to jump. *The leopard sprang on its prey.*

springbok springboks

NOUN A **springbok** is a small South African antelope which moves in leaps.

sprinkle sprinkles, sprinkling, sprinkled

VERB If you **sprinkle** a liquid or powder over something, you scatter it over it.

sprint sprints, sprinting, sprinted

VERB To **sprint** means to run fast over a short distance.

sprout sprouts, sprouting, sprouted

VERB **1** When something **sprouts**, it starts to grow.

NOUN **2 Sprouts** are small round green vegetables.

See *Vegetables* on page 256.

sprung

VERB **Sprung** is the past participle of **spring**.

spun

VERB **Spun** is the past tense of **spin**.

spurt spurts, spurting, spurted

VERB When a liquid or flame **spurts** out, it comes out quickly in a powerful stream. *Blood spurted from his arm.*

spy spies, spying, spied
NOUN **1** A **spy** is a person sent to find out secret information about a country or organization.
VERB **2** If you **spy** on someone, you watch them secretly.

square squares
NOUN **1** A **square** is a shape with four equal sides and four right angles.
See *Colours and flat shapes* on page 271.
NOUN **2** The **square** of a number is the number multiplied by itself. For example, the square of 3, written 3^2, is 3×3.
ADJECTIVE **3 Square** is used before units of length when talking about the area of something. *The room measures 25 square metres.*

squash squashes, squashing, squashed
VERB **1** If you **squash** something, you press it so that it loses its shape.
NOUN **2** If there is a **squash** in a place, there are a lot of people pressed against each other.
NOUN **3 Squash** is a drink made from fruit juice, sugar, and water.

squat squats, squatting, squatted
VERB If you **squat**, you crouch down, balancing on your feet with your legs bent.

squawk squawks, squawking, squawked
VERB When a bird **squawks**, it makes a loud harsh noise.

squeak squeaks, squeaking, squeaked
VERB If something **squeaks**, it makes a short high-pitched sound.

squeal squeals, squealing, squealed
VERB When things or people **squeal**, they make a long high-pitched sound.

squeeze squeezes, squeezing, squeezed
VERB **1** When you **squeeze** something, you press it firmly from two sides.

VERB **2** When you **squeeze** something into a small amount of time or space, you manage to fit it in.

squirrel squirrels
NOUN A **squirrel** is a small furry animal with a long bushy tail.

squirt squirts, squirting, squirted
VERB If a liquid **squirts**, it comes out of a narrow opening in a thin fast stream.

stable stables
NOUN A **stable** is a building in which horses are kept.

stack stacks, stacking, stacked
NOUN **1** A **stack** of things is a pile of them, one on top of the other.
VERB **2** If you **stack** things, you arrange them one on top of the other in a pile.

stadium stadiums
NOUN A **stadium** is a large place where you go to watch games.

staff
NOUN The **staff** of an organization are the people who work for it.

stag stags
NOUN A **stag** is an adult male deer.

stage stages
NOUN **1** A **stage** is a part of a process that lasts for a period of time. *The final stage is really difficult.*
NOUN **2** In a theatre, the **stage** is a raised platform where the actors perform.

stagger staggers, staggering, staggered
VERB **1** If someone **staggers**, they walk unsteadily.
VERB **2** If something **staggers** you, it amazes you.

a b c d e f g h i j k l m n o p q r **Ss** t u v w x y z

stain

stain stains

NOUN A **stain** is a mark on something that is difficult to remove.

stair stairs

NOUN A **stair** is one of a set of steps in a building going from one floor to another.

staircase staircases

NOUN A **staircase** is a set of stairs.

stake stakes

NOUN A **stake** is a pointed wooden post that can be hammered into the ground and used as a support.

stale staler, stalest

ADJECTIVE **Stale** food or air is not fresh.

stalk stalks, stalking, stalked

NOUN 1 A **stalk** is the main stem of a plant.

VERB 2 To **stalk** a person or animal means to follow them slowly and quietly.

stall stalls

NOUN 1 A **stall** is a large table on which there are goods for sale.

PLURAL NOUN 2 In a theatre, the **stalls** are the seats at the lowest level, in front of the stage.

stallion stallions

NOUN A **stallion** is an adult male horse.

stammer stammers, stammering, stammered

VERB When someone **stammers**, they hesitate and repeat some sounds when they speak.

stamp stamps, stamping, stamped

NOUN 1 A **stamp** is a small piece of gummed paper which you stick on a letter or parcel before posting it.

VERB 2 If you **stamp**, you lift your foot and put it down hard on the ground.

stand stands, standing, stood

VERB 1 When you **stand**, your body is upright and you are on your feet.

VERB 2 If a letter **stands for** a particular word, it is an abbreviation of that word. *So you're J Smith. What does J **stand for?***

VERB 3 If you cannot **stand** something, you cannot bear it. *I can't **stand** that boy.*

standard standards

NOUN 1 A **standard** is how good something is. *This is not up to your usual **standard**.*

ADJECTIVE 2 Something which is **standard** is usual, and not special or extra. *Power steering is now a **standard** feature on this car.*

stank

VERB **Stank** is the past tense of **stink**.

star stars, starring, starred

NOUN 1 A **star** is a large ball of burning gas in space that appears as a point of light in the sky at night.

NOUN 2 A **star** is also a shape with four, five or more points sticking out in a regular pattern.

See Colours and flat shapes on page 271.

NOUN 3 A **star** is also a famous person in entertainment or sport.

VERB 4 If an actor or actress **stars** in a film, they have one of the most important parts in it.

starch

NOUN **Starch** is a substance that gives you energy. It is found in foods such as bread and potatoes.

stare stares, staring, stared

VERB If you **stare** at something, you look at it for a long time.

starfish starfishes or starfish

NOUN A **starfish** is a flat, star-shaped sea animal with five limbs.

starling starlings
NOUN A **starling** is a common European bird with shiny dark feathers.

start starts, starting, started
VERB **1** To **start** means to begin.
VERB **2** If someone **starts** a machine or car, they use the controls to make it work.

startle startles, startling, startled
VERB If something **startles** you, it frightens you by making a sudden movement or noise.

starve starves, starving, starved
VERB When people or animals **starve**, they suffer a great deal from lack of food and sometimes die.

state states, stating, stated
NOUN **1** The **state** of someone or something is how they are. *Have you seen the state of the garden?*
NOUN **2** A **state** is a country, or a part of a country making some of its own laws.
VERB **3** If you **state** something, you say it clearly and formally.
in a state PHRASE If you are **in a state**, you are nervous or upset.

statement statements
NOUN A **statement** is something you say or write when you give facts or information in a formal way.

station stations
NOUN **1** A **station** is a building where trains or buses stop for passengers.
NOUN **2** A **station** is also a building for people such as the police or fire brigade.

stationary
ADJECTIVE If something like a vehicle is **stationary**, it is not moving.

stationery
NOUN **Stationery** is paper, pens, envelopes and other equipment used for writing.

statue statues
NOUN A **statue** is a large sculpture of a person or animal.

stay stays, staying, stayed
VERB **1** If you **stay** in a place, you do not move away from it.
VERB **2** If you **stay** with someone, you live in their house for a while.

steady steadier, steadiest
ADJECTIVE **1** If something such as a ladder is **steady**, it is firm and does not shake or move about.
ADJECTIVE **2** A **steady** look or voice is calm and controlled.
steadily ADVERB

steak steaks
NOUN A **steak** is a thick slice of meat or fish.

steal steals, stealing, stole, stolen
VERB To **steal** means to take something which does not belong to you, and keep it.

steam
NOUN **Steam** is the hot vapour formed when water boils.

steel
NOUN **Steel** is a strong metal made mostly from iron.

steep steeper, steepest
ADJECTIVE Something such as a road or hill that is **steep** slopes sharply.

steeple steeples
NOUN A **steeple** is a church tower with a high pointed top.

steer steers, steering, steered
VERB When someone **steers** something like a car or cycle, they make it go in the direction they want.

stem **stems**

NOUN The **stem** of a plant is the long thin centre part.

stencil **stencils**

NOUN A **stencil** is a thin sheet with a cut-out pattern. Ink or paint passes through the stencil to form a pattern on the surface below.

step **steps**

NOUN **1** A **step** is the movement you make when you lift your foot and put it down in a different place.

NOUN **2** A **step** is also a raised flat surface which you use to move from one level to another.

stereo **stereos**

NOUN A **stereo** is a machine that plays sound from tapes or CDs, with the sound coming through two speakers.

stern **sterner, sternest**

ADJECTIVE Someone who is **stern** is serious and expects to be obeyed.

stew **stews**

NOUN A **stew** is a meal which you make by cooking meat, fish or vegetables slowly for a long time.

stick **sticks, sticking, stuck**

NOUN **1** A **stick** is a long thin piece of wood.

VERB **2** If you **stick** a pointed object, such as a drawing pin, into something, you push it in.

VERB **3** If you **stick** two things together, you fix them with something like glue.

VERB **4** If something like a drawer **sticks**, it cannot be moved.

sticker **stickers**

NOUN A **sticker** is a small piece of paper that you can stick on to a surface. It has writing or a picture on one side.

sticky **stickier, stickiest**

ADJECTIVE Something that is **sticky**, like jam or glue, can stick to other things.

stiff **stiffer, stiffest**

ADJECTIVE **1** Something that is **stiff** is quite hard or firm. *Use a stiff broom to sweep up the leaves.*

ADJECTIVE **2** If a person is **stiff**, their muscles or joints hurt when they move.

stile **stiles**

NOUN A **stile** is a kind of fixed gate with a step on each side. It is made so that people can get into a field without letting animals out.

still **stiller, stillest**

ADVERB **1** You say **still** when something is the same as it was before. *I've still got a headache.*

ADVERB OR ADJECTIVE **2** Still means staying in the same position without moving. *He wouldn't sit still.*

stilt **stilts**

NOUN **Stilts** are two long pieces of wood or metal on which people walk.

sting **stings, stinging, stung**

VERB If a creature or plant **stings** you, it pricks your skin and hurts you.

stink **stinks, stinking, stank, stunk**

VERB Something that **stinks** smells bad.

stir **stirs, stirring, stirred**

VERB If you **stir** a liquid, you move it around with a spoon or a stick.

stitch **stitches, stitching, stitched**

VERB If you **stitch** fabric, you push a needle and thread in and out through it.

stocking **stockings**

NOUN **Stockings** are long pieces of thin clothing that cover a woman's legs and feet.

stole

VERB **Stole** is the past tense of **steal**.

stolen

VERB **1 Stolen** is the past participle of **steal**.

ADJECTIVE **2** If something is **stolen**, it has been taken away from its owner. *The police found the **stolen** bike.*

stomach **stomachs**

NOUN Your **stomach** is the part of your body that holds food when you have eaten it.

stone **stones**

NOUN **1 Stone** is a hard dry material that is dug out of the ground. It is often used for building houses and walls.

NOUN **2** A **stone** is a small piece of rock.

NOUN **3** The **stone** in a fruit such as a plum is the large seed in the centre.

NOUN **4** A **stone** is a unit of weight equal to just over six kilograms.

stony **stonier, stoniest**

ADJECTIVE **Stony** ground is rough and contains a lot of stones.

stood

VERB **Stood** is the past tense of **stand**.

stool **stools**

NOUN A **stool** is a seat with legs but no back.

stoop **stoops, stooping, stooped**

VERB If you **stoop**, you bend your body down from the waist, usually so that you can pick something up.

stop **stops, stopping, stopped**

VERB **1** If you **stop** what you are doing, you no longer do it.

VERB **2** If you **stop** somewhere, you stay there for a short while.

store **stores, storing, stored**

VERB **1** When you **store** things, you put them away and keep them until they are wanted.

NOUN **2** A **store** is a large shop.

storey **storeys**

NOUN A **storey** is all the rooms on one floor of a building.

stork **storks**

NOUN A **stork** is a large bird with a long beak and long legs.

storm **storms**

NOUN A **storm** is bad weather with heavy rain and strong winds. Often there is thunder and lightning.
stormy ADJECTIVE

story **stories**

NOUN A **story** tells you about things that have happened. It can be about something real or something made up.

stout **stouter, stoutest**

ADJECTIVE **1** Someone **stout** is rather fat.

ADJECTIVE **2** Things such as branches that are **stout** are thick and strong.

stove **stoves**

NOUN A **stove** is a piece of equipment for heating a room or for cooking.

straight **straighter, straightest**

ADJECTIVE **1** Something which is **straight** does not bend or curve. You use a ruler to draw a straight line.

ADVERB **2 Straight** can mean immediately and directly. *We promised to go **straight** to school.*

straighten **straightens, straightening, straightened**

VERB If you **straighten** something, you make it straight, or neat and tidy.

strain **strains, straining, strained**

VERB **1** If you **strain** to do something, you try too hard.

VERB **2** To **strain** food means to pour away the liquid from it.

VERB **3** If you **strain** a muscle, you injure it by moving awkwardly.

a
b
c
d
e
f
g
h
i
j
k
l
m
n
o
p
q
r
Ss
t
u
v
w
x
y
z

strange

strange stranger, strangest
ADJECTIVE **1** Something that is **strange** is odd or unexpected.
ADJECTIVE **2** A **strange** place is one you have never been to before.

stranger strangers
NOUN A **stranger** is a person you do not know.

strap straps
NOUN A **strap** is a strip of something like leather which is used to carry something around, or to fasten things together.

straw straws
NOUN **1** Straw is dried stalks of cereal such as wheat.
NOUN **2** A **straw** is a thin tube of paper or plastic, which you drink through.

strawberry strawberries
NOUN A **strawberry** is a small red fruit. It is soft and juicy and has tiny yellow seeds on its skin.
See *Fruit* on page 257.

stray strays, straying, strayed
VERB **1** If people or animals **stray**, they wander away from where they are supposed to be.
ADJECTIVE **2** A **stray** dog or cat is one that has wandered away from home.

stream streams
NOUN **1** A **stream** is a small river.
NOUN **2** A **stream** is also a steady flow of something like liquid or traffic.

street streets
NOUN A **street** is a road in a town or village, usually with buildings along it.

strength
NOUN **Strength** is how strong something is.

stretch stretches, stretching, stretched
VERB **1** If you **stretch**, you hold out part of your body as far as you can.
VERB **2** If you **stretch** something, you pull it so that it becomes longer or wider.
NOUN **3** A **stretch** of land or water is an area of it.

strict stricter, strictest
ADJECTIVE **1** Someone who is **strict** makes you behave well.
ADJECTIVE **2** A **strict** rule or law is one that must be obeyed.

stride strides, striding, strode
VERB **1** To **stride** along means to walk quickly with long steps.
NOUN **2** A **stride** is a long step.

strike strikes, striking, struck
VERB **1** To **strike** someone or something means to hit them.
VERB **2** When a clock **strikes**, it rings a bell to show what the time is.
VERB **3** If someone **strikes** a match, they make a flame or sparks with it.
NOUN **4** A **strike** is when workers refuse to go on working.

string strings
NOUN **1** String is thin rope.
NOUN **2** On a musical instrument like a guitar, the **strings** are the parts that you touch to make the sounds.

strip strips, stripping, stripped
NOUN **1** A **strip** of paper, cloth or other material is a long narrow piece of it.
VERB **2** If you **strip**, you take off all your clothes.

stripe stripes
NOUN A **stripe** is a coloured line on something.

strode
VERB **Strode** is the past tense of **stride**.

stroke strokes, stroking, stroked
VERB If you **stroke** something, you move your hand gently over it.

stroll strolls, strolling, strolled
VERB To **stroll** means to walk along slowly in a relaxed way.

strong stronger, strongest

ADJECTIVE **1** If you are **strong**, you can work hard and carry heavy things.

ADJECTIVE **2** Objects or materials that are **strong** will not break easily.

ADJECTIVE **3** Wind or water currents that are **strong** move very fast.

ADJECTIVE **4** Smells and flavours that are **strong** are easily noticed.

struck

VERB **Struck** is the past tense of **strike**.

structure structures

NOUN A **structure** is something that has been built.

struggle struggles, struggling, struggled

VERB **1** If you **struggle** to do something, you try hard to do it but find it difficult.

VERB **2** If you **struggle** when you are being held by something or someone, you twist and kick to try and get free.

stubborn

ADJECTIVE Someone who is **stubborn** is determined to do what they want.

stuck

VERB **1** **Stuck** is the past tense of **stick**.

ADJECTIVE **2** If you are **stuck**, you cannot carry on because it is too difficult.

student students

NOUN A **student** is a person who is studying at a university or college.

studio studios

NOUN **1** A **studio** is a room where a photographer or artist works.

NOUN **2** A **studio** is also a place where films, television programmes or other recordings are made.

study studies, studying, studied

VERB **1** If you **study** a subject, you spend time learning about it.

VERB **2** If you **study** something, you look at it carefully.

NOUN **3** A **study** is a room for writing and studying.

stuff stuffs, stuffing, stuffed

NOUN **1** You can talk about a substance or group of things as **stuff**.

VERB **2** If you **stuff** something with objects, you fill it with them.

stuffy stuffier, stuffiest

ADJECTIVE If it is **stuffy** in a room, there is not enough fresh air in it.

stumble stumbles, stumbling, stumbled

VERB If you **stumble** when you are walking, you trip and almost fall.

stump stumps

NOUN A **stump** is the small part of something, such as a tree, that remains when most of it has been removed.

stun stuns, stunning, stunned

VERB **1** If you are **stunned** by something, you are very surprised by it.

VERB **2** To **stun** a person or animal means to knock them unconscious by hitting them on the head.

stung

VERB **Stung** is the past tense of **sting**.

stunk

VERB **Stunk** is the past participle of **stink**.

stupid stupider, stupidest

ADJECTIVE Someone who is **stupid** does things that are not at all sensible.

stupidly ADVERB

sturdy sturdier, sturdiest

ADJECTIVE Someone or something that is **sturdy** is strong and firm.

a
b
c
d
e
f
g
h
i
j
k
l
m
n
o
p
q
r
Ss
t
u
v
w
x
y
z

stutter stutters

NOUN Someone who has a **stutter** finds it difficult to speak smoothly and often repeats sounds.

sty sties

NOUN A **sty** is a hut with a yard where pigs are kept.

style styles

NOUN The **style** of something is its design. *I'd like shoes in a different **style**.*

sub-

PREFIX **Sub-** is used at the beginning of words that have "under" as part of their meaning, for example "submarine" (meaning underwater).
See *Prefixes* on page 264.

subheading subheadings

NOUN A **subheading** is a heading which is less important than the main heading. *We'll have "animals" as a main heading, and "mammals" as a **subheading**.*

subject subjects

NOUN **1** A **subject** is a particular thing that people study at school or college, for example science or drawing.
NOUN **2** The **subject** of a piece of writing or a conversation is the thing or person being talked about.
NOUN **3** In grammar, the **subject** is the word or words representing a person or thing doing the action. For example, in the sentence "My cat caught a bird", "my cat" is the subject.

submarine submarines

NOUN A **submarine** is a ship that can travel under water.

substance substances

NOUN Any solid, powder, liquid or paste can be called a **substance**.

subtract subtracts, subtracting, subtracted

VERB If you **subtract** one number from another, you take away the first number from the second. The symbol you use for subtract is –.

subtraction

NOUN **Subtraction** is taking one number away from another.

suburb suburbs

NOUN A **suburb** is an area of a town or city that is away from its centre.

subway subways

NOUN A **subway** is a footpath that goes underneath a road.

succeed succeeds, succeeding, succeeded

VERB If you **succeed**, you manage to do what you set out to do.

success

NOUN **Success** is managing to do something that you set out to do.

successful

ADJECTIVE If you are **successful**, you achieve what you wanted to achieve.

such

ADVERB You can use **such** to emphasize something. *She's **such** a nice girl.*
such as PHRASE You can use **such as** to introduce examples of something. *I like team games **such as** football and rounders.*

suck sucks, sucking, sucked

VERB If you **suck** something, you hold it in your mouth and pull at it with your cheeks and tongue, usually to get liquid out of it.

sudden
ADJECTIVE Something that is **sudden** happens quickly and unexpectedly.
suddenly ADVERB

suffer suffers, suffering, suffered
VERB If someone is **suffering**, they feel pain or sadness.

suffix suffixes
NOUN A **suffix** is a group of letters which is added to the end of a word to form a new word, for example "-able" or "-ful".
See *Suffixes on page 265.*

sugar
NOUN **Sugar** is a sweet substance used to sweeten food and drinks.

suggest suggests, suggesting, suggested
VERB If you **suggest** something to someone, you give a plan or an idea for them to think about.
suggestion NOUN

suit suits, suiting, suited
NOUN **1** A **suit** is a matching jacket and trousers or skirt.

VERB **2** If something **suits** you, it is right for you.

suitable
ADJECTIVE Something that is **suitable** for a particular purpose is right for it. *Are these shoes **suitable** for running?*

suitcase suitcases
NOUN A **suitcase** is a case that you carry clothes in when you are travelling.

sulk sulks, sulking, sulked
VERB If you **sulk**, you are silent and bad-tempered for a while because you are annoyed about something.

sultana sultanas
NOUN A **sultana** is a dried white grape.

sum sums
NOUN **1** A **sum** is an amount of money.
NOUN **2** In maths, the **sum** is the answer or total that you get when you add numbers. *The **sum** of 2 and 3 is 5.*

summarize summarizes, summarizing, summarized;
also spelt **summarise**
VERB To **summarize** something means to give a short account of its main points.

summary summaries
NOUN If you give a **summary** of something, you give the main points.

summer summers
NOUN **Summer** is the season between spring and autumn.

summit summits
NOUN The **summit** of a mountain is its top.

sun suns
NOUN The **sun** is the star that gives us heat and light.

sunburn
NOUN **Sunburn** is sore skin on someone's body when they have been in the sun for too long.

Sunday Sundays
NOUN **Sunday** is the day between Saturday and Monday.

sundial sundials
NOUN A **sundial** is an object that uses the sun to tell the time. It has a pointer that casts a shadow on a flat base marked with the hours.

sunflower

sunflower **sunflowers**
NOUN A **sunflower** is a tall plant with large yellow flowers.

sung
VERB **Sung** is the past participle of **sing**.

sunglasses
PLURAL NOUN **Sunglasses** are glasses with dark lenses that you wear to protect your eyes from the sun.

sunk
VERB **Sunk** is the past participle of **sink**.

sunlight
NOUN **Sunlight** is the bright light produced when the sun is shining.
sunlit ADJECTIVE

sunny **sunnier, sunniest**
ADJECTIVE When the weather is **sunny**, the sun is shining brightly.

sunrise **sunrises**
NOUN **Sunrise** is the time in the morning when the sun comes up.

sunset **sunsets**
NOUN **Sunset** is the time in the evening when the sun goes down.

sunshine
NOUN **Sunshine** is the bright light produced when the sun is shining.

super
ADJECTIVE **Super** means very nice or very good. *We've just seen a **super** film.*

super-
PREFIX **Super-** is added to words to describe something that is larger or better, for example "supermarket".
*See **Prefixes** on page 264.*

superlative **superlatives**
NOUN In grammar, the **superlative** is the form of an adjective which has "the most" of that adjective. For example, "fattest" is the superlative of "fat".
*See **Adjective** on page 263.*

supermarket **supermarkets**
NOUN A **supermarket** is a large shop which sells all kinds of food and things for the house.

supersonic
ADJECTIVE A **supersonic** aircraft can travel faster than the speed of sound.

superstitious
ADJECTIVE People who are **superstitious** believe in things like magic and powers that bring good or bad luck.

supper **suppers**
NOUN **Supper** is a meal or snack eaten in the evening.

supply **supplies, supplying, supplied**
VERB **1** If someone **supplies** you with something, they provide you with it.
NOUN **2** A **supply** of something is the amount of it which someone has. *The water **supply** is getting very low.*

support **supports, supporting, supported**
VERB **1** If you **support** someone, you want them to do well.
VERB **2** If something **supports** an object, it holds it up firmly.

suppose **supposes, supposing, supposed**
VERB **1** If you **suppose** that something is true, you think that it is likely to be true.
CONJUNCTION **2** You can use **suppose** or **supposing** when you are thinking about doing something. ***Supposing** we just left without saying anything, what do you think would happen?*
I suppose PHRASE You can say **I suppose** when you are not certain about something. *Yes, **I suppose** he could come.*

sure

ADJECTIVE **1** If you are **sure** something is true, you believe it is true.

ADJECTIVE **2** If something is **sure** to happen, it will definitely happen.

ADJECTIVE **3** If you are **sure** of yourself, you are very confident.

make sure PHRASE If you **make sure** of something, you check it. *Can you **make sure** we locked up properly?*

surf surfs, surfing, surfed

NOUN **1** Surf is the white foam that forms on the top of waves when they break.

VERB **2** When you **surf**, you ride towards the shore on top of a large wave while standing on a special board.

VERB **3** When you **surf** the Internet, you go from website to website.

surface surfaces

NOUN The **surface** of something is the top or outside area of it.

surgeon surgeons

NOUN A **surgeon** is a doctor who performs operations.

surgery surgeries

NOUN **1** Surgery is medical treatment in which part of the patient's body is cut open.

NOUN **2** A **surgery** is a room or building where a doctor or dentist works.

surname surnames

NOUN Your **surname** is the name you share with other members of your family.

surprise surprises

NOUN A **surprise** is something unexpected.

surrender surrenders, surrendering, surrendered

VERB If someone **surrenders**, they stop fighting and agree that they have lost.

surround surrounds, surrounding, surrounded

VERB If something **surrounds** something else, it is all round it.

surroundings

PLURAL NOUN Your **surroundings** are the area around you.

survey surveys

NOUN **1** A **survey** of something is a detailed examination of it, often in the form of a report.

VERB **2** A **survey** is also a set of questions to find out what people think about things.

survive survives, surviving, survived

VERB If someone **survives**, they continue to live after being close to death.

suspect suspects, suspecting, suspected

VERB If you **suspect** someone of doing something wrong, you think they have done it.

suspense

NOUN Suspense is excitement or worry caused by having to wait for something.

suspicious

ADJECTIVE **1** If you are **suspicious** of someone, you do not trust them.

ADJECTIVE **2** If something is **suspicious**, it makes you feel something is wrong.

swallow swallows, swallowing, swallowed

VERB **1** When you **swallow** food or drink, it goes down your throat.

NOUN **2** A **swallow** is a small bird with pointed wings and a long forked tail.

a
b
c
d
e
f
g
h
i
j
k
l
m
n
o
p
q
r
Ss
t
u
v
w
x
y
z

swam

VERB **Swam** is the past tense of **swim**.

swamp **swamps**

NOUN A **swamp** is an area of extremely wet land.

swan **swans**

NOUN A **swan** is a large white bird with a long neck that lives on rivers and lakes.

swap **swaps, swapping, swapped**

VERB If you **swap** something, you give it to someone and receive something else from them in exchange.

swarm **swarms**

NOUN A **swarm** is a large group of bees or other insects flying together.
See **Collective nouns** on page 262.

sway **sways, swaying, swayed**

VERB When people or things **sway**, they lean or swing slowly from side to side.

sweat

NOUN **Sweat** is the salty liquid which comes from your skin when you are hot.

sweater **sweaters**

NOUN A **sweater** is a knitted piece of clothing covering your upper body and arms.

sweatshirt **sweatshirts**

NOUN A **sweatshirt** is a piece of clothing made of thick cotton. It covers your upper body and arms.

sweep **sweeps, sweeping, swept**

VERB If you **sweep** a floor or a path, you clean it by pushing a broom over it.

sweet **sweeter, sweetest; sweets**

ADJECTIVE **1** Food or drink that is **sweet** has a taste of sugar.

PLURAL NOUN **2 Sweets** are things such as chocolates and toffees.

NOUN **3** A **sweet** can be something that is eaten after the main part of a meal.

sweet corn

NOUN **Sweet corn** is a long stalk covered with juicy yellow seeds that can be eaten as a vegetable.
See **Vegetables** on page 256.

swell **swells, swelling, swelled or swollen**

VERB If something **swells**, it becomes larger and rounder than usual.

swept

VERB **Swept** is the past tense of **sweep**.

swerve **swerves, swerving, swerved**

VERB If something that is moving **swerves**, it suddenly changes direction.

swift **swifter, swiftest**

ADJECTIVE Something that is **swift** can move very quickly.

swim **swims, swimming, swam, swum**

VERB When you **swim**, you use your arms and legs to move through water.

swimming

NOUN **Swimming** is the activity of moving yourself through water.

swimming costume **swimming costumes**

NOUN A **swimming costume** is the clothing worn by a woman or girl when she goes swimming.

swimming pool **swimming pools**

NOUN A **swimming pool** is a place made for people to swim in.

swimming trunks

PLURAL NOUN **Swimming trunks** are shorts worn by a man or boy when they go swimming.

swing swings, swinging, swung

VERB **1** If something **swings**, it keeps moving backwards and forwards, or from side to side, while it is hanging.
NOUN **2** A **swing** is a seat that hangs from a frame and moves backwards and forwards when you sit on it.

switch switches, switching, switched

NOUN **1** A **switch** is a small control for a piece of equipment such as a light or radio.
VERB **2** To **switch** is to change one thing for another. *I switched to another school when I moved house.*

swollen

ADJECTIVE Something that is **swollen** has swelled up.

swoop swoops, swooping, swooped

VERB When a bird **swoops**, it suddenly flies downwards in a smooth curve.

swop

Swop is another spelling of **swap**.

sword swords

NOUN A **sword** is a weapon with a long blade and a short handle.

swum

VERB **Swum** is the past participle of **swim**.

swung

VERB **Swung** is the past tense of **swing**.

sycamore sycamores

NOUN A **sycamore** is a tree that has large five-pointed leaves.

syllable syllables

NOUN Each beat in a word is a **syllable**. For example, "cat" has one syllable, and "cattle" has two.

symbol symbols

NOUN A **symbol** is a sign or mark that stands for something else. For example, the symbol + stands for "plus".

symmetrical

ADJECTIVE If something is **symmetrical**, it has two halves that are exactly the same, except that one half is like a reflection of the other half.

symmetry

NOUN **1** **Symmetry** is when one half of something is exactly like a mirror image of the other half.
NOUN **2** The **line of symmetry** is the dividing line between two symmetrical halves.

sympathy

NOUN If you feel **sympathy** for someone who is unhappy, you are sorry for them.

synagogue synagogues

NOUN A **synagogue** is a building where Jewish people pray.

synonym synonyms

NOUN **Synonyms** are words that have the same or similar meaning. The words "nice" and "pleasant" are synonyms. See *Synonyms* on page 266.

syrup

NOUN **Syrup** is a thick sweet liquid made by boiling sugar with water.

system systems

NOUN **1** A **system** is a way of doing something. *I've got a new system for organizing my toys.*
NOUN **2** You can refer to a set of equipment as a **system**, for example a central heating system.

a
b
c
d
e
f
g
h
i
j
k
l
m
n
o
p
q
r
Ss
t
u
v
w
x
y
z

Tt

table tables

NOUN **1** A **table** is a piece of furniture with a flat top for putting things on.

NOUN **2** A **table** is also a set of facts or figures arranged in rows or columns.

tablet tablets

NOUN A **tablet** is a small round pill made of powdered medicine.

table tennis

NOUN **Table tennis** is a game for two or four people. You use bats to hit a small hollow ball over a low net across a table.

tackle tackles, tackling, tackled

VERB **1** If you **tackle** a difficult task, you deal with it in a determined way.

VERB **2** If you **tackle** someone in a game such as football, you try to get the ball away from them.

tactful

ADJECTIVE A **tactful** person is careful not to hurt someone else's feelings.

tactfully ADVERB

tadpole tadpoles

NOUN **Tadpoles** are small water animals that grow into frogs or toads. They have long tails and round black heads.

tail tails

NOUN **1** A **tail** is the part of an animal, bird or fish that grows out of the end of its body.

NOUN **2** The back part of a plane is called the **tail**.

take takes, taking, took, taken

VERB **1** If you **take** something, you put your hand round it and carry it. *Let me take your coat.*

VERB **2** If someone **takes** you somewhere, you go there with them.

VERB **3** If a person **takes** something that does not belong to them, they steal it.

VERB **4** If you **take away** one number or amount from another, you find out how much is left.

talcum powder

NOUN **Talcum powder**, or **talc**, is a soft powder which you put on your skin to help dry it and make it smell nice.

tale tales

NOUN A **tale** is a story.

talent talents

NOUN **Talent** is the natural ability a person has to do something well.

talk talks, talking, talked

VERB When you **talk**, you say things to someone.

talkative

ADJECTIVE Someone who is **talkative** talks a lot.

tall taller, tallest

ADJECTIVE **1** Someone who is **tall** is higher than a lot of other people.

ADJECTIVE **2** You use **tall** to say how high somebody or something is. *My little brother is only one metre tall.*

tally tallies

NOUN A **tally** is a record of amounts which you add to as you go along.

tame tamer, tamest

ADJECTIVE A **tame** animal is not afraid of humans and will not hurt them.

tan

NOUN If someone has a **tan**, their skin has become darker than it usually is because they have been in the sun.

tangle tangles, tangling, tangled

NOUN **1** A **tangle** is a mass of things such as hairs or fibres that are knotted or coiled together and are hard to separate.
VERB **2** If something is **tangled**, it is twisted in knots.

tank tanks

NOUN **1** A **tank** is a large container for liquid or gas.
NOUN **2** A **tank** is also a vehicle for soldiers which moves on tracks. Tanks are covered with strong metal armour, and have guns or rockets.

tanker tankers

NOUN A **tanker** is a ship, truck or railway vehicle for carrying gas or liquid.

tap taps, tapping, tapped

NOUN **1** A **tap** is a handle which controls the flow of gas or liquid from a pipe.
VERB **2** If you **tap** something, you hit it lightly.

tape tapes

NOUN **1** Tape is a strip of sticky material which you use to stick things together.
NOUN **2** A **tape** is a long thin magnetic strip that you can record sounds or pictures on.

tape measure tape measures

NOUN A **tape measure** is a strip of plastic or metal that is marked in centimetres or inches. It is used to measure things.

tape recorder tape recorders

NOUN A **tape recorder** is a machine that records and plays sound on tape.

tar

NOUN Tar is a thick black substance that is used for making roads.

target targets

NOUN A **target** is something that people aim at and try to hit.

tart tarts

NOUN A **tart** is a piece of pastry filled with jam or fruit.

task tasks

NOUN A **task** is a piece of work which has to be done.

tassel tassels

NOUN A **tassel** is a tuft of loose threads tied by a knot and used for decoration.

taste tastes, tasting, tasted

NOUN **1** Your sense of **taste** is your ability to recognize the flavour of things in your mouth.
VERB **2** When you **taste** food, you take a little bit to see what it is like.

tasty tastier, tastiest

ADJECTIVE Something that is **tasty** has a pleasant flavour.

taught

VERB **Taught** is the past tense of **teach**.

tax taxes

NOUN Tax is money that people have to pay to the government.

taxi taxis

NOUN A **taxi** is a car that people pay to be driven somewhere in.

tea teas

NOUN **1** Tea is a drink made by pouring boiling water onto the dried leaves of the tea plant.
NOUN **2** Tea is also an afternoon meal.

tea bag tea bags

NOUN A **tea bag** is a small paper bag with tea leaves in it which is put in boiling water to make tea.

teach teaches, teaching, taught

VERB If someone **teaches** you something, they tell or show you how to do it.

teacher teachers

NOUN A **teacher** is a person whose job is to help people learn.

a
b
c
d
e
f
g
h
i
j
k
l
m
n
o
p
q
r
s
Tt
u
v
w
x
y
z

a
b
c
d
e
f
g
h
i
j
k
l
m
n
o
p
q
r
s

Tt

u
v
w
x
y
z

team **teams**

NOUN A **team** is a number of people working or playing together.

teapot **teapots**

NOUN A **teapot** is a container for making tea. It has a lid, a handle and a spout.

tear **tears, tearing, tore, torn**

(*rhymes with* **fear**) NOUN **1** Tears are the drops of liquid that come out of your eyes when you cry.

(*rhymes with* **fair**) VERB **2** If you **tear** something, such as paper or fabric, you pull it apart.

tease **teases, teasing, teased**

VERB If someone **teases** you, they make fun of you.

teaspoon **teaspoons**

NOUN A **teaspoon** is a small spoon used for stirring drinks.

technology

NOUN **Technology** is the practical use of science in areas such as industry, farming or medicine.

teddy bear **teddy bears**

NOUN A **teddy bear** is a child's soft toy which looks like a friendly bear.

teenager **teenagers**

NOUN A **teenager** is someone from 13 to 19 years of age.

teeth

NOUN **Teeth** is the plural of **tooth**.

telephone **telephones**

NOUN A **telephone**, or **phone**, is an instrument for talking to someone else who is in another place.

telescope **telescopes**

NOUN A **telescope** is an instrument for making objects that are far away look nearer and larger.

television **televisions**

NOUN A **television** is a machine that receives signals through the air or on cable and changes them into pictures and sounds.

tell **tells, telling, told**

VERB **1** If you **tell** someone something, you let them know about it.
VERB **2** If someone **tells** you to do something, they say you must do it.
VERB **3** If you **tell** the time, you find out what the time is by looking at a clock.

temper

NOUN **1** Someone's **temper** is how cheerful or how angry they are feeling.
NOUN **2** If you lose your **temper**, you become angry.

temperature **temperatures**

NOUN The **temperature** of something is how hot or cold it is.

temple **temples**

NOUN A **temple** is a building used for the worship of a god in various religions.

temporary

ADJECTIVE Something that is **temporary** only lasts for a short time.

tempt **tempts, tempting, tempted**

VERB If something **tempts** you, you want to do it but you think it might be wrong.
tempting ADJECTIVE

tender

ADJECTIVE **1** Someone who is **tender** shows gentle and caring feelings.
ADJECTIVE **2** Meat or other food which is **tender** is very easy to cut or chew.

tennis

NOUN **Tennis** is a game for two or four players in which a ball is hit over a net.

tense **tenser, tensest; tenses**

ADJECTIVE **1** If you are **tense**, you are nervous and cannot relax.
NOUN **2** The **tense** of a verb is the form which shows whether you are talking about the past, present or future.

tent tents

NOUN A **tent** is a shelter made of canvas or nylon, held up by poles and ropes.

tentacle tentacles

NOUN The **tentacles** of an animal, such as an octopus, are its long thin arms.

term terms

NOUN A **term** is one of the periods that each year is divided into at school.

terrace terraces

NOUN A **terrace** is a row of houses joined together.

terrible

ADJECTIVE Something **terrible** is serious and unpleasant.
terribly ADVERB

terrify terrifies, terrifying, terrified

VERB If something **terrifies** you, it makes you feel extremely frightened.

territory territories

NOUN **1** The **territory** of a country is the land that it controls.
NOUN **2** An animal's **territory** is an area that it considers its own and defends when other animals try to enter it.

terror

NOUN **Terror** is great fear or panic.

test tests, testing, tested

VERB **1** If someone **tests** something, they try to find out whether it works properly.
NOUN **2** A **test** is something you have to do to show how much you know.

tetrahedron tetrahedrons or tetrahedra

NOUN A **tetrahedron** is a solid shape with four triangular faces.
See *Solid shapes* on page 271.

text texts

NOUN **Text** is any written material.

textbook textbooks

NOUN A **textbook** is a book about a particular subject for students to use.

than

PREPOSITION OR CONJUNCTION You use **than** to link two things that you are comparing. *She's older **than** me.*

thank thanks, thanking, thanked

VERB You **thank** people when you are grateful for something they have done.

that those

ADJECTIVE **1** You use **that** or **those** to describe something which is not the nearest one. *Give me **that** book, please.*
PRONOUN **2** You can use **that** or **those** to refer to people or things which have already been mentioned. *What about going by bus? Is **that** a good idea?*

thatched

ADJECTIVE A **thatched** roof is one made of straw or reeds.

thaw thaws, thawing, thawed

VERB When something that is frozen **thaws**, it melts.

theatre theatres

NOUN A **theatre** is a building where you go to see a play or show.

their

ADJECTIVE **Their** refers to something belonging or relating to people or things that have already been mentioned. *Leave it to Sam and Joe. It's **their** problem.*

them

PRONOUN **Them** refers to people or things which have already been mentioned. *I don't want any sprouts. I don't like **them**.*

theme themes

NOUN A **theme** is the main idea in a piece of writing, painting, film or music.

themselves

PRONOUN If people do something **themselves**, no one else does it. *My parents had to educate **themselves**.*

then

ADVERB **Then** refers to a particular time in the past or future. *I left the room **then**.*

there

ADVERB **1 There** means in, at, or to that place. *He's sitting over **there**.*

PRONOUN **2 There** is used to say that something exists or does not exist. *Are **there** any more crisps?*

therefore

ADVERB **Therefore** means as a result. *It was raining, **therefore** we stayed indoors.*

thermometer **thermometers**

NOUN A **thermometer** is an instrument that measures temperature.

thesaurus **thesauruses**

NOUN A **thesaurus** is a book in which words with similar meanings are grouped together.

these

ADJECTIVE OR PRONOUN **These** is the plural of **this**.

thick **thicker, thickest**

ADJECTIVE **1** An object that is **thick** is deeper through than other things of the same kind. *I'll have a **thick** slice, please.*

ADJECTIVE **2** Something that is **thick** is made up of a lot of things growing closely together. *She has long **thick** hair.*

ADJECTIVE **3 Thick** liquids do not flow easily.

thief **thieves**

NOUN A **thief** is a person who steals something.

thigh **thighs**

NOUN Your **thighs** are the top parts of your legs above your knees.

thin **thinner, thinnest**

ADJECTIVE **1** Something that is **thin** is much narrower than it is long. *The witch's nose was long and **thin**.*

ADJECTIVE **2** A **thin** person weighs less than most people of the same height.

ADJECTIVE **3** Something such as paper or cloth that is **thin** has only a small distance between front and back.

ADJECTIVE **4 Thin** liquids are watery.

thing **things**

NOUN **1** A **thing** is an object, rather than an animal or human being.

PLURAL NOUN **2** Your **things** are your clothes or possessions.

think **thinks, thinking, thought**

VERB **1** When you **think**, you use your mind to consider ideas or problems.

VERB **2** If you say you **think** something is true, you mean you believe it is true but you are not sure.

third person

NOUN In grammar, the **third person** refers to a person, thing or group. It is expressed as "he", "she", "it", or "they".

thirsty

ADJECTIVE If you are **thirsty**, you feel that you need to drink something.

thirstily ADVERB

this **these**

ADJECTIVE **1 This** is used to refer to someone or something that is nearby. *Would you like to borrow **this** book?*

PRONOUN **2** You can use **this** to introduce someone. ***This** is Ranjit.*

thistle **thistles**

NOUN A **thistle** is a wild plant with prickly leaves and purple flowers.

thorn **thorns**

NOUN A **thorn** is one of the sharp points on the stem of a plant such as a rose.

thorough

ADJECTIVE **1** Someone who is **thorough** is always careful in their work.
ADJECTIVE **2** A **thorough** action is one that is done carefully and completely. *The doctor gave him a thorough examination.*
thoroughly ADVERB

those

ADJECTIVE OR PRONOUN **Those** is the plural of **that**.

though

CONJUNCTION **1** You say **though** before something that makes another part of the sentence rather surprising. *She didn't take a coat, though it was raining.*
CONJUNCTION **2** You can use **though** to mean if. *It looks as though you were right.*

thought thoughts

VERB **1 Thought** is the past tense of **think**.
NOUN **2** A **thought** is an idea that you have in your mind.
NOUN **3 Thought** is the action of thinking carefully about something.

thoughtful

ADJECTIVE **1** If someone is **thoughtful**, they are thinking a lot.
ADJECTIVE **2** A **thoughtful** person remembers what other people want or need, and tries to be kind to them.
thoughtfully ADVERB

thoughtless

ADJECTIVE If you are **thoughtless**, you do not think about what other people feel.

thousand

A **thousand** is the number 1000.

thread threads, threading, threaded

NOUN **1** A **thread** is a long fine piece of cotton, silk, nylon or wool.
VERB **2** When you **thread** a needle, you put thread through the hole in the top.

threat threats

NOUN A **threat** is a warning that something unpleasant may happen.

threaten threatens, threatening, threatened

VERB If someone **threatens** you, they say that something unpleasant may happen if you do not do what they want.

three-dimensional

ADJECTIVE A **three-dimensional** or **3D** object or shape is not flat. It has height or depth as well as length and width.
See *Solid shapes* on page 271.

threw

VERB **Threw** is the past tense of **throw**.

thrill thrills

NOUN A **thrill** is a sudden feeling of great excitement or pleasure.
thrilling ADJECTIVE

throat throats

NOUN **1** Your **throat** is the back of your mouth and the top part of the passages inside your neck.
NOUN **2** The front part of your neck is also called your **throat**.

throb throbs, throbbing, throbbed

VERB **1** If a part of your body **throbs**, you feel a series of strong beats or dull pains.
VERB **2** If something **throbs**, it vibrates and makes a loud rhythmic noise.

throne thrones

NOUN A **throne** is a special chair used by kings and queens on important occasions.

through

PREPOSITION **Through** means moving from one side of something to the other. *We found a path through the woods.*

throw

throw throws, throwing, threw, thrown
VERB If you **throw** an object that you are holding, you send it through the air.

thrush thrushes
NOUN A **thrush** is a songbird with a brown back and a pale spotted chest.

thrust thrusts, thrusting, thrust
VERB If you **thrust** something somewhere, you push or move it there quickly with a lot of force.

thud thuds
NOUN A **thud** is a dull sound, such as a heavy object makes when it falls onto a carpet.

thumb thumbs
NOUN Your **thumb** is the short thick finger on the side of your hand.

thump thumps, thumping, thumped
VERB If you **thump** something, you hit it hard, usually with your fist. *He shouted and thumped the table.*

thunder
NOUN **Thunder** is the loud noise that you hear after a flash of lightning in a storm.

thunderstorm thunderstorms
NOUN A **thunderstorm** is a storm with thunder, lightning and heavy rain.

Thursday Thursdays
NOUN **Thursday** is the day between Wednesday and Friday.

tick ticks
NOUN A **tick** is a sign to show that something is correct.

ticket tickets
NOUN A **ticket** is a small piece of card or paper that shows that you have paid for something such as a train ride.

tickle tickles, tickling, tickled
VERB When you **tickle** someone, you move your fingers lightly over their body to make them laugh.

tide tides
NOUN The **tide** is the regular change in the level of the sea on the shore.

tidy tidier, tidiest; tidies, tidying, tidied
ADJECTIVE **1** Something that is **tidy** is neat and well arranged.
VERB **2** When you **tidy** a room, you put things away in their proper place.
tidily ADVERB

tie ties, tying, tied
NOUN **1** A **tie** is a long narrow piece of cloth that is worn round the neck.
NOUN **2** A **tie** in a race or competition is when two people have the same result.
VERB **3** If you **tie** an object to something, you fasten it with something such as string.

tiger tigers
NOUN A **tiger** is a large wild cat that lives in Asia. Its fur is usually orange with black stripes.

tight tighter, tightest
ADJECTIVE **1** Clothes that are **tight** fit too closely to your body.
ADJECTIVE **2** Something that is **tight** is firmly fastened and difficult to move.

tights
PLURAL NOUN **Tights** are a piece of clothing made of thin material that fit closely over your hips, legs and feet.

tile tiles
NOUN A **tile** is a small thin piece of something such as slate or carpet, that is used to cover surfaces.

till tills
PREPOSITION OR CONJUNCTION **1 Till** means the same as until. *Wait till morning... Wait till I get back.*
NOUN **2** A **till** is a drawer or box in a shop or bank where money is kept.

tilt **tilts, tilting, tilted**
VERB If you **tilt** something, you make it slope.

timber
NOUN **Timber** is wood used for building, and making furniture.

time
NOUN **1** **Time** is what is measured in seconds, minutes, hours, days and years. *See Time on page 268.*
NOUN **2** If it is **time** to do something, that thing ought to be done now.

times
NOUN **1** **Times** is used after numbers to say how often something happens.
NOUN **2** In maths, **times** is used to link numbers that are multiplied together. *Four times three is twelve.*

timetable **timetables**
NOUN A **timetable** is a list of the times when things happen, or when trains and buses go.

timid
ADJECTIVE A **timid** person is not brave.

tin **tins**
NOUN **1** **Tin** is a soft silvery-white metal.
NOUN **2** A **tin** is a metal container with a lid, for storing food.

tingle **tingles, tingling, tingled**
VERB When part of your body **tingles**, you feel a slight prickling or stinging.

tinkle **tinkles, tinkling, tinkled**
VERB If something **tinkles**, it makes a sound like a small bell ringing.

tinned
ADJECTIVE **Tinned** food has been preserved by being sealed in a tin.

tin opener **tin openers**
NOUN A **tin opener** is something you use for opening tins of food.

tiny **tinier, tiniest**
ADJECTIVE Something that is **tiny** is very small.

tip **tips, tipping, tipped**
VERB **1** If you **tip** an object, you move it so that it is no longer straight. *She tipped her chair back and almost fell over.*
NOUN **2** The **tip** of something long and narrow is the end of it.

tiptoe **tiptoes, tiptoeing, tiptoed**
VERB If you **tiptoe** somewhere, you walk there very quietly on your toes.

tired
ADJECTIVE If you are **tired**, you feel that you want to rest or sleep.

tissue **tissues**
NOUN A **tissue** is a piece of soft paper that you can use as a handkerchief.

title **titles**
NOUN **1** A **title** is the name of something such as a book or film.
NOUN **2** Someone's **title** is a name such as Mr, Mrs or Sir, that goes in front of their own name.

toad **toads**
NOUN A **toad** is an amphibian. It looks like a frog but it has a drier skin and lives mostly on land. *See Amphibians on page 259.*

toadstool **toadstools**
NOUN A **toadstool** is a type of poisonous fungus.

toast
NOUN **Toast** is a slice of bread made brown and crisp by heating.

toboggan **toboggans**
NOUN A **toboggan** is a vehicle for travelling on snow. It has a flat seat, with two metal or wooden runners.

a b c d e f g h i j k l m n o p q r s **Tt** u v w x y z

today

a
b
c
d
e
f
g
h
i
j
k
l
m
n
o
p
q
r
s

Tt

u
v
w
x
y
z

today
ADVERB **Today** is the day that is happening now.

toddler toddlers
NOUN A **toddler** is a small child who has only just learned to walk.

toe toes
NOUN Your **toes** are the five parts at the end of your foot which you can move.

toffee toffees
NOUN A **toffee** is a sticky, chewy sweet made from butter and sugar.

together
ADVERB **1** If two people do something **together**, they both do it.
ADVERB **2** If two things happen **together**, they happen at the same time.

toilet toilets
NOUN **1** A **toilet** is a bowl connected to a drain and fitted with a seat. You use it to get rid of waste matter from your body.
NOUN **2** A **toilet** is also a small room containing a toilet.

told
VERB **Told** is the past tense of **tell**.

tomato tomatoes
NOUN A **tomato** is a soft, small red fruit. It can be cooked or eaten raw in salads.
See *Fruit* on page 257.

tomorrow
ADVERB **Tomorrow** is the day after today.

ton tons
NOUN A **ton** is a unit of weight equal to about 1000 kilograms.

tongue tongues
NOUN Your **tongue** is the soft, moving part inside your mouth. You use your tongue for tasting, eating and speaking.

tongue twister tongue twisters
NOUN A **tongue twister** is a sentence or expression which is difficult to say properly. For example, "She sells seashells on the seashore" is a tongue twister.

tonight
ADVERB **Tonight** is the evening of today or the night that follows today.

tonne tonnes
NOUN A **tonne** is a metric measure of weight. It is equal to 1000 kilograms.

too
ADVERB **1 Too** means also, or as well. *I was there **too**.*
ADVERB **2 Too** also means more than is needed. *I've had **too** much to eat.*

took
VERB **Took** is the past tense of **take**.

tool tools
NOUN A **tool** is anything that you use to help you do something, such as a hammer.

tooth teeth
NOUN **1** A **tooth** is one of the hard white objects in your mouth. You use your teeth for biting and chewing food.
NOUN **2** The **teeth** of a comb, saw or zip are the parts that stick out in a row.

toothbrush toothbrushes
NOUN A **toothbrush** is a small brush that you use for cleaning your teeth.

toothpaste
NOUN **Toothpaste** is a substance which you use to clean your teeth.

top tops
NOUN **1** The **top** of something is its highest point, part or surface.
NOUN **2** The **top** of a bottle, jar or tube is its cap or lid.

topic topics
NOUN A **topic** is a particular subject that you write or talk about.

torch **torches**

NOUN A **torch** is a small electric lamp which you can carry in your hand.

tore

VERB **Tore** is the past tense of **tear**.

torn

VERB **Torn** is the past participle of **tear**.

tornado **tornadoes** or **tornados**

NOUN A **tornado** is a very strong wind that moves round in a circle and can cause a lot of damage.

tortoise **tortoises**

NOUN A **tortoise** is a slow-moving reptile with a hard thick shell.
See *Reptiles* on page 259.

toss **tosses, tossing, tossed**

VERB 1 If you **toss** something, you throw it lightly and carelessly.
VERB 2 If something **tosses**, it keeps moving from side to side.

total **totals**

NOUN 1 A **total** is the number you get when you add several numbers together.
ADJECTIVE 2 **Total** means complete.
*The party was a **total** success.*

touch **touches, touching, touched**

VERB 1 If you **touch** something, you feel it with your hand.
VERB 2 If two things are **touching**, there is no space between them.

tough **tougher, toughest**

ADJECTIVE Something that is **tough** is strong and difficult to cut, tear or break.

tour **tours**

NOUN A **tour** is a journey to visit interesting places.

tourist **tourists**

NOUN A **tourist** is a person who visits places for pleasure and interest.

tournament **tournaments**

NOUN A **tournament** is a competition in which lots of matches are played, until just one person or team is left.

tow **tows, towing, towed**

VERB If a vehicle **tows** another vehicle, it pulls it along behind.

towards

PREPOSITION 1 If you move **towards** something, you go in that direction.
PREPOSITION 2 If you give money **towards** something, you help pay for it.

towel **towels**

NOUN A **towel** is a piece of soft thick cloth that you use to dry yourself with.

tower **towers**

NOUN A **tower** is a tall narrow building or a tall part of a building.

town **towns**

NOUN A **town** is a place with a lot of streets and buildings where people live and work.

toy **toys**

NOUN A **toy** is something you play with, such as a doll or a model car.

trace **traces, tracing, traced**

VERB 1 If you **trace** something such as a map, you copy it by covering it with a piece of thin paper and drawing over the lines underneath.
VERB 2 If you **trace** something, you find it after looking for it.

track **tracks**

NOUN 1 A **track** is a rough narrow road or path.
NOUN 2 A **track** is also a special road or path that is used for racing.
NOUN 3 A railway **track** is a strip of ground with rails that trains travel on.

tracksuit **tracksuits**

NOUN A **tracksuit** is a loose warm suit of trousers and a top, worn for outdoor sports.

a
b
c
d
e
f
g
h
i
j
k
l
m
n
o
p
q
r
s
Tt
u
v
w
x
y
z

tractor

tractor **tractors**

NOUN A **tractor** is a vehicle with large rear wheels. Tractors are used on farms for pulling or lifting things.

trade

NOUN **Trade** is the buying and selling of goods or services. Trade can be between people, companies or countries.

trademark **trademarks**

NOUN A **trademark** is a name or symbol that a manufacturer always uses on its products. It is usually protected by law so that nobody else can use it.

tradition **traditions**

NOUN A **tradition** is something that people have done or believed in for a long time.
traditional ADJECTIVE
traditionally ADVERB

traffic

NOUN **Traffic** is the movement of vehicles on the road, in the air or on water.

traffic light **traffic lights**

NOUN **Traffic lights** are special signals to control the flow of traffic. Red lights mean stop and green lights mean go.

traffic warden **traffic wardens**

NOUN A **traffic warden** is a person who makes sure that cars are parked correctly.

tragedy **tragedies**

NOUN 1 A **tragedy** is an event or situation that is very sad.
NOUN 2 A **tragedy** is also a serious play, that usually ends with the death of the main character.
tragic ADJECTIVE

trail **trails, trailing, trailed**

NOUN 1 A **trail** is a rough path across open country or through forests.
NOUN 2 A **trail** is also the scent, footprints and other signs that people and animals leave behind them.
VERB 3 If you **trail** something or it **trails**, it drags along behind you.

trailer **trailers**

NOUN 1 A **trailer** is a vehicle pulled by a car, used for carrying things.
NOUN 2 A **trailer** can also be a series of short pieces from a film or television programme in order to advertise it.

train **trains, training, trained**

NOUN 1 A **train** is a number of carriages or trucks which are joined together and pulled by an engine along a railway.
VERB 2 If someone **trains** you to do a job, they teach you the skills you need.
VERB 3 If you **train** a dog, you teach it to behave properly.

trainer **trainers**

NOUN 1 A **trainer** is a person who coaches people in sports such as boxing.
NOUN 2 **Trainers** are special shoes people wear for running or jogging.

tram **trams**

NOUN A **tram** is a vehicle which runs on rails along the street.

trampoline **trampolines**

NOUN A **trampoline** is something that is used for jumping on. It is made of strong cloth held into a frame by springs.

transfer **transfers, transferring, transferred**

VERB If you **transfer** something, you move it to a different place or position.

translate **translates, translating, translated**
VERB If you **translate** something, you put the words into a different language.
translation NOUN

translucent
ADJECTIVE If something is **translucent**, light passes through it so that it glows.

transparent
ADJECTIVE If something is **transparent**, it lets light through and you can see through it.

transplant **transplants**
NOUN A **transplant** is an operation to put part of one person's body into another person.

transport
NOUN **Transport** is using vehicles to move people and things from one place to another.

trap **traps, trapping, trapped**
NOUN **1** A **trap** is something that is specially made to catch animals.
VERB **2** If a person is **trapped**, they cannot escape.

trap door **trap doors**
NOUN A **trap door** is a small door in a floor or ceiling.

trapeze **trapezes**
NOUN A **trapeze** is a bar hung from a high place by ropes. People swing from trapezes in circuses.

travel **travels, travelling, travelled**
VERB If you **travel**, you go from one place to another.
traveller NOUN

tray **trays**
NOUN A **tray** is a flat object with raised edges, used for carrying food or drinks.

treacherous
ADJECTIVE **1** A person who is **treacherous** cannot be trusted.
ADJECTIVE **2** If something like the sea is **treacherous**, it is dangerous.

treacle
NOUN **Treacle** is a thick sweet sticky liquid made from sugar.

tread **treads, treading, trod, trodden**
VERB If you **tread** on something, you walk on it or step on it.

treasure **treasures**
NOUN **Treasure** is valuable things such as jewels or paintings.

treat **treats, treating, treated**
VERB **1** If you **treat** someone in a certain way, you behave that way towards them. *My uncle* **treats** *me as if I'm five.*
VERB **2** If someone **treats** a person who is ill, they help them get well again.
NOUN **3** A **treat** is something enjoyable.

tree **trees**
NOUN A **tree** is a large plant with a hard woody trunk, branches and leaves.

tremble **trembles, trembling, trembled**
VERB If you **tremble**, you shake slightly, because you are frightened or cold.

trespass **trespasses, trespassing, trespassed**
VERB To **trespass** means to go on someone else's land without asking.

trial **trials**
NOUN **1** A **trial** is when you try something out to see if it works.
NOUN **2** In law, a **trial** is a time in court. People decide whether a person is guilty of a crime.

triangle **triangles**
NOUN A **triangle** is a flat shape with three straight sides and three angles.
triangular ADJECTIVE
See **Colours and flat shapes** *on page 271.*

a b c d e f g h i j k l m n o p q r s **Tt** u v w x y z

tribe **tribes**

NOUN A **tribe** is a group of people of the same race, customs and language, who are ruled by one chief.

trick **tricks, tricking, tricked**

NOUN **1** A **trick** is a clever or skilful act that someone does to entertain people.
VERB **2** If a person **tricks** someone, they deceive them.

trickle **trickles, trickling, trickled**

VERB When a liquid **trickles**, it flows slowly in small amounts.

tricycle **tricycles**

NOUN A **tricycle** is a vehicle similar to a bicycle, but with three wheels.

tried

VERB **Tried** is the past tense of **try**.

tries

VERB **Tries** is a present tense form of **try**.

trifle **trifles**

NOUN **Trifle** is a cold pudding made of layers of sponge, fruit, jelly and custard.

trigger **triggers**

NOUN A **trigger** is a small lever on a gun, which is pulled to fire the gun.

trim **trims, trimming, trimmed**

VERB If a person **trims** something, such as a hedge or your hair, they cut off small amounts of it to make it neat.

trip **trips, tripping, tripped**

NOUN **1** A **trip** is a journey to a place and back again.
VERB **2** If you **trip**, you catch your foot on something and fall over.

triumph **triumphs**

NOUN A **triumph** is a great success.

triumphant

ADJECTIVE Someone who is **triumphant** feels extremely happy because they have been very successful.

trod

VERB **Trod** is the past tense of **tread**.

trolley **trolleys**

NOUN A **trolley** is a small cart on wheels used for carrying heavy objects.

troops

PLURAL NOUN **Troops** are soldiers.

trophy **trophies**

NOUN A **trophy** is a cup or shield given to the winner of a competition.

tropical

ADJECTIVE **Tropical** means to do with the tropics, which are the hottest part of the world, near the equator.

trot **trots, trotting, trotted**

VERB When a horse **trots**, it moves at a speed a little faster than a walk.

trouble **troubles**

NOUN **Trouble** is something that worries or bothers you.

trough **troughs**

NOUN A **trough** is a long narrow container which holds food or drink for farm animals.

trousers

PLURAL NOUN **Trousers** are a piece of clothing for the body from the waist down, with a separate part for each leg.

trout

NOUN A **trout** is a fish that lives in lakes and rivers.

trowel **trowels**

NOUN A **trowel** is a small garden tool with a curved and pointed blade used for planting or weeding.

truant **truants**

NOUN A **truant** is a child who stays away from school without permission.

truce truces

NOUN A **truce** is an agreement between two people or groups to stop fighting or quarrelling for a time.

truck trucks

NOUN **1** A **truck** is a large motor vehicle which is open at the back. Trucks are used for carrying heavy loads.

NOUN **2** A **truck** is also an open vehicle used for carrying things on a railway.

trudge trudges, trudging, trudged

VERB If you **trudge**, you walk with slow heavy steps.

true truer, truest

ADJECTIVE **1** A **true** story or statement is based on facts and is not made up.

ADJECTIVE **2** **True** feelings are sincere.

truly ADVERB

trumpet trumpets

NOUN A **trumpet** is a brass musical instrument that you blow into.

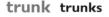

trunk trunks

NOUN **1** The **trunk** of a tree is its main stem, from which the branches grow.

NOUN **2** An elephant's **trunk** is its long flexible nose.

NOUN **3** A **trunk** is also a large box with a lid used for storing things.

trust trusts, trusting, trusted

VERB If you **trust** someone, you believe that they are honest and will not do anything to hurt you.

truth

NOUN The **truth** is the facts about something or someone, rather than things that are imagined or made up.

truthful

ADJECTIVE A **truthful** person is honest and tells the truth.

truthfully ADVERB

try tries, trying, tried

VERB **1** If you **try** to do something, you do your best to do it.

VERB **2** If you **try** something, you test it to see what it is like.

T-shirt T-shirts

NOUN A **T-shirt** is a simple short-sleeved cotton shirt with no collar.

tub tubs

NOUN A **tub** is a round container for food.

tube tubes

NOUN **1** A **tube** is a round hollow pipe.

NOUN **2** A **tube** is also a container with a cap at one end that you squeeze to get the contents out.

tuck tucks, tucking, tucked

VERB If you **tuck** something, you put the end of it under or into something else. *He **tucked** his shirt into his trousers.*

Tuesday Tuesdays

NOUN **Tuesday** is the day after Monday and before Wednesday.

tuft tufts

NOUN A **tuft** of something, such as hair, is a bunch of it growing closely together.

tug tugs, tugging, tugged

VERB If you **tug** something, you give it a quick strong pull.

tug-of-war

NOUN A **tug-of-war** is a sport in which two teams pull against each other on opposite ends of a rope.

tulip tulips

NOUN A **tulip** is a spring flower shaped like an upside-down bell.

tumble tumbles, tumbling, tumbled

VERB If you **tumble**, you fall over and over.

tuna

NOUN **Tuna** are large edible fish that live in warm seas.

tune tunes

NOUN A **tune** is a series of musical notes that are nice to listen to.

a
b
c
d
e
f
g
h
i
j
k
l
m
n
o
p
q
r
s
Tt
u
v
w
x
y
z

tunnel

tunnel **tunnels**
NOUN A **tunnel** is a long passage under the ground or through a hill.

turkey **turkeys**
NOUN A **turkey** is a large bird that is kept on a farm for its meat.

turn **turns, turning, turned**
VERB **1** When you **turn**, you move so that you are facing a different way.
VERB **2** When you **turn** something, you move it round.
VERB **3** When something **turns into** something else, it becomes that thing. *When water freezes, it **turns into** ice.*
NOUN **4** If people take **turns** to do something, they do it one after the other.

turnip **turnips**
NOUN A **turnip** is a round root vegetable with a white or yellow skin.
See *Vegetables* on page 256.

turquoise
ADJECTIVE Something **turquoise** is a blue-green colour.
See *Colours* on page 271.

turtle **turtles**
NOUN A **turtle** is a large reptile with a thick shell. It lives mostly in the sea.
See *Reptiles* on page 259.

tusk **tusks**
NOUN **Tusks** are long pointed teeth that some animals have. For example, elephants and walruses have tusks.

TV **TVs**
NOUN TV is an abbreviation of **television**.

twice
ADVERB **Twice** means two times.

twig **twigs**
NOUN A **twig** is a small thin branch of a tree or bush.

twilight
NOUN **Twilight** is the time after sunset when it is just getting dark.

twin **twins**
NOUN If two people are **twins**, they have the same mother and were born on the same day.

twinkle **twinkles, twinkling, twinkled**
VERB If something **twinkles**, it shines with little flashes.

twirl **twirls, twirling, twirled**
VERB If something **twirls**, or if you twirl it, it spins round and round.

twist **twists, twisting, twisted**
VERB **1** When you **twist** something, you turn one end in the opposite direction to the other.
VERB **2** When something **twists**, it moves or bends into a strange shape.

two-dimensional
ADJECTIVE Something that is **two-dimensional**, or **2D**, is a flat shape. For example, a circle is two-dimensional.
See *Colours and flat shapes* on page 271.

tying
VERB **Tying** is a present tense form of **tie**.

type **types, typing, typed**
NOUN **1** **Type** means kind or sort. *What type of plant is it?*
VERB **2** If you **type** words, you use a computer or typewriter.

typhoon **typhoons**
NOUN A **typhoon** is a storm with extremely strong winds.

typical
ADJECTIVE Something that is **typical** is what you would expect.

tyre **tyres**
NOUN A **tyre** is a thick ring of rubber fitted round each wheel of a vehicle.

Uu

ugly uglier, ugliest
ADJECTIVE Someone or something that is **ugly** is not pleasant to look at.

umbrella umbrellas
NOUN An **umbrella** is a shelter from the rain. It consists of a folding frame covered in thin cloth, attached to a long stick.

un-
PREFIX **Un-** is added to the beginning of a word to make it mean the opposite, for example "happy" → "unhappy".
See Prefixes on page 264.

unable
ADJECTIVE If you are **unable** to do something, you cannot do it.

unaware
ADJECTIVE If you are **unaware** of something, you do not know about it.

unbearable
ADJECTIVE Something **unbearable** is so unpleasant, painful or upsetting you feel you cannot stand it.

unbelievable
ADJECTIVE **1** Something **unbelievable** is extremely great or surprising. *She showed* **unbelievable** *courage.*
ADJECTIVE **2 Unbelievable** can also be used to describe something that is so unlikely you cannot believe it.

unbreakable
ADJECTIVE Something that is **unbreakable** cannot be broken.

uncertain
ADJECTIVE If you are **uncertain**, you are not sure what to do.

uncle uncles
NOUN Your **uncle** is the brother of one of your parents, or your aunt's husband.

uncomfortable
ADJECTIVE If you are **uncomfortable**, you do not feel easy.

uncommon
ADJECTIVE Something **uncommon** does not often happen, or is not often seen.

unconscious
ADJECTIVE Someone who is **unconscious** is unable to see, hear or feel anything that is going on. This is usually because they have fainted or have been badly injured.

under
PREPOSITION **1 Under** means below or beneath.

PREPOSITION **2 Under** can also mean less than. *Children* **under** *five can go in free.*

under-
PREFIX **1 Under-** is added to the beginning of a word to form a new word meaning under the thing mentioned, for example "ground" → "underground".
PREFIX **2 Under-** can also be used as a prefix to mean not enough. *The hungry rabbit was* **underfed**.
See Prefixes on page 264.

underground

underground

ADJECTIVE **1** Something **underground** is below the surface of the ground.

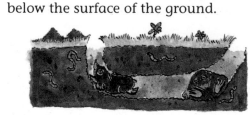

NOUN **2** The **underground** is a railway that runs in tunnels under some cities.

undergrowth

NOUN **Undergrowth** is bushes or plants growing together under the trees in a forest or jungle.

underline underlines, underlining, underlined

VERB If you **underline** a word or sentence, you draw a line under it.

underneath

PREPOSITION OR ADVERB **Underneath** means below or beneath. *They found the missing card* **underneath** *the table... They couldn't move the car because their cat was* **underneath**.

understand understands, understanding, understood

VERB If you **understand** something, you know what it means.

underwear

NOUN Your **underwear** is the clothing that you wear next to your skin under your other clothes.

undo undoes, undoing, undid, undone

VERB If you **undo** something that is tied up, you untie it.

undress undresses, undressing, undressed

VERB When you **undress**, you take off your clothes.

uneasy

ADJECTIVE If you are **uneasy**, you are worried that something is wrong.

unemployed

ADJECTIVE Someone who is **unemployed** does not have a job.

uneven

ADJECTIVE Something that is **uneven** does not have a flat, smooth surface.

unexpected

ADJECTIVE Something that is **unexpected** surprises you.
unexpectedly ADVERB

unfair

ADJECTIVE If you think that something is **unfair**, it does not seem right or reasonable to you.
unfairly ADVERB

unfortunate

ADJECTIVE **1** Someone who is **unfortunate** is unlucky.
ADJECTIVE **2** If you say something is **unfortunate**, you mean you wish it had not happened.
unfortunately ADVERB

unfriendly

ADJECTIVE Someone who is **unfriendly** is not kind to you.

ungrateful

ADJECTIVE If someone is **ungrateful**, they are not thankful for something that has been given to them or done for them.

unhappy unhappier, unhappiest

ADJECTIVE Someone who is **unhappy** is sad or miserable.
unhappily ADVERB

unhealthy unhealthier, unhealthiest

ADJECTIVE **1** Someone who is **unhealthy** is often ill.
ADJECTIVE **2** Something that is **unhealthy** is likely to cause illness.

unicorn unicorns

NOUN A **unicorn** is an imaginary animal like a white horse with a horn in the middle of its forehead.

uniform **uniforms**

NOUN A **uniform** is a special set of clothes that is worn by people to show that they belong to the same group.

unique

ADJECTIVE If something is **unique**, it is the only one of its kind.

unit **units**

NOUN **1** A **unit** is an amount that is used for measuring things. For example, a second is a unit of time.

NOUN **2** In maths, the number of ones is the number of **units**. *The number 37 has 3 tens and 7 units*.

unite **unites, uniting, united**

VERB If people **unite**, they work as a group.
united ADJECTIVE

universe

NOUN The **universe** is the whole of space including all the stars and planets.

university **universities**

NOUN A **university** is a place where people can carry on their education when they have left school.

unkind

ADJECTIVE Someone who is **unkind** is rather cruel and unpleasant.

unleaded

ADJECTIVE **Unleaded** petrol has a smaller amount of lead in it, in order to reduce the pollution from vehicles.

unless

CONJUNCTION You use **unless** to introduce a condition which is necessary for something else to happen. *I won't come unless you invite me.*

unlike

PREPOSITION If one thing is **unlike** another, the two things are different.

unlikely

ADJECTIVE If something is **unlikely**, it is probably not true or probably will not happen.

unload **unloads, unloading, unloaded**

VERB If people **unload** something, such as a lorry, they take the load off it.

unlock **unlocks, unlocking, unlocked**

VERB If you **unlock** something, such as a door, you open it with a key.

unlucky

ADJECTIVE Someone who is **unlucky** has bad luck.
unluckily ADVERB

unnatural

ADJECTIVE Something **unnatural** is strange because it is not usual. *There was an unnatural stillness.*
unnaturally ADVERB

unnecessary

ADJECTIVE Something that is **unnecessary** is not needed.

unpack **unpacks, unpacking, unpacked**

VERB When you **unpack**, you take everything out of a suitcase, bag or box.

unpleasant

ADJECTIVE Something that is **unpleasant** is rather nasty and not enjoyable.

unpopular

ADJECTIVE Someone or something that is **unpopular** is disliked by most people.

unsafe

ADJECTIVE If something like a building or a machine is **unsafe**, it is dangerous.

unselfish

ADJECTIVE People who are **unselfish** care more about other people than they do about themselves.

a
b
c
d
e
f
g
h
i
j
k
l
m
n
o
p
q
r
s
t
Uu
v
w
x
y
z

a b c d e f g h i j k l m n o p q r s t

Uu

v w x y z

untidy   untidier, untidiest

ADJECTIVE **1** Someone who is **untidy** does not care whether things are neat and well arranged.

ADJECTIVE **2** An **untidy** place is not neat or well arranged.

untie   unties, untying, untied

VERB If you **untie** something, you undo the knots in the string around it.

until

PREPOSITION OR CONJUNCTION **Until** means up to a certain time. *The shop was open until midnight... He waited until the dog was asleep.*

untrue

ADJECTIVE Something that is **untrue** is false and not based on facts.

unusual

ADJECTIVE Someone or something that is **unusual** is different from the ordinary.

up

PREPOSITION OR ADVERB **1** Up means towards or in a higher place. *She ran up the stairs... It was high up in the mountains.*

ADVERB **2** If an amount of something goes **up**, it increases. *The price of butter has gone up.*

upper-case

ADJECTIVE **Upper-case** letters are capital letters. See **lower-case**.

upright

ADJECTIVE If you are **upright**, you are standing up straight.

uproar   uproars

NOUN An **uproar** is a lot of noise and shouting.

upset   upsets, upsetting, upset

VERB **1** If someone **upsets** something, they turn it over by accident. *He upset a tin of paint on the carpet.*

ADJECTIVE **2** If you are **upset**, you are unhappy or disappointed.

upside down

ADJECTIVE Something that is **upside down** has been turned so that the part that should be at the top is at the bottom.

upstairs

ADVERB **1** If you go **upstairs** in a building, you go up to a higher floor.

ADVERB **2** Someone or something that is **upstairs** is on a higher floor than you.

up-to-date

ADJECTIVE Something that is **up-to-date** is new or modern.

urgent

ADJECTIVE Something that is **urgent** needs to be done at once.

use   uses, using, used

VERB If you **use** something, you do something with it that helps you.

used

VERB Something that **used** to be done was done in the past.

used to PHRASE If you are **used to** something, you are familiar with it and have often experienced it.

useful

ADJECTIVE If something is **useful**, it helps you in some way.

useless

ADJECTIVE If something is **useless**, you cannot use it.

usual

ADJECTIVE Something that is **usual** happens, or is done or used, most often.

usually

ADVERB If something **usually** happens, it happens most often.

Vv

vacant

ADJECTIVE Somewhere that is **vacant** has nobody in it.

vaccination   vaccinations

NOUN A **vaccination** is an injection that stops you getting an illness.

vacuum cleaner   vacuum cleaners

NOUN A **vacuum cleaner** is an electric machine which cleans by sucking up dirt.

vagina   vaginas

NOUN The **vagina** is an opening in a woman's body through which babies pass when they are being born.

vague   vaguer, vaguest

ADJECTIVE Things that are **vague** are not definite or clear. *He had a **vague** feeling he should be doing something.*

vain

ADJECTIVE A **vain** person is too proud of how they look or what they can do.

valley   valleys

NOUN A **valley** is a low piece of land between hills. Valleys often have rivers flowing through them.

valuable

ADJECTIVE **1** Things that are **valuable** are worth a lot of money.

ADJECTIVE **2** Help or advice that is **valuable** is very useful.

value

NOUN **1** The **value** of something is its importance or usefulness.

NOUN **2** The **value** of something such as jewellery is the amount of money that it is worth.

vampire   vampires

NOUN In horror stories, **vampires** are creatures that suck the blood of living people.

van   vans

NOUN A **van** is a vehicle larger than a car but smaller than a lorry. Vans are used for carrying goods.

vandal   vandals

NOUN A **vandal** is someone who damages something useful or beautiful on purpose and for no good reason.

vanilla

NOUN **Vanilla** is a flavouring for food. It comes from the pods of a tropical plant.

vanish   vanishes, vanishing, vanished

VERB If something **vanishes**, it disappears suddenly.

vapour   vapours

NOUN **Vapour** is a mass of tiny drops of water or other liquids in the air, which appear as clouds, mist or fumes.

variety   variety

NOUN A **variety** of things is lots of different types.

various

ADJECTIVE You say **various** to mean several different things of one kind. *There were **various** questions she wanted to ask.*

vase   vases

NOUN A **vase** is a kind of jar used as an ornament, or to hold cut flowers.

vast

ADJECTIVE Something that is **vast** is extremely large.

a
b
c
d
e
f
g
h
i
j
k
l
m
n
o
p
q
r
s
t
u
Vv
w
x
y
z

vegetable

vegetable **vegetables**

NOUN **Vegetables** are plants, or parts of plants such as leaves, that can be eaten.
See *Vegetables* on page 256.

vegetarian **vegetarians**

NOUN A **vegetarian** is a person who does not eat meat or fish.

vehicle **vehicles**

NOUN A **vehicle** is a machine such as a car or bus that carries people or things from place to place.

veil **veils**

NOUN A **veil** is a piece of thin soft cloth that some women wear over their face or head.

vein **veins**

NOUN A **vein** is a tube inside the body which carries blood to the heart.

velvet

NOUN **Velvet** is a material which has soft short threads on one side.

verb **verbs**

NOUN In grammar, a **verb** is a word that expresses actions and states, for example "take" and "run".
See *Verb* on page 263.

verdict **verdicts**

NOUN In a law court, a **verdict** is whether a prisoner is guilty or not guilty.

verse **verses**

NOUN 1 **Verse** is another word for poetry.
NOUN 2 A **verse** is one of the parts that a poem or song is divided into.

version **versions**

NOUN A **version** of something is a form of it in which some details are different from earlier or later forms. *This is a different version of my story.*

vertex **vertexes** or **vertices**

NOUN 1 The **vertex** of something is its highest point.

NOUN 2 The **vertex** can also be the corner point of a polygon or polyhedron. For example, a triangle has three vertices and a cuboid has eight.

vertical

ADJECTIVE Something that is **vertical** stands straight up from a flat surface. See **horizontal**.

very

ADVERB **Very** is used before words to make them stronger. *He had **very** bad dreams.*

vessel **vessels**

NOUN A **vessel** is a ship or boat.

vest **vests**

NOUN A **vest** is a piece of underwear for the top half of the body.

vet **vets**

NOUN A **vet** is a person whose job is to look after sick and injured animals. Vet is an abbreviation of **veterinary surgeon**.

via

PREPOSITION If you go **via** a particular place, you go through it to get to somewhere else. *We go to Cambridge **via** the Dartford Tunnel.*

viaduct **viaducts**

NOUN A **viaduct** is a long high bridge that carries a road or railway across a valley.

vibrate **vibrates, vibrating, vibrated**

VERB If something **vibrates**, it shakes with a very slight, very quick movement.

vicious

ADJECTIVE Someone or something that is **vicious** is cruel and violent.

victim victims

NOUN A **victim** is someone who has been harmed or injured by someone or something.

victory victories

NOUN A **victory** is a success in a battle or competition.

video videos, videoing, videoed

NOUN **1** A **video** is a machine that records television programmes so that you can watch them later.

NOUN **2** A **video** is also a tape that you use to record television programmes.

NOUN **3** A **video** is also a taped recording of a film that you can watch on your television set.

VERB **4** If you **video** something, you record it on tape so that you can watch it later.

view views

NOUN The **view** from a window or a high place is everything that can be seen from there.

village villages

NOUN A **village** is a small group of houses and other buildings in a country area.

vine vines

NOUN A **vine** is a climbing plant that produces grapes.

vinegar

NOUN **Vinegar** is a sharp-tasting liquid that is used to add taste to some foods, and is also used for pickling.

violence

NOUN **Violence** is behaviour that is meant to hurt or kill people.

violent

ADJECTIVE **1** Someone who is **violent** uses force to hurt or kill people.

ADJECTIVE **2** Something that is **violent** happens suddenly and with great force. A **violent** earthquake shook the city.

violently ADVERB

violet violets

NOUN A **violet** is a small plant with purple or white flowers.

violin violins

NOUN A **violin** is a musical instrument with four strings. It is held under the chin and played with a bow.

virtual

ADJECTIVE **Virtual** means something that is very like a real thing but is not actually the same. *What he said was a* ***virtual*** *lie.*

virtual reality

NOUN **Virtual reality** is an image created by a computer that looks real to the person using it.

virus viruses

NOUN **1** A **virus** is a tiny germ which you cannot see without a microscope. Viruses can cause diseases.

NOUN **2** A disease caused by a virus can also be called a **virus**.

visible

ADJECTIVE Something that is **visible** can be seen.

visibly ADVERB

vision visions

NOUN **1** Vision is the ability to see clearly. *Your* ***vision*** *will be better if you wear glasses.*

NOUN **2** A **vision** is a picture in your mind.

visit visits, visiting, visited

VERB If you **visit** a person or a place, you go to see them.

visitor visitors

NOUN A **visitor** is someone who is visiting a person or place.

vital
ADJECTIVE If something is **vital** when you are doing something, you will not succeed without it. *It is **vital** to get the measurements exactly right.*

vitamin **vitamins**
NOUN A **vitamin** is one of the substances which you need to stay healthy. There are vitamins in many kinds of food.

vivid
ADJECTIVE **1** A **vivid** colour is very bright.
ADJECTIVE **2** Memories or descriptions that are **vivid** are clear and remain firmly fixed in your mind.
vividly ADVERB

vixen **vixens**
NOUN A **vixen** is a female fox.

vocabulary
NOUN Someone's **vocabulary** is the total number of words in a language that they know.

voice **voices**
NOUN **1** Someone's **voice** is the sound they make when they speak or sing.
NOUN **2** In grammar, the active **voice** and the passive voice refer to the relation between a verb and its subject. For example, the sentence "Tom hit the ball" is in the active voice, and "The ball was hit by Tom" is in the passive voice. See **active** and **passive**.

volcano **volcanoes**
NOUN A **volcano** is a mountain with a hole called a crater in the top. Sometimes hot melted rock, gas, steam and ash burst from the crater.

volume **volumes**
NOUN **1** A **volume** is a book.
NOUN **2** The **volume** of something is the amount of space that it takes up.

NOUN **3** The **volume** of something, such as a radio or television, is how loud or quiet its sound is. *He played his radio at full **volume**.*

voluntary
ADJECTIVE **1** **Voluntary** actions are ones that you offer to do, rather than being asked to or made to.
ADJECTIVE **2** **Voluntary** work is done by people who are not paid for what they do.
voluntarily ADVERB

volunteer **volunteers, volunteering, volunteered**
VERB **1** If you **volunteer** to do something, you offer to do it without expecting any reward.
NOUN **2** A **volunteer** is someone who does work for which they are not paid.

vote **votes, voting, voted**
VERB **1** If you **vote**, you make a choice, usually by raising your hand or writing on a piece of paper. *We **voted** for Tim as group leader.*
VERB **2** If you **vote** that a particular thing should happen, that is what you suggest. *I **vote** we all go swimming.*

voucher **vouchers**
NOUN A **voucher** is a ticket or piece of paper that can be used instead of money.

vowel **vowels**
NOUN In the English language, the letters a, e, i, o and u are **vowels**. See **consonant**.

voyage **voyages**
NOUN A **voyage** is a long journey on a ship or in a spacecraft.

vulture **vultures**
NOUN A **vulture** is a large bird which feeds on dead animals. Vultures live in hot countries.

wade wades, wading, waded
VERB To **wade** means to walk through fairly shallow water.

wafer wafers
NOUN A **wafer** is a thin crisp biscuit.

wag wags, wagging, wagged
VERB When a dog **wags** its tail, it waves it from side to side because it is happy.

wagon wagons
NOUN **1** A **wagon** is a strong cart for carrying heavy loads. Wagons are usually pulled by a horse or tractor.
NOUN **2** A **wagon** is also a railway truck.

wail wails, wailing, wailed
VERB If someone **wails**, they make a long crying noise.

waist waists
NOUN Your **waist** is the narrow middle part of your body, just below your chest.

wait waits, waiting, waited
VERB If you **wait**, you spend time before something happens.

wake wakes, waking, woke, woken
VERB When you **wake**, you stop sleeping.

walk walks, walking, walked
VERB When you **walk**, you move along by putting one foot in front of the other.

wall walls
NOUN **1** A **wall** is one of the vertical sides of a building or a room.
NOUN **2** A **wall** can also be used to divide or go round an area of land.

wallet wallets
NOUN A **wallet** is a small flat case that fits in a pocket. It is used to hold things such as paper money and credit cards.

wallpaper wallpapers
NOUN **Wallpaper** is thick coloured or patterned paper that is used for covering and decorating the walls of a room.

walnut walnuts
NOUN A **walnut** is a nut with a wrinkled shape and a light brown shell.

walrus walruses
NOUN A **walrus** is a mammal that lives in the sea and looks like a large seal. It has coarse whiskers and two long tusks.

wand wands
NOUN A **wand** is a long thin rod that magicians wave when they are performing tricks and magic.

wander wanders, wandering, wandered
VERB If you **wander**, you walk around without going in any particular direction.

want wants, wanting, wanted
VERB If you **want** something, you wish for it or need it.

war wars
NOUN A **war** is a period of fighting between countries.

wardrobe wardrobes
NOUN A **wardrobe** is a tall cupboard where you can hang your clothes.

warehouse warehouses
NOUN A **warehouse** is a large building which is used to store things.

warm warmer, warmest
ADJECTIVE **1** Something that is **warm** has some heat but not enough to be hot.
ADJECTIVE **2** Clothes and blankets that are **warm** are made of a material that stops you feeling cold.

a
b
c
d
e
f
g
h
i
j
k
l
m
n
o
p
q
r
s
t
u
v
Ww
x
y
z

warmth

warmth

NOUN **Warmth** is a comfortable amount of heat.

warn warns, warning, warned

VERB If you **warn** someone, you tell them about a danger or problem that they might meet.

warning warnings

NOUN A **warning** is something that tells you about a possible problem or danger.

warren warrens

NOUN A **warren** is a group of holes in the ground which rabbits live in. The holes are connected by tunnels.

wary warier, wariest

ADJECTIVE If you are **wary** about something, you are careful because you are not sure about it.

warily ADVERB

wash washes, washing, washed

VERB If you **wash** something, you clean it with soap and water.

washable

ADJECTIVE Clothes or materials that are **washable** can be washed in water without being damaged.

washing

NOUN **Washing** is clothes, towels and bedding that need to be washed.

washing machine washing machines

NOUN A **washing machine** is a machine for washing clothes in.

washing-up

NOUN If you do the **washing-up**, you wash things such as plates, pans and knives after a meal.

wasp wasps

NOUN A **wasp** is a flying insect with yellow and black stripes across its body. Wasps can sting.

waste wastes, wasting, wasted

VERB **1** If you **waste** something, such as time or money, you use too much of it on something that is not important.
NOUN **2** Waste is material that is no longer wanted. This is often because the useful part of it has been taken out.

watch watches, watching, watched

NOUN **1** A **watch** is a small clock that you can wear on your wrist.
VERB **2** If you **watch** something, you look at it carefully to see what happens.

water waters, watering, watered

NOUN **1** Water is a clear liquid that all living things need in order to live.
VERB **2** If you **water** a plant or animal, you give it water to drink.

waterfall waterfalls

NOUN A **waterfall** is water that flows over the edge of a cliff to the ground below.

waterlogged

ADJECTIVE Land that is **waterlogged** is so wet the soil cannot contain any more water.

waterproof

ADJECTIVE A material that is **waterproof** does not let water pass through it.

watertight

ADJECTIVE Something that is **watertight** is closed so tightly that it does not allow water to pass through.

wave waves, waving, waved
VERB **1** If you **wave**, you move your hand in the air, to say hello or goodbye.
VERB **2** If something **waves**, it moves gently up and down or from side to side. *The flags **waved** in the wind.*
NOUN **3** A **wave** is a raised line of water on the surface of the sea caused by wind or tides.
NOUN **4** A **wave** is also a gentle curving shape in someone's hair.

wax
NOUN **Wax** is a solid, slightly shiny substance, made of fat or oil. It is used to make candles and polish.

way ways
NOUN **1** A **way** of doing something is how it can be done.
NOUN **2** The **way** to a particular place is the direction you have to go to get there.

weak weaker, weakest
ADJECTIVE **1** People or animals that are **weak** do not have much strength or energy.
ADJECTIVE **2** If an object or part of an object is **weak**, it could break easily.
ADJECTIVE **3** Drinks, such as tea or coffee, that are **weak** do not have a strong taste.

wealthy wealthier, wealthiest
ADJECTIVE Someone who is **wealthy** has a lot of money.

weapon weapons
NOUN A **weapon** is an object such as a gun or missile which is used to hurt or kill people in a fight or war.

wear wears, wearing, wore, worn
VERB **1** When you **wear** things, such as clothes, you have them on your body.
VERB **2** When something **wears out**, it has been used so much that it cannot be used any more.

weary wearier, weariest
ADJECTIVE If you are **weary**, you are tired.
wearily ADVERB

weather
NOUN The **weather** is what it is like outside, for example raining, sunny or windy.
See Weather words on page 269.

weave weaves, weaving, wove, woven
VERB When someone **weaves** cloth, they make it by crossing threads over and under each other, using a machine called a loom.

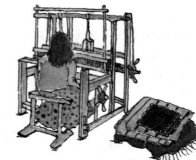

web webs
NOUN **1** A **web** is a fine net made by a spider to catch flies.
NOUN **2** The **web** is short for the World Wide Web, which is where information can be stored on the Internet.

webbed
ADJECTIVE **Webbed** feet have the toes connected by a piece of skin.

website websites
NOUN A **website** is a group of pages on the Internet which contain information about a particular subject.

wedding weddings
NOUN A **wedding** is when a man and woman become husband and wife.

Wednesday Wednesdays
NOUN **Wednesday** is the day between Tuesday and Thursday.

weed weeds
NOUN A **weed** is any wild plant that grows where it is not wanted. Weeds grow strongly and stop other plants growing properly.

week weeks
NOUN A **week** is a period of seven days.

a
b
c
d
e
f
g
h
i
j
k
l
m
n
o
p
q
r
s
t
u
v
Ww
x
y
z

weekend **weekends**

NOUN A **weekend** is Saturday and Sunday.

weep **weeps, weeping, wept**

VERB If someone **weeps**, they cry.

weigh **weighs, weighing, weighed**

VERB **1** If something **weighs** a particular amount, that is how heavy it is.

VERB **2** If you **weigh** something, you use scales to measure how heavy it is.

weight

NOUN The **weight** of something is its heaviness. Weight and mass are connected. Weight is usually measured in grams and kilograms. See **mass**.

weird **weirder, weirdest**

ADJECTIVE Something that is **weird** seems strange and peculiar.

welcome **welcomes, welcoming, welcomed**

VERB If you **welcome** someone, you speak to them in a friendly way when they arrive.

well **better, best; wells**

ADJECTIVE **1** If you are **well**, you are healthy.

ADVERB **2** If you do something **well**, you do it to a high standard.

NOUN **3** A **well** is a deep hole in the ground that has been dug to reach water or oil.

wellington **wellingtons**

NOUN **Wellingtons** are long waterproof rubber boots.

went

VERB **Went** is the past tense of **go**.

wept

VERB **Wept** is the past tense of **weep**.

west

NOUN The **west** is one of the four main points of the compass. It is the direction in which you look to see the sun set. See **compass point**.

western ADJECTIVE

wet **wetter, wettest**

ADJECTIVE **1** If something is **wet**, it is covered in water or some other liquid.

ADJECTIVE **2** If the weather is **wet**, it is raining.

ADJECTIVE **3** If something such as ink or cement is **wet**, it has not yet dried.

whale **whales**

NOUN A **whale** is a huge mammal that lives in the sea. Whales breathe through an opening in the top of their head.

what

ADJECTIVE OR PRONOUN **1** **What** is used in questions. *What time is it? What is your name?*

PRONOUN **2** You can use **what** to refer to information about something. *I don't know **what** you mean.*

what about PHRASE You say **what about** at the beginning of a question when you are making a suggestion or offer. *What about a sandwich?*

wheat

NOUN **Wheat** is a cereal plant grown for its grain, which is used to make flour.

wheel **wheels**

NOUN A **wheel** is a circular object which turns round on a rod fixed to its centre. Wheels are fitted under things such as cars, bicycles and prams so that they can move along.

wheelbarrow **wheelbarrows**

NOUN A **wheelbarrow** is a small cart with a single wheel at the front.

wheelchair **wheelchairs**

NOUN A **wheelchair** is a chair with large wheels for use by people who find walking difficult or impossible.

when

ADVERB **1** You use **when** to ask what time something happened or will happen. *When are you leaving?*

CONJUNCTION **2** You use **when** to refer to a certain time. *I met him when we were at school together.*

where

ADVERB **1** You use **where** to ask questions about place. *Where is my book?*

CONJUNCTION **2** You use **where** to talk about the place in which something is situated or happening. *I don't know where we are.*

whether

CONJUNCTION You can use **whether** instead of **if**. *I don't know whether I can go.*

which

ADJECTIVE **1** You use **which** to ask for information about something when there are two or more possibilities. *Which room are you in?*

PRONOUN **2** You also use **which** when you are going to say more about something you have already mentioned. *We have a car which is dropping to bits.*

while

CONJUNCTION **1** If something happens **while** something else is happening, the two things happen at the same time.

NOUN **2** A **while** is a period of time. *She had to wait a little while.*

whimper whimpers, whimpering, whimpered

VERB When children or animals **whimper**, they make soft unhappy sounds, as if they are about to cry.

whine whines, whining, whined

VERB To **whine** is to make a long high-pitched noise because you are unhappy about something.

whip whips, whipping, whipped

VERB If you **whip** cream or eggs, you beat them until they are thick and frothy or stiff.

whirl whirls, whirling, whirled

VERB When something **whirls**, it turns round very fast.

whirlpool whirlpools

NOUN A **whirlpool** is a small place in a river or the sea where the water is moving quickly round and round, so that anything floating near it is pulled into its centre.

whirlwind whirlwinds

NOUN A **whirlwind** is a tall column of air which spins round and round very quickly.

whirr whirrs, whirring, whirred

VERB When something like a machine **whirrs**, it makes a series of low sounds so fast that it seems like one sound.

whisk whisks, whisking, whisked

VERB If you **whisk** something like cream, you stir it very fast.

whisker whiskers

NOUN The **whiskers** of an animal such as a cat or mouse are the long stiff hairs near its mouth.

whisper whispers, whispering, whispered

VERB When you **whisper**, you talk very quietly, using your breath and not your voice.

whistle whistles, whistling, whistled

NOUN **1** A **whistle** is a small metal tube which makes a loud sound when you blow it.

VERB **2** When you **whistle**, you make a loud high noise by using a whistle or by forcing your breath out between your lips.

white

white whiter, whitest; whites
ADJECTIVE **1** Something that is **white** is the colour of milk.
See *Colours on page 271.*
ADJECTIVE **2** If someone goes **white**, their face becomes very pale because they are afraid, shocked or ill.
NOUN **3** The **white** of an egg is the transparent liquid surrounding the yolk.

who
PRONOUN **1** You use **who** when you are asking about someone. *Who told you?*
PRONOUN **2** You use **who** at the beginning of a clause when you want to say more about someone you have just mentioned. *I've got a brother **who** wants to be a vet.*

whole wholes
NOUN **1** The **whole** of something is all of it. *It was the only pair in the **whole** of Brighton.*
ADJECTIVE **2** You use **whole** to describe all of something. *Take the **whole** cake.*
ADJECTIVE **3** **Whole** means in one piece.

whose
PRONOUN **1** You use **whose** to ask who something belongs to. *Whose book is this?*
PRONOUN **2** You use **whose** in front of information relating to a person or thing you have just mentioned. *That's the girl **whose** mother is a lawyer.*

why
ADVERB **1** You use **why** in questions when you ask about the reason for something. *Why did you do that?*
ADVERB **2** You also use **why** to talk about the reasons for something. *She wondered **why** he was there.*

wicked
ADJECTIVE Someone or something **wicked** is very bad.

wide wider, widest
ADJECTIVE **1** Something that is **wide** measures a lot from one side to the other.
ADVERB **2** If you open something **wide**, you open it a long way.

widow widows
NOUN A **widow** is a woman whose husband has died. See **widower**.

widower widowers
NOUN A **widower** is a man whose wife has died. See **widow**.

width widths
NOUN The **width** of something is the distance from one side to the other.

wife wives
NOUN A man's **wife** is the woman he is married to.

wig wigs
NOUN A **wig** is a false head of hair. People wear wigs because they are bald, or to cover their own hair.

wigwam wigwams
NOUN A **wigwam** is a kind of tent used by some North American Indians.

wild wilder, wildest
ADJECTIVE **1** **Wild** animals, birds and plants live in natural surroundings and are not looked after by people.
ADJECTIVE **2** **Wild** behaviour is excited and not controlled.

wildlife
NOUN **Wildlife** means wild animals and plants.

will
VERB **1** You use **will** to form the future tense. *Robin **will** be quite annoyed.*
VERB **2** You use **will** when asking or telling someone to do something. *Will you do me a favour?*

willing
ADJECTIVE **1** If you are **willing** to do something, you are ready and happy to do it if someone wants you to.

ADJECTIVE **2** A **willing** person is someone who does things cheerfully.

willow **willows**

NOUN A **willow** is a tree with long thin branches and narrow leaves that likes to grow near water.

win **wins, winning, won**

VERB **1** If you **win** a race or game, you do better than the others taking part.
VERB **2** If you **win** a prize, you get it as a reward for doing something well.

wind **winds, winding, wound**

(*rhymes with* **tinned**) NOUN **1** A **wind** is a current of air that moves across the earth's surface.
(*rhymes with* **mind**) VERB **2** If a road or river **winds**, it has lots of bends in it.
(*rhymes with* **mind**) VERB **3** When you **wind** something round something else, you wrap it round several times.

windmill **windmills**

NOUN A **windmill** is a building with large sails on the outside, which turn as the wind blows. This works a machine that grinds corn to make flour.

window **windows**

NOUN A **window** is a space in a wall or vehicle. It has glass in it so that light can come in and you can see through.

windscreen **windscreens**

NOUN The **windscreen** of a vehicle is the glass window at the front.

windy **windier, windiest**

ADJECTIVE If it is **windy**, the wind is blowing hard.

wine **wines**

NOUN **Wine** is a strong drink usually made from the juice of grapes.

wing **wings**

NOUN **1** The **wings** of a bird or insect are the two limbs on its body that it uses for flying.
NOUN **2** The **wings** of an aeroplane are the long flat parts sticking out of its sides, which support it in the air.

wink **winks, winking, winked**

VERB When you **wink**, you close one eye for a moment. *She winked to show that she was joking.*

winner **winners**

NOUN If someone or something wins a prize, race or competition, they are the **winner**.

winter **winters**

NOUN **Winter** is the season between autumn and spring.

wipe **wipes, wiping, wiped**

VERB If you **wipe** something, you rub its surface lightly to remove dirt or liquid.

wire **wires**

NOUN **Wire** is a long, thin, flexible piece of metal which can be used to make or fasten things or to carry an electric current.

wise **wiser, wisest**

ADJECTIVE Someone who is **wise** can use their experience and knowledge to make sensible decisions.
wisdom NOUN

wish **wishes, wishing, wished**

VERB **1** If you **wish** that something would happen, you would like it to happen.
NOUN **2** A **wish** is the act of wishing for something you would like to happen.

witch **witches**

NOUN In fairy stories, a witch is a woman who has magic powers. See **wizard**.

a
b
c
d
e
f
g
h
i
j
k
l
m
n
o
p
q
r
s
t
u
v
Ww
x
y
z

with

PREPOSITION 1 If you are **with** someone, you are in their company. *I was there **with** Mum and Dad.*

PREPOSITION 2 With can mean using or having. *She worked **with** a big brush.*

wither withers, withering, withered

VERB If a plant **withers**, it shrivels up and dies.

within

PREPOSITION 1 Within means not going outside certain limits. *Stay **within** the school grounds.*

PREPOSITION 2 Within can also mean before a period of time has passed. *You must write back **within** ten days.*

without

PREPOSITION 1 Without means not having or using. *You can't get in **without** a key.*

PREPOSITION 2 Without can mean not in someone's company. *He went **without** me.*

PREPOSITION 3 Without can also mean that something does not happen. *She rang three times **without** an answer.*

witness witnesses, witnessing, witnessed

NOUN 1 A **witness** is someone who has seen an event such as an accident and can describe what happened.

VERB 2 If you **witness** an event, you see it happen.

wizard wizards

NOUN In fairy stories, a **wizard** is a man who has magic powers. See **witch**.

wobble wobbles, wobbling, wobbled

VERB If something **wobbles**, it makes small movements from side to side.

woke

VERB Woke is the past tense of **wake**.

woken

VERB Woken is the past participle of **wake**.

wolf wolves

NOUN A **wolf** is a wild animal that looks like a large dog. Wolves live in a group called a pack.

woman women

NOUN A **woman** is an adult female human being. See **man**.

won

VERB Won is the past tense of **win**.

wonder wonders, wondering, wondered

VERB 1 If you **wonder** about something, you wish you knew more about it.

VERB 2 If you **wonder** what to do about something, you are not sure what to do about it.

NOUN 3 Wonder is a feeling of great and pleasant surprise.

wonderful

ADJECTIVE If something is **wonderful**, it makes you feel very happy.

won't

VERB Won't is a contraction of **will not**.

wood woods

NOUN 1 Wood is the substance which forms the trunks and branches of trees.

NOUN 2 A **wood** is a large area of trees growing near each other.

wooden

ADJECTIVE Something that is **wooden** is made of wood.

woodpecker woodpeckers

NOUN A **woodpecker** is a bird with a long sharp beak. It drills holes in trees to find insects.

Ww

woodwork

NOUN **1** The **woodwork** in a house is all the parts that are made of wood, such as the doors and window frames.

NOUN **2** Woodwork is making things out of wood.

woof woofs

NOUN Woof is the noise that a dog makes when it barks.

wool

NOUN **1** Wool is the hair that grows on sheep and on some other animals.

NOUN **2** Wool is also the yarn spun from the wool of animals which is used to knit, weave, and make things like clothes, blankets and carpets.

woollen

ADJECTIVE Something that is **woollen** is made from wool.

woolly woollier, woolliest

ADJECTIVE Something that is **woolly** is made of wool, or looks like wool.

word words

NOUN A **word** is a set of sounds or letters that has a meaning. A word can be written or spoken. When it is written, there are no spaces between the letters.

word processor word processors

NOUN A **word processor** is a computer which is used to store and print words that are typed into it.

wore

VERB Wore is the past tense of **wear**.

work works, working, worked

VERB **1** When you **work**, you spend time and energy doing something useful.

VERB **2** People who **work** have a job that they are paid to do.

VERB **3** If something **works**, it does what it is supposed to do.

work out works out, working out, worked out

VERB **1** If you **work out** the answer to a problem, you find the answer.

VERB **2** If you **work out**, you do exercises to make your body fit and strong.

world worlds

NOUN The **world** is the planet we live on.

worm worms

NOUN A **worm** is a small animal with a long thin body. Worms have no bones and no legs. They live in the soil.

worn

VERB **1** Worn is the past participle of **wear**.

ADJECTIVE **2** Something that is **worn** is damaged or thin because it is old and has been used a lot.

worry worries, worrying, worried

VERB If you **worry**, you keep thinking about problems or about unpleasant things that might happen.

worse

ADJECTIVE **1** Worse is the comparative form of **bad**.

ADJECTIVE **2** If someone who is ill gets **worse**, they are more ill than before.

worship worships, worshipping, worshipped

VERB If you **worship** a god, you show your respect by praying and singing hymns.

worst

ADJECTIVE Worst is the superlative form of **bad**.

worth

ADJECTIVE **1** If something is **worth** a particular amount of money, it could be sold for that amount.

ADJECTIVE **2** If something is **worth** doing, it is enjoyable or useful. *That film is worth seeing.*

would

VERB **1** You use **would** to say what someone thought was going to happen. *We were sure it would rain.*

VERB **2** You also use **would** to say you want something to happen. *I would like to know how they do that.*

a
b
c
d
e
f
g
h
i
j
k
l
m
n
o
p
q
r
s
t
u
v
Ww
x
y
z

wound

wound **wounds**
(*rhymes with* **round**) VERB **1** Wound is the past tense of **wind**.
(*said* **woond**) NOUN **2** A **wound** is an injury to your body, especially a cut in your skin.

wove
VERB Wove is the past tense of **weave**.

woven
VERB Woven is the past participle of **weave**.

wrap **wraps, wrapping, wrapped**
VERB When you **wrap** something, you cover it tightly with something like paper.

wrapping **wrappings**
NOUN **Wrapping** is the material used to cover and protect something.

wreath **wreaths**
NOUN A **wreath** is an arrangement of flowers and leaves, often in the shape of a circle.

wreck **wrecks, wrecking, wrecked**
VERB **1** If someone or something **wrecks** something, they destroy it completely.
VERB **2** If a ship is **wrecked**, it is so badly damaged that it can no longer sail.
NOUN **3** A **wreck** is a vehicle that has been badly damaged in an accident.

wren **wrens**
NOUN A **wren** is a tiny brown bird.

wrestle **wrestles, wrestling, wrestled**
VERB If you **wrestle** with someone, you fight them by holding or throwing them, but not hitting them.

wriggle **wriggles, wriggling, wriggled**
VERB When you **wriggle**, you twist and turn your body with quick movements.

wring **wrings, wringing, wrung**
VERB If you **wring** a wet piece of cloth, you squeeze the water out of it by twisting it.

wrinkle **wrinkles**
NOUN **1** A **wrinkle** is a line in someone's skin, especially on their face, that forms as they grow old.
NOUN **2** A **wrinkle** is also a raised fold in something like cloth or thin paper.

wrinkled
ADJECTIVE If something is **wrinkled**, it has folds or lines in it.

wrist **wrists**
NOUN Your **wrist** is the part of your body between your hand and your arm, which bends when you move your hand.

write **writes, writing, wrote, written**
VERB **1** When you **write**, you use a pen or pencil to make words, letters or numbers.
VERB **2** If you **write** something such as a poem or a story, you create it.
VERB **3** When you **write** to someone, you tell them about something in a letter.

writing
NOUN **1** **Writing** is something that has been written or printed.
NOUN **2** Your **writing** is the way you write with a pen or pencil.

written
VERB Written is the past participle of **write**.

wrong
ADJECTIVE **1** Something that is **wrong** is not correct.
ADJECTIVE **2** If there is something **wrong** with a machine, vehicle, or piece of equipment, it is not working properly.
ADJECTIVE **3** If a person does something **wrong**, they do something bad.

wrote
VERB Wrote is the past tense of **write**.

wrung
VERB Wrung is the past tense of **wring**.

a
b
c
d
e
f
g
h
i
j
k
l
m
n
o
p
q
r
s
t
u
v
Ww
x
y
z

Xx

X-ray X-rays

NOUN An **X-ray** is a ray that can pass through some solid materials. X-rays are used by doctors to examine bones or organs inside people's bodies.

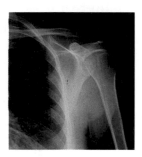

xylophone xylophones

NOUN A **xylophone** is a musical instrument made of wooden bars of different lengths which are arranged in a row. You play a xylophone by hitting the bars with special hammers.

Yy

yacht yachts

NOUN A **yacht** is a large boat with sails or a motor. Yachts are used for racing or for pleasure trips.

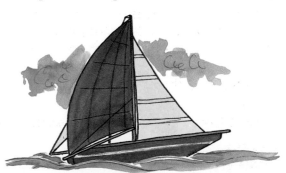

yam yams

NOUN A **yam** is a root vegetable which grows in tropical regions.

yard yards

NOUN **1** A **yard** is a unit of length equal to just under one metre.
NOUN **2** A **yard** is also an enclosed area that is usually next to a building.

yarn yarns

NOUN **Yarn** is thread made from something such as wool or cotton. It is used for knitting or making cloth.

yawn yawns, yawning, yawned

VERB When you **yawn**, you open your mouth wide and take in more air than usual. You often yawn when you are tired or bored.

a
b
c
d
e
f
g
h
i
j
k
l
m
n
o
p
q
r
s
t
u
v
w
x

z

year **years**

NOUN A **year** is a period of time. It is equal to 12 months, or 52 weeks, or 365 days.

yeast

NOUN **Yeast** is a kind of fungus that is used to make bread rise. It is also used in making drinks such as beer.

yell **yells, yelling, yelled**

VERB If you **yell**, you shout loudly. People sometimes yell if they are excited, angry, or in pain.

yellow

ADJECTIVE Something that is **yellow** is the colour of lemons or egg yolks. See *Colours* on page 271.

yelp **yelps, yelping, yelped**

VERB If people or animals **yelp**, they give a sudden short cry. This is often because they are frightened or in pain.

yes

You say **yes** to agree with someone, to say that something is true, or to accept something.

yesterday

ADVERB **Yesterday** is the day before today.

yet

ADVERB **1** You say **yet** when you mean up till now. *She hasn't come yet.*

ADVERB **2** If something should not be done **yet**, it should be done later. *Don't switch it off yet.*

CONJUNCTION **3** You can use **yet** to introduce something which is rather surprising. *He doesn't like maths, yet he always does well.*

yew **yews**

NOUN A **yew** is an evergreen tree with thin, dark green leaves. Some yew trees have red berries.

yogurt **yogurts**; also spelt **yoghurt**

NOUN **Yogurt** is a slightly sour, thick liquid food made from milk.

yolk **yolks**

NOUN A **yolk** is the yellow part in the middle of an egg.

young **younger, youngest**

ADJECTIVE **1** A **young** person, animal or plant has not been alive for very long.

NOUN **2** The **young** of an animal are its babies.

your

ADJECTIVE **Your** means belonging or relating to the person or group of people that someone is speaking to. *Your teacher seems nice.*

yourself **yourselves**

PRONOUN If you do something **yourself**, no one else does it. *If you do that, you'll hurt yourself.*

by yourself PHRASE If you are **by yourself**, you are on your own. *What are you doing here all by yourself?*

youth **youths**

NOUN **1** A **youth** is a boy or young man.

NOUN **2** Your **youth** is the time in your life when you are young.

yo-yo **yo-yos**

NOUN A **yo-yo** is a round wooden or plastic toy attached to a piece of string. You play by making the yo-yo rise and fall on the string.

Zz

zap zaps, zapping, zapped
VERB **1** If you **zap** something or somebody in a computer game, you get rid of them.

VERB **2** To **zap** also means to keep changing channels on the television.

zebra zebras
NOUN A **zebra** is a type of African wild horse with black and white stripes over its body.

zebra crossing zebra crossings
NOUN A **zebra crossing** is a place where you can cross the road safely. The road is marked with black and white stripes.

zero zeros
1 Zero is the number 0.

NOUN **2** Zero is also the freezing point of water, 0°C.

zigzag zigzags
NOUN A **zigzag** is a line which keeps changing direction sharply.

zinc
NOUN **Zinc** is a bluish-white metal which is used to make other metals, or to cover other metals such as iron to stop them rusting.

zip zips
NOUN A **zip** is a long narrow fastener with two rows of teeth that are closed or opened by a small clip pulled between them.

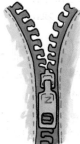

zone zones
NOUN A **zone** is an area of land or sea that is considered to be different from the areas around it. *My dad wants to turn the garden into a cat-free* **zone**.

zoo zoos
NOUN A **zoo** is a park where wild animals are kept so that people can look at them or study them.

zoom zooms, zooming, zoomed
VERB **1** To **zoom** somewhere means to go there very quickly.

VERB **2** If a camera **zooms** in on a person or thing being photographed, it gives a close-up picture of them.

a
b
c
d
e
f
g
h
i
j
k
l
m
n
o
p
q
r
s
t
u
v
w
x
y
z

Zz

Vegetables

celery

garlic

broccoli

aubergine

cabbage

radish

cauliflower

cucumber

lettuce

courgette

asparagus

onion

pea

potato

beetroot

turnip

mangetout

pepper

bean

parsnip

sprout

spinach

sweet potato

sweet corn

carrot

leek

apple

avocado

tomato

cherry

kiwi fruit

grape

grapefruit

lime

pear

plum

passion fruit

orange

lemon

mango

peach

strawberry

raspberry

melon

banana

pineapple

Your body

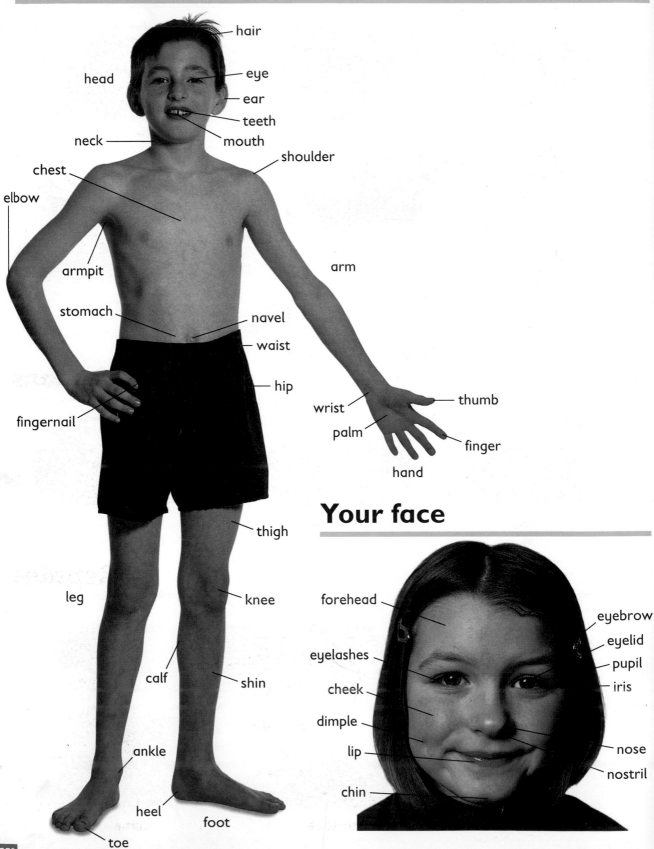

hair

head

eye

ear

teeth

mouth

neck

chest

shoulder

elbow

armpit

arm

stomach

navel

waist

hip

fingernail

wrist

thumb

palm

finger

hand

thigh

leg

knee

calf

shin

ankle

heel

foot

toe

Your face

forehead

eyebrow

eyelid

pupil

iris

eyelashes

cheek

dimple

lip

nose

nostril

chin

Insects

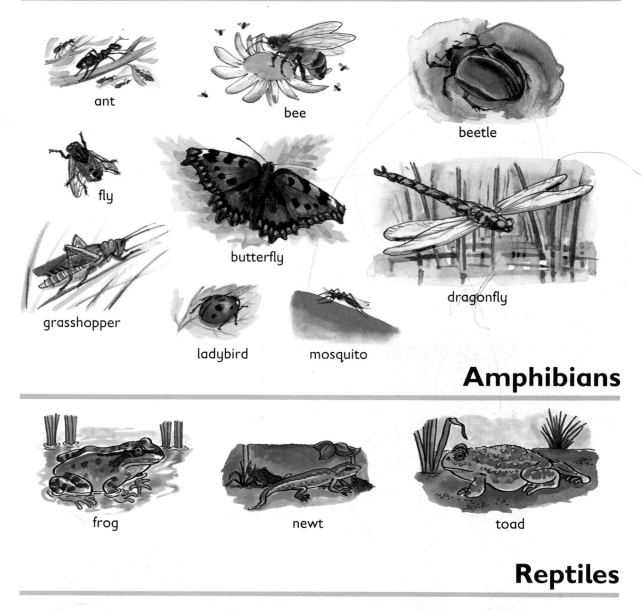

ant

bee

beetle

fly

butterfly

dragonfly

grasshopper

ladybird

mosquito

Amphibians

frog

newt

toad

Reptiles

alligator

crocodile

lizard

snake

tortoise

turtle

Young animals

bear and cub

cat and kitten

deer and fawn

goat and kid

goose and gosling

hare and leveret

horse and foal

kangaroo and joey

pig and piglet

rabbit and kitten

seal and calf or pup

sheep and lamb

tiger and cub

swan and cygnet

whale and calf

More young animals

bird and chick

chicken and chick

cow and calf

dog and puppy

duck and duckling

elephant and calf

fox and cub

lion and cub

wolf and cub

Words we use a lot

a	began	for	home	must	said	this	when
about	being	from	how	my	saw	three	where
after	but	get	I	name	say	to	which
again	by	go	if	next	seen	too	who
all	came	goes	in	no	she	took	why
along	can	going	is	not	should	two	will
am	can't	got	it	now	so	up	with
an	come	had	its	of	some	upon	woman
and	coming	hadn't	it's	off	suddenly	us	would
another	could	has	just	okay	take	very	wouldn't
are	couldn't	hasn't	last	on	than	want	yes
aren't	did	have	made	once	that	was	you
as	didn't	haven't	make	one	the	wasn't	your
at	do	he	man	or	their	way	
away	does	heard	many	our	them	we	
back	doesn't	her	may	out	then	went	
be	don't	here	me	over	there	were	
because	every	him	more	people	these	weren't	
been	first	his	much	put	they	what	

Silent letters

Each of these words has a silent letter. Can you think of any other words like these?

clim**b**	**k**nit
colum**n**	**k**nock
com**b**	**k**not
dou**b**t	**k**now
ghost	lam**b**
gnat	s**c**issors
gnaw	s**w**ord
gnome	**w**rap
hour	**w**riggle
knee	**w**rite
knife	

Confusable words

These words have different meanings but are easy to mix up.

its (belongs to it)
it's (it is)

The dog wagged its tail.
It's not funny.

loose
lose

My tooth's loose.
Don't lose your pen.

passed
past

I passed my test.
It's ten past three.

their (belongs to them)
they're (they are)
there

The girls counted their money.
They're going to the shop.
There are 26 chairs in this room.
Put your bag down there.

than
then (at that time)

I am shorter than you.
Then I heard footsteps.

too
two
to

Can I come too? This is too hard.
I'd like two cakes.
I want to swim. Let's go to the beach.

whose (belongs to whom)
who's (who is or who has)

Whose bag is this?
Who's that?
I know who's been sending you notes.

Parts of speech

Noun

A **noun** is a person, place, thing or idea.
There are different types of noun.

cat

cats

A noun can be **singular**, which means one …

… or **plural**, which means more than one.

Common nouns name people, places, things, or ideas in general. For example, "boy", "dog", "school", "computer" and "happiness" are common nouns.

Proper nouns are the names of particular people, places or things. They start with a capital letter. For example, "Ben", "France" and "Buckingham Palace" are proper nouns.

Collective nouns

A **collective noun** names a group of things.

a **bunch** of grapes

a **clutch** of eggs

a **pack** of wolves

a **flock** of sheep

a **litter** of puppies

a **herd** of cows

a **pride** of lions

a **school** of dolphins

a **shoal** of fish

a **swarm** of bees

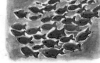

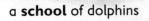

Pronoun

A **pronoun** is used to replace a noun.

I	me	my	mine	myself
you	you	your	yours	yourself, yourselves
he, she, it	him, her, it	his, her, its	his, hers, its	himself, herself, itself
we	us	our	ours	ourselves
they	them	their	theirs	themselves

Personal pronouns are used for a person or thing that has already been named, for example "me", "her", "you", "it". *John jumped for the ball. He caught it!*

Possessive pronouns show that a noun belongs to a person or thing that has already been named, for example, "my", "their", "his", "our". *The bird flapped its wings.*

Adjective

An **adjective** describes a noun. For example, "tall", "happy" and "lucky" are all adjectives.

Some adjectives have a **comparative** and a **superlative** form. In most cases, these forms are made by adding "-er" or "-est" to the adjective.

adjective	comparative (more)	superlative (most)
tall	taller	tallest
hot	hotter	hottest
good	better	best
lucky	luckier	luckiest

Verb

A **verb** is an action word. It tells you what people and things do. For example, "sleep", "think" and "play" are all verbs.

Verbs have different forms called **tenses**. A tense shows whether you are talking about the past, present or future.

past	present	future
I *played*	I *play*	I *will play*
	I *am playing*	

Adverb

An **adverb** tells you more about a verb. For example, "shyly", "brightly" and "happily" are all adverbs. Many adverbs end in the suffix "-ly".

How did Mary and Brian talk?
   *They talked **loudly**.*

Other adverbs tell you "where", "when", or "how often" something happens.

where: outside, inside, here, there
when: today, soon, immediately
how often: never, frequently, often, always

Punctuation

A B C	A **capital letter** is used at the beginning of a sentence and for proper nouns.	*My brother Jim lives in New Zealand.*
.	You put a **full stop** at the end of a sentence.	*This is a sentence.*
?	You put a **question mark** at the end of a question.	*Can you come to my party?*
,	You use a **comma** to separate parts of a sentence or items on a list.	*She brought sandwiches, crisps, apples and juice to the picnic.*
!	You use an **exclamation mark** at the end of a sentence to show a strong feeling.	*Wow!*
'	An **apostrophe** is used in contractions and to show belonging.	*I didn't mean to break my brother's toy.*
" " ' '	**Speech marks** show where speech begins and ends.	*"I like your hair," she said.*
-	You use a **hyphen** to join together words or parts of words.	*I'm left-handed.*
( )	**Brackets** are used to show that something is not part of the main text.	*My cousin (the one from America) is coming to stay.*
—	A **dash** can be used instead of brackets, or to show a change of subject.	*My best friend – besides you – is George.*
:	You can use a **colon** for several things, for example in front of a list.	*You will need the following: strong walking boots, a map and a compass.*
;	A **semicolon** is used to separate different parts of a sentence or list, or to show a pause.	*The pizza choices are: cheese; onions, peppers and mushrooms; ham and pineapple; pepperoni; or sausage.*

Prefixes

A **prefix** is a group of letters added to the beginning of a word to make a new word.

prefix	meaning	example	prefix	meaning	example
anti-	opposite of, against	anticlockwise	over-	too much	oversleep
			poly-	many	polygon
co-	together	copilot	pre-	before	prehistoric
de-	take away	decode	re-	again	rearrange
dis-	opposite of	disappear	semi-	half	semicircle
ex-	former	ex-husband	sub-	under, part of	subheading
micro-	very small	microscope	super-	larger, more than	supersonic
mid-	middle	midnight			
mini-	smaller	minibus	un-	not	unlucky
mis-	wrong	misspell	under-	under or not enough	underground
non-	not	non-fiction			

A **suffix** is a letter or group of letters added to the end of a word to make a new word.

Some suffixes can change nouns into other nouns:

-hood   child → child**hood**

-ist   art → art**ist**   science → scient**ist**

-ship   friend → friend**ship**

Some suffixes can make nouns feminine:

-ess   lion → lion**ess**   prince → prin**cess**

Some suffixes can form a diminutive (a small word):

-ette   disk → disk**ette**

Some suffixes can change nouns or verbs into adjectives:

-able   comfort → comfort**able**   enjoy → enjoy**able**

-al   music → music**al**

-ary   imagine → imagin**ary**

-ful   help → help**ful**

-ible   sense → sens**ible**

-ic   angel → angel**ic**   drama → dramat**ic**

-ish   child → child**ish**

-ive   act → act**ive**   persuade → persuas**ive**

-less   care → care**less**

-like   life → life**like**

-ous   poison → poison**ous**

-worthy trust → trust**worthy**

-y   thirst → thirs**ty**

Some suffixes can change adjectives into adverbs:

-ally   automatic → automatic**ally**

-ly   slow → slow**ly**   happy → happi**ly**

Some suffixes can change verbs or adjectives into nouns:

-ment   advertise → advertise**ment**   enjoy → enjoy**ment**

-ness   ill → ill**ness**   happy → happi**ness**

-sion   divide → divi**sion**

-tion   add → addi**tion**   invite → invita**tion**

Some suffixes can change nouns into verbs:

-ate   illustration → illustr**ate**

Synonyms

Synonyms are words that have the same, or almost the same, meaning.
Here are some useful synonyms for everyday words.

angry
furious, mad, annoyed, outraged, indignant

bad
a bad person – wicked, nasty
a bad child – naughty, spiteful, defiant
bad food – rotten, decayed
a bad pain – severe
bad news – distressing, grave, terrible

big
huge, large, enormous, gigantic, vast, colossal

good
a good dog – well-behaved
a good painting – fine
a good film – enjoyable
a good worker – able, clever

happy
cheerful, content, delighted, glad, pleased, thrilled

kind
kind of person or thing – type, class, group

level
grade, position, stage

lots or **a lot**
plenty, a great deal, heaps, loads, many, a large amount, masses, piles

lovely
a lovely day – pleasant, glorious, sunny, splendid
a lovely meal – tasty, scrumptious, delicious
a lovely person – warm, kind, helpful, friendly
a lovely time – enjoyable, great, fantastic, wonderful, fabulous

nasty
a nasty person – unkind, rude, unpleasant
a nasty taste – horrible, foul, disgusting, awful

nice
nice food – delicious
a nice person – kind, helpful, pleasant
a nice view – lovely

rough
a rough road – bumpy, stony
a rough sea – choppy, stormy

small
a small problem – unimportant, trivial
a small child – little, tiny, young
a small room – cramped, cosy, modest

What else can you say?

The word "said" is useful, but here are some more interesting words that you can use to describe speech.

answer
reply, respond, retort, admit, agree

ask
enquire, demand, beg, query, wonder

said
announced, whispered, shouted, stammered, mumbled, yelled, shrieked, screamed, cried, murmured, remarked, declared, groaned, snarled, whimpered, admitted

Antonyms

Antonyms are words that have the opposite meaning.

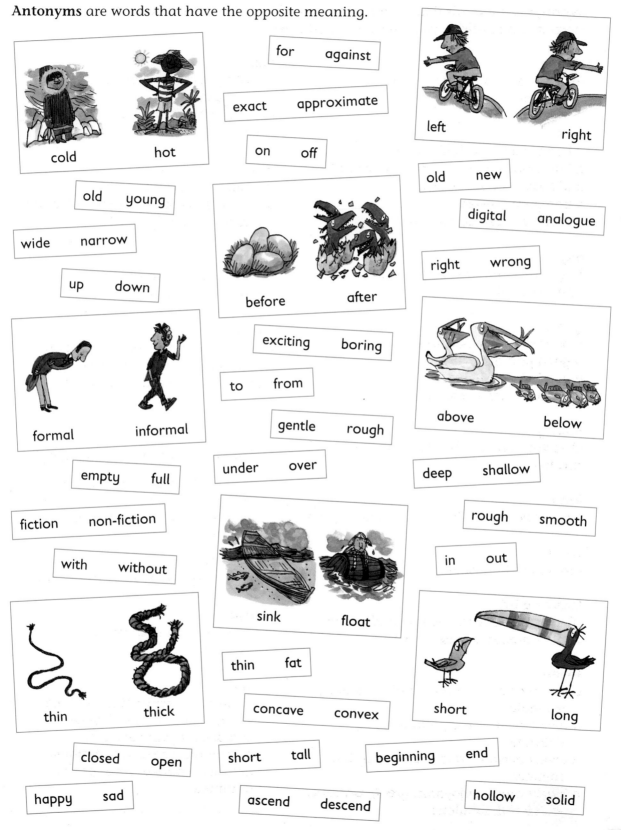

cold   hot

for   against

exact   approximate

on   off

left   right

old   new

old   young

digital   analogue

wide   narrow

right   wrong

up   down

before   after

exciting   boring

formal   informal

to   from

above   below

gentle   rough

empty   full

under   over

deep   shallow

fiction   non-fiction

rough   smooth

with   without

in   out

sink   float

thin   fat

short   long

thin   thick

concave   convex

closed   open

short   tall

beginning   end

happy   sad

ascend   descend

hollow   solid

Time

9:50 a.m.

10 minutes to 10

7:25 p.m.

25 minutes past 7

Telling time

a.m.

p.m.

o'clock

half past

quarter past

quarter to

analogue

digital

clock

watch

timer

More time words

yesterday
today
tomorrow

calendar
date
weekend
holiday
birthday

second
minute
hour
day
week
fortnight
month
year
leap year
decade
century
millennium

dawn
morning
midday
noon
afternoon
dusk
evening
night
midnight

bedtime
daytime
dinnertime
playtime

Months
January
February
March
April
May
June
July
August
September
October
November
December

How often?
never
once
twice
sometimes
often
usually
always

Days
Monday
Tuesday
Wednesday
Thursday
Friday
Saturday
Sunday

Seasons
spring
summer
autumn
winter

Weather words

bright   sunny   dry   breeze   clear   hot

freezing cold icy snow frost

dry   hot   drought   sun

cloudy chilly foggy drizzle misty

rain   windy   wet   sleet   cool

hail lightning gale storm thunder

showers rainbow sunshine warm breeze

269

Measures

Length
millimetre (mm)
centimetre (cm)
metre (m)
kilometre (km)
mile

Mass or weight
gram (g)
half-kilogram
kilogram (kg)

Capacity
millilitre (ml)
half-litre
litre (l)
pint (pt)

Abbreviations

a.m.	in the morning
°C	degrees Celsius
CD	compact disc (such as a music CD)
CD-ROM	a CD that is played on a computer (an abbreviation of "compact disc read-only memory")
cm	centimetre
cm²	square centimetre
DIY	do-it-yourself
Dr	Doctor
DVD	digital video disc *or* digital versatile disc
etc.	"et cetera", which means "and so on" in Latin
EU	European Union
g	gram
GP	general practitioner (a doctor)
ICT	information and communications technology
IT	information technology
kg	kilogram
km	kilometre
l	litre
m	metre
ml	millilitre
MP	Member of Parliament

Mr	a title used before a man's name
Mrs	a title used before the name of a married woman
Ms	a title used before a woman's name
OAP	old age pensioner
p	pence
p.	page
PC	personal computer *or* police constable
PE	physical education
p.m.	in the afternoon or evening
pp.	pages
PS	PS is written at the end of a letter, before an extra message (an abbreviation of "postscript")
PTO	please turn over
RSVP	please reply (an abbreviation of the French phrase "répondez s'il vous plaît")
SOS	a Morse code signal for help, especially used by ships or planes (sometimes said to be an abbreviation of "save our souls")
TV	television
UFO	unidentified flying object
VIP	very important person
www	World Wide Web

Colours and flat shapes (2D)

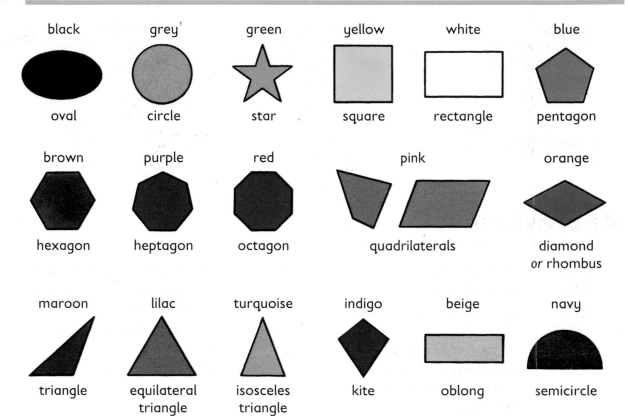

black — oval
grey — circle
green — star
yellow — square
white — rectangle
blue — pentagon

brown — hexagon
purple — heptagon
red — octagon
pink — quadrilaterals
orange — diamond *or* rhombus

maroon — triangle
lilac — equilateral triangle
turquoise — isosceles triangle
indigo — kite
beige — oblong
navy — semicircle

Solid shapes (3D)

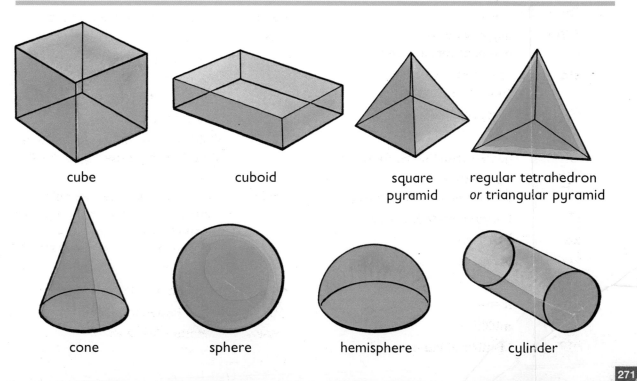

cube

cuboid

square pyramid

regular tetrahedron *or* triangular pyramid

cone

sphere

hemisphere

cylinder

Number bank

0	zero	30	thirty	1st	first
1	one	31	thirty-one	2nd	second
2	two	40	forty	3rd	third
3	three	41	forty-one	4th	fourth
4	four	50	fifty	5th	fifth
5	five	51	fifty-one	6th	sixth
6	six	60	sixty	7th	seventh
7	seven	61	sixty-one	8th	eighth
8	eight	70	seventy	9th	ninth
9	nine	71	seventy-one	10th	tenth
10	ten	80	eighty	11th	eleventh
11	eleven	81	eighty-one	12th	twelfth
12	twelve	90	ninety	13th	thirteenth
13	thirteen	91	ninety-one	14th	fourteenth
14	fourteen	100	one hundred	15th	fifteenth
15	fifteen	101	one hundred and one	16th	sixteenth
16	sixteen	150	one hundred and fifty	17th	seventeenth
17	seventeen	200	two hundred	18th	eighteenth
18	eighteen	1000	one thousand	19th	nineteenth
19	nineteen	10 000	ten thousand	20th	twentieth
20	twenty	100 000	one hundred thousand	21st	twenty-first
21	twenty-one	1 000 000	one million		

Fractions

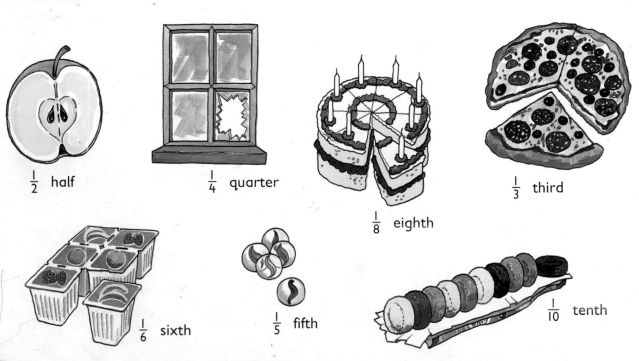

$\frac{1}{2}$ half

$\frac{1}{4}$ quarter

$\frac{1}{8}$ eighth

$\frac{1}{3}$ third

$\frac{1}{6}$ sixth

$\frac{1}{5}$ fifth

$\frac{1}{10}$ tenth